Pat Butcher is athletics correspondent for the *Financial Times*. He has made two television documentaries, *Arabian Knight, the Enigma of Saïd Aouita* and *Race for Kenya*, an exploration of the genetic and cultural reasons for East African running success. He once ran a mile in 4 min. 09.4 sec.

THE PERFECT DISTANCE

OVETT AND COE: THE RECORD-BREAKING RIVALRY

Pat Butcher

PHOENIX

For Mum and Dad

A PHOENIX PAPERBACK

First published in Great Britain in 2004
by Weidenfeld & Nicolson
This paperback edition published in 2005
by Phoenix,
an imprint of Orion Books Ltd,
Orion House, 5 Upper St Martin's Lane,
London WC2H 9EA

1 3 5 7 9 10 8 6 4 2

A CIP catalogue record for this book
is available from the British Library

ISBN 0 75381 900 7

Typeset in Great Britain by
Butler and Tanner Ltd, Frome and London

Printed and bound in Great Britain by
Clays Ltd, St Ives plc

www.orionbooks.co.uk

Total recall only happens in fiction. The events described here stretch back over three decades and more, and memory is not always reliable. Forgetting and fabricating are not always intentional, as the debates over retrieved memory suggest. In an interview more than twenty years ago with former 10,000 metres world record holder David Bedford, he broke off from recalling one of his feats to say, 'It's like we're talking about another person'. It was his version of L. P. Hartley's observation in *The Go-Between* – 'The past is a foreign country: they do things differently there.'

Steve Ovett and Sebastian Coe, whom I cannot thank enough for their trust and their time, did things very differently – differently from each other, and differently from everyone else. Since I was there much of the time, this is an attempt to be a go-between – between them and you and that foreign country where they performed with such distinction.

I have used Mel Watman's invaluable *Coe & Ovett File* (taken from *Athletics Weekly* reports and interviews) as an aide-mémoire and as a source for the occasional contemporary quote. I have similarly used David Miller's early volumes with and on Sebastian Coe, *Running Free* and *Coming Back*; and the autobiography *Ovett*, with John Rodda, as well as *Steve Ovett* by Simon Turnbull. But since this current volume is mostly from primary sources, any blame accruing is entirely mine.

My thanks to the three score and more of my other interviewees whose demonstrable pleasure in recalling their involvement, however peripheral in a golden era for the sport, was so gratifying.

Thanks too to my agent John Saddler, whose idea this volume was in the first place; to my editor Ian Preece; to my family, friends and colleagues for their support; to Kenth Andersson, Jörg Wenig and Andy Edwards for their help with translations; to Kevin Grogan and James O'Brien for their advice on specific chapters, and especially to Kevin for reminding me that Homer was the first athletics writer.

Pat Butcher, London 2004

Contents

... even so close behind him was Odysseus treading in his footprints before the dust could settle there, and Ajax could feel his breath on the back of his head as he ran swiftly on

Homer, *The Iliad*

Illustrations

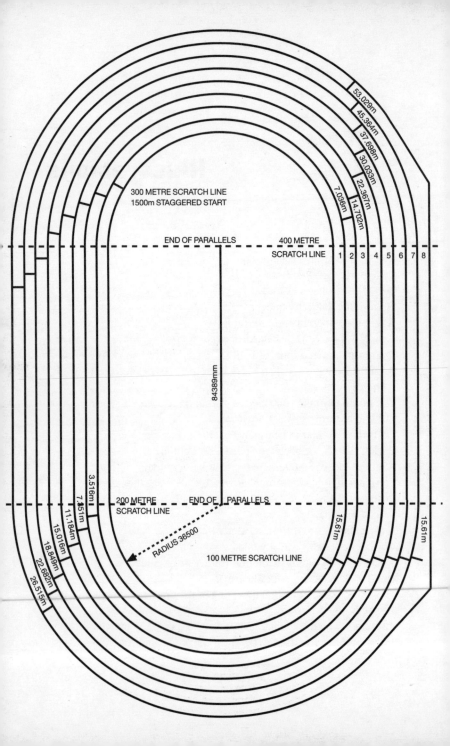

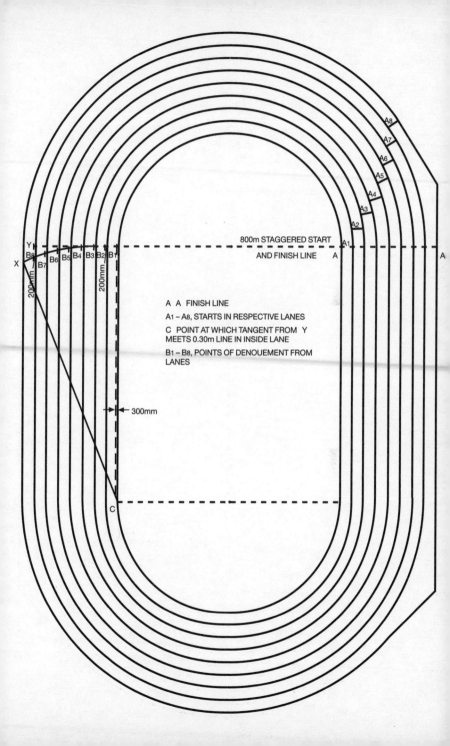

800m STAGGERED START
AND FINISH LINE

A A FINISH LINE
A1 – A8, STARTS IN RESPECTIVE LANES
C POINT AT WHICH TANGENT FROM Y
MEETS 0.30m LINE IN INSIDE LANE
B1 – B8, POINTS OF DENOUEMENT FROM
LANES

300mm

The Great Tradition

They said you could hear the roar out in Santa Monica, a good ten miles away. Yet the three men easing away from their pursuers at the centre of the cauldron were only dimly aware of the crescendo. They were edging towards their own limits. And the howls of close to a hundred thousand spectators, most of them now on their feet in the sun-drenched stadium had as little impact as the advice from the millions at home yelling at their televisions. The British public had never seen anything like it. Nor had the rest of the world. It was a sporting moment for the ages, worthy of nearby Hollywood. It was the penultimate bend of the 1500 metres, the Olympic Games' blue riband event, and the predatory trio moving swiftly up to the shoulder of the unwilling pacemaker were all Brits. They were the finest flowering of the Great Tradition.

Sebastian Coe, the defending champion, was leading. His lifelong rival, his nemesis, Steve Ovett, was bringing up the rear. Sandwiched between them was Steve Cram, the youngster who would eventually upstage them both as the best miler in the world. The eyes blinked, the cameras clicked, and for a sublime moment frozen in time this was the apotheosis of the institution that was the rivalry between Coe and Ovett. A dozen years had elapsed since they had ploughed through the fields of west London, each unaware of the other, each dreaming of a moment like this. Four years had gone by since they had 'swapped'

Olympic titles in Moscow. They were just forty seconds from the finish line, moments away from triumph for one and a race to a hospital bed for the other. Nothing would ever be the same again.

2

Rivals

A quarter of a century ago, Britain was a nation divided. It was not the split between those who loved the newly elected Prime Minister Margaret Thatcher with a strange passion, and those who hated her with visceral contempt. It was not the ever-widening gulf between the haves and the have-nots. It was not the traditional rift between the north and south. But it was all of those, and more. It was Steve Ovett versus Sebastian Coe.

Although they had met, unknown to each other, in a schoolboy race in 1972, the rivalry between Coe and Ovett began in earnest in 1978. Since Ovett, already a star, had not spoken to the media since 1975, he was portrayed as brash, arrogant, a bully-boy. Moreover, his behaviour in races did little to dispel the image. He was ruthless towards his opponents, whom he seemed to taunt, firstly by tracking them with contemptuous ease as they tried to pull away, then by gliding past them, barely acknowledging their presence, and ultimately by waving casually as he crossed the line – first, of course – with a grin on his unstrained face. Curiously, for the press who loathed him, the crowds loved him.

Then Coe appeared, as if from nowhere. And he quickly became equally good on the track, but in a different way: he dominated races right from the gun. Belying his frail frame, Coe would shoot to the front from the off, daring anyone to follow. They could not. He became so good that his only opponent became the clock. Pacemakers were enlisted to ease his path, and he shattered world records with graceful ease. What's more, he was a darling with the media. Well spoken, eloquent, the only problem was that he could be a little stiff at times, but then he was still young. There were a few who detected an element of smugness, but they were dismissed as the 'Ovett camp'. It was like that. You were either for Ovett, or you were for Coe. There were no agnostics. But the story was not quite what it seemed.

Ovett and Coe. Coe and Ovett. They were as distinct as Apollo and Dionysus, and as famous as Laurel and Hardy, and for the longest, brightest moment in the history of track and field athletics, they were as familiar as bacon and eggs. In fact, whatever your breakfast, you could barely open your newspaper in the decade following the Montreal Olympics of 1976 without finding something about one or the other. Or both. For they were inextricably linked. And have remained so.

Ovett and Coe. The Tough and the Toff. Coe, slight, elegant, intense, fear of failure investing his every move. Ovett, the barrel-chested bruiser, strolling around the track like the very incarnation of Kipling's dictum to accept victory and defeat with equal panache. Hollywood could not have conceived it better. Sebastian Coe, looking and sounding as if he had sauntered off the pages of an Anthony Powell novel, or stepped off the set of *Chariots of Fire*. Steve Ovett, in contrast was the comic-book anti-hero. His alter-ego was Alf Tupper, the 1950s icon of 'Tough of the Track' in *The Rover*. They were the sparring, inseparable twins of the premier Olympic sport. Their stand-offs in Moscow 1980 and Los Angeles 1984 relegated the rest of the Olympic Games to a side-show. They kept us on the edges of our seats, either in the stadium or in front of the television, for the best part of ten years.

Between them they won three golds, two silvers and a bronze at the Olympics, and a sackful of European and Commonwealth medals. Together they tore up the middle-distance record books, setting close to a score of new standards, and elevating athletics from a once-every-four-years Olympic occasion to a daily feast of professional excellence. They were the moving forces for an unprecedented period of British hegemony in international middle-distance running, a decade when British athletes won every major international title at 1500 metres, and held every world record from 800 to 5000 metres.

They may not have been the first to receive payment for running, but they created the sport as we know it today. And they did it by clambering from the most ordinary of English beginnings to the most extraordinary international finale – a riveting and desolating climax in front of 100,000 spectators and a TV audience of hundreds of millions in the rococo splendour of the Coliseum in Los Angeles.

They were the beginning and the end of an era in more ways than one. Amateur athletics had been born a century before them, out of the corruption of professional match races, where 'fixing' was common, as was running under assumed names. But the last gasp of that colourful era came in the mid-1880s, with two equally dominant characters, the professional runners or 'pedestrians' Walter George, a Wiltshire pharmacist, and Wille Cummings, a publican from Preston. They were Coe and Ovett a century beforehand, and they ran two series of three races, which resulted in a world mile record that lasted for thirty years.

A hundred years later, the amateurism with which an Oxbridge elite had rescued athletics and given it a Corinthian veneer had become redundant; and the era of Thatcherism ushered in the new professional sport. Ovett and Coe were in the vanguard of that transformation; indeed, their rivalry virtually created the new professionalism. By the late seventies, athletics was practised in over 200 countries. It had more world-wide penetration than any other sport, including football. And, as with football, Britain, which had created athletics as a 'modern' sport, had been gradually pushed further and further into the background, while the superpowers – the USA and the Soviet Union – were using the Olympic arena as their Cold War battleground. Yet, in the wake of a single bronze medal for Britain at the Montreal Olympics in 1976, two athletes from the same tiny island were suddenly dominating the sports news, not only of athletics but of every sport world-wide.

Prime Minister Harold Wilson was convinced that had England

beaten Germany in the 1970 Football World Cup, he would have won the election which followed. Coe and Ovett did provoke a similar 'feel-good' factor, way beyond their sport, and in a manner which was accessible to everyone. In an era of strife and social division, they gave Britons something to be proud of, and something that the rest of the world could immediately identify with – excellence. Again and again and again. They rebuffed challenges from all-comers, Americans, Russians and the newly emerging Africans, who now carry all before them, yet still talk about Ovett and Coe in hushed terms, as the men they set out to emulate. In 2001, Alan Webb became the first US schoolboy to break four minutes for a mile in almost thirty years. His inspiration was a photograph on his bedroom wall. It is the snapshot with which we opened this story, of Coe and Ovett (and Cram) going into the final lap of the Olympic 1500 metres in the Los Angeles Coliseum, the year before Webb was born.

Their attitudes, origins and very ways of competing contributed to the polar perceptions which made the rivalry so exciting and interesting to the millions around the world who hung on their every result. They were nature and nurture writ large, the 'natural' versus the 'mechanical'. And they pushed middle-distance running – the main focus of athletics – into a new dimension, a golden age. In Britain, they were the principal peaks which drew up a mountain range of middle-distance talent around them – Steve Cram, Dave Moorcroft, Peter Elliott, Jack Buckner, Tom McKean, Tim Hutchings. And in peripheral events, we had the giant figures in the wider athletics world, too: Daley Thompson, Allan Wells, Tessa Sanderson and, later, Linford Christie. But all these great talents were no more than minor planets revolving around a binary system – two suns, two stars – Steve Ovett and Sebastian Coe.

3

The Tough

Considering the importance accorded to genetic inheritance nowadays, it would hardly seem that Steven Michael James Ovett had the most auspicious start in life. Born in Brighton on 9 October 1955, he was the son of a roof tiler with a serious smoking problem and his sixteen-year-old wife. But Steve Ovett was a massive and precocious athletic talent, with a startling range. As a fifteen-year-old, he ran the 400 metres in under 50 seconds, to win the English Youths title; by the time he was seventeen, and less than twenty years after Roger Bannister's mind-expanding 'first', he ran a 4-minute mile; he then won the English National Under-20 cross-country championships over 10 kilometres by almost a minute. He was, it seems, marked for greatness right from the gun.

'I suppose I was lucky to be born really,' Ovett mused to me once, 'given the attitudes back then [in the mid-fifties], I could just as easily have been aborted.' There's a possibility to ponder. However, shortly after Steve's birth, his father Alan, known universally as Mick, went into the Royal Air Force to do his national service. He did a bit of sprinting in the RAF, but any benefits would have been more than offset by his smoking, at least a couple of packs a day, which he kept up even through a later heart-attack and subsequent triple bypass operation.

Gay Ovett, née James, cannot have had an easy time as a teenage bride and mother. She had been an only child herself, the daughter of a local undertaker and a housewife, and it was with them that she and baby Steve lived while Mick was in the RAF. It may have been Mick's absence in young Steve's early years which engendered the closeness the child shared with 'Pop', his paternal grandfather Albert. Pop had started the family stall, which still exists on Brighton Open Market, just off the London Road. Steve helped out there in his early teens, working for 80p an hour, according to his uncle Dave.

The mutual affection between Pop and young Steve resulted in an unusual move when the child was just four. Dave Ovett, the youngest of the three brothers – Mick was the middle one – recalls how it happened. Dave, instantly recognisable despite the stockier figure, with his Ovett male-pattern baldness, broke off from selling the eggs and bacon on the Ovetts' stall to perch on a makeshift coffee table, where the traders take their smoke breaks. 'My dad was working here one day,' he recalls, 'and I think Steve was only just over four, and one of the stall-holders said, "Albert, your grandson is sitting up the top of the market." He'd come along the main road, and waited for his granddad. And my dad took him home, and he lived with him after that.'

He was to live with his grandparents for the best part of a decade, but his parents lived close by – Mick was back at home after three years in the RAF – and he would see them almost daily. His sister Sue was two years younger, and a brother, Nicky, would be born another seven years later. But Steve was effectively brought up as an only child, with all the affection that an older couple could bestow. As he acknowledges, Pop doted on him. And the old man would have a lot to be proud of when Steve started running.

By 1960, Mick was firmly ensconced on the market stall, which involved very long days. He would be up at five to go to the wholesale market, then prepare the wares on the stall, work there all day, and not return home until six or later. When Gay was not pregnant or caring for infants, she worked in the market café. Later, she would manage the Rotunda Café in nearby Preston Park, where a bronze statue of her son at his emaciated best – or in the style of Giacometti – now faces out towards London Road, the route to Crystal Palace, site of many of his popular victories.

Mick was, by all accounts a fairly laid-back man, who never-theless took the duty of care for his family very seriously. He was the breadwinner, but also a caring and supportive father. Much later, in 1976, he would drop his market commitments and fly off at a moment's notice to Montreal when he realised from a depressed phone call that his twenty-year-old son needed the support that the British team was not offering a young athlete in his first Olympic Games.

For all that she had a husband and three children, Gay Ovett seems to have been a solitary person who did not suffer fools gladly – a trait her first-born would inherit. Nor was she slow to make her distaste felt, in language that owed much to the market environment. Uncle Dave says, 'She was an odd one. She didn't like anybody. But she was good to him [Steve]. She was devoted, he never went without nothing. That was her life, wasn't it?'

Ovett's detractors always point to an early manifestation of his innate contrariness, his admission that his first running experience came when he broke a milk bottle over a youthful peer's head and 'legged it'. He returned home to find the irate mother of his victim and swift retribution from Mick. But, fittingly, Pop was the first to see the glimmer of the young Ovett's talent. As Uncle Dave recalls, 'You always knew when my dad was coming, because you could hear him whistling round the corner. Anyway, he'd been to see Steve in the junior 60-metre dash at school. I heard him whistling, and he comes round the corner with such a face on him. I said, "What's the matter, did he win?" "Did he win?" he says. "The gun went, and those little pair of legs went like that, and he was away. He won easy." That was that. That's how it all started.'

Despite suffering from dyslexia, which was barely recognised back in the early sixties, Ovett passed the 11-plus to go to Varndean Grammar School, on the outskirts of Brighton. It was not far from his home; nor from Preston Park, where he would first train; nor from Withdean Stadium, where he would have his first club races. In fact, everything was close, primarily his family. The Ovett world revolved around a tiny nexus, yet he would draw enormous strength from it over the coming years.

And there was Brighton to enjoy. The seaside town had long been a magnet for people from London and the rest of the south. Later, in a flight of literary allusion, a Scandinavian journalist would compare the assumed hardman Ovett to the psychotic Pinky Brown in Graham Greene's *Brighton Rock*. But Ovett's Brighton was a life-enhancing place, as he recalls: 'I was so lucky, I had a wonderful youth in Brighton. It was a fabulous town to grow up in, from the Regency debauchery coming to the swinging sixties, the seventies, the mods, the rockers, the eighties. It was probably one of the greatest times to be a child, be an adolescent, so I had all that, I had all the facilities that Brighton had, the promenade to run along, the Downs to race and train on. I loved it.'

The first serious steps towards competitive running came in 1968, and they were anything but tentative. While the athletics world was gearing up for the Olympic Games in Mexico City, a youngster who would be one of the stars of the show twelve years later took his first strides towards Olympic glory. It was his first school sports day at Varndean, and, in his own words, 'Ovett Junior won everything.'

What's more, this was not simply running events. Ovett won the high jump and the long jump as well. In fact, he would go on to set Sussex county junior records, one of which, for the long jump (6.28 metres) lasted for close to twenty years. This catholicism is not uncommon in good young athletes; they seem to excel in all events. But the jumps are interesting for what was to come later. For both Ovett and Seb Coe excelled at something called a 'sargent jump'. This is a gym exercise where you stand side-on to a wall, stretch your closer arm upwards, and make a fingertip mark on the wall. You then crouch and do a standing jump upwards, and tap the wall at the apogee of the jump. According to veteran coach, Frank Horwill, a seminal figure in the development of the British Milers' Club, both Ovett and Coe were far above the norm as youngsters. This bounding capacity is crucial when developed in middle-distance runners. As Horwill recalls, 'Twenty-three inches difference [between the lower and upper marks] is considered astounding. They went through the bloody roof, both Coe and

Ovett. They could nearly touch the ceiling. In other words, the twenty-three inches was almost thirty-three. That showed enormous elastic leg strength. All good 800-metre runners have above-average elastic leg strength. They also have the ability to hop. I think Seb Coe would do twenty-five metres in eight hops. Ten was considered good on each leg. Nine is very good. But eight is like a kangaroo.'

A few more excursions like the annual school sports day persuaded the ever-attentive Ovett parents, Mick especially, that their talented son should join the local athletics club. Brighton & Hove AC was one of the better clubs in Britain, and still is. It has the considerable advantage of a well-run municipal stadium, formerly Withdean, now Brighton Sports Arena, and runs a wide variety of teams, from juniors through to veterans, with track and field events, road-racing and cross-country running. But, like most clubs, the organisation is largely, if not wholly dependent on amateurs and volunteers. Even nowadays, professional athletics is for the very few.

Ovett soon impressed the older club members, but no more so than many other talented youngsters at the time. Reg Hook was the Brighton club president, and he was also a photographer and journalist for the Brighton *Argus*. He would be involved with the Ovetts in both capacities during the Brighton years. Hook still lives in Patcham, a village on the outskirts of Brighton, a few streets away from where the Ovetts lived, and a mile from Preston Park. He recalls, 'I suppose he was thirteen, possibly only twelve, when he joined the club. He looked good. He was a tall, lanky athlete, long stride and naturally stylish, light on his feet. But you get athletes like this. They are good for a couple of years, and then they don't appear, or they don't fulfil their promise. Steve was one of those who did, and he made an immediate impression.'

The admiration was not reciprocated, unfortunately. Mick Ovett and his young son were underwhelmed by their reception at Withdean Stadium, where they were pretty much left to their own devices. So much so that Mick began his son's development with some rudimentary coaching of his own. Sensibly, though, Mick soon acknowledged that he didn't know enough, and he asked at the club if anyone would coach his fourteen-year-old. Tony Tilbury was the team manager at the time, and asked his brother Barry to take a look at Ovett. Barry had recently moved about forty miles away, to Walton on Thames, but he had seen Steve win a cross-country race in Brighton's Stanmer Park just the weekend before and had been impressed enough to agree.

Barry Tilbury lives in a village not far west of Heathrow Airport nowadays, and he still coaches local athletes. A wiry man in his mid-sixties, he is the archetypal coach. I had to wade into his hallway through boxes of magazines and running kit. Pride of place in his living room, where the walls are covered with photos of athletes, is his computer, on which are his stats and training programmes, and articles for various running magazines, none of which pay, of course. He's a coach, he doesn't mind. All he needs is an occasional thank-you from the athletes he trains, and a bit of recognition.

Unfortunately, Tilbury is suffering from a degenerative cognitive condition, and occasionally names and locations escape him, but the further back the incident, the better he remembers it, and he has various aides-mémoire, like letters and training schedules, to jog the failing memory. One thing that was not dampened was his enthusiasm. Like I said, he's a coach.

After work one midweek day in early 1970, Tilbury drove to Brighton to visit the Ovett household. 'The father said, "What do you think he could do in the future?" Now I understand when I look at people how good they are, and I said, "I can't tell exactly what it might be, but I think he will get to the Olympics." '

This was more than satisfactory to Mick and Gay, and they agreed to let Tilbury coach young Ovett. The majority of the time, Mick would supervise local sessions laid out by Tilbury, and Ovett would occasionally go to Walton, stay with Tilbury, and train with the other youngsters at the local club. Whether the Ovetts believed Tilbury's prescient forecast or not, they did their son a big favour. One thing that is obvious from the training and racing schedules, and from our conversation, is that Tilbury is not a believer in pushing youngsters too hard. That is a sure recipe for disaster, and a potential early end to a career. More than half of the winners of the Under-17 English national cross-country title never make it past twenty as elite runners. At this stage, Ovett was still running in sprints, 100 and 200 metres, as much as he was competing over 400 and 800 metres.

Tilbury's meticulous racing log for the early teenage Ovett is telling. During the two years that Ovett trained under Tilbury's guidance, the youngster improved from 2 minutes, 9 seconds for 800 metres, to 1 minute 55.3 seconds, which was a UK record for a fifteen-year-old. Steve's uncle Dave has an interesting tale from those early years, one which reflects both the young Ovett's talent and the incredulity which that talent engendered in time-serving officials. The extended Ovett family was very supportive, once they knew that they had a potential champion in their ranks. In early May 1970, Ovett ran an 800 metres at Crawley, a few miles inland from Brighton. The family travelled up for the race. The records state that Ovett won in 2 minutes 1 second, after a first lap of 57 seconds. But Uncle Dave remembers it differently. 'Mick came over a bit annoyed. "Do you know what?" he said. "They've clocked him at two minutes dead, and they won't give him two minutes, because they said that he's too young to run two minutes. Nobody can do that at fourteen." ' The matter was rectified two weeks later at Walton track, where Tilbury coached. Ovett won another 800 metres. After a slightly speedier first lap of 56.5 seconds, he was clocked at exactly 2 minutes. So that settled that.

As far as Ovett's character was concerned, Tilbury recalls a well-behaved youngster who did everything that his coach asked. Tilbury was already convinced that Ovett was going to be an 800/1500 metres runner and was obviously inculcating that belief in the youngster, too. But, first, he was to prove himself at the shorter track distances. Although he was still running 100s and 200s, which would be invaluable for that devastating 'kick' finish for which he would become famous, he would lose as many sprints as he won. But as soon as it got to 400 metres, one lap of the track, his strength would tell. And it was at 400 metres that he had his first national success. In early July 1970, the Ovett family packed up the car, got relief for the market stall, and drove the 200 miles to Solihull in the West Midlands.

The English Schools Athletics Championships are legendary throughout the national athletics community. They are the cradle of the sport, with over 50 per cent of Britain's elite athletes since the 1950s coming through their ranks. They are also awesome in their organisation, with hundreds of qualifying heats being run with military precision. On the other hand, if a battalion of teachers can't organise a timetable, who can? They are the initial goal of every youngster aspiring to become an Olympic champion. As proof, Britain's Olympic gold medals in Moscow were forged largely in the English (or National) Schools Championships. Ovett, Coe and Daley Thompson (Allan Wells, a late developer was the sole exception) all competed, and won, at the English Schools.

Ovett's road to Olympia began in the heart of England. Solihull was once one of the richest boroughs in Britain, thanks to the Rover car factory. But the British car industry was in rapid decline, and the Midlands had suffered badly by the early seventies. In contrast, British middle-distance running, which had been in decline for a decade or more, was getting its first proper view of a youngster who would usher in a golden age. Aged fourteen and nine months Ovett was entered for the Boys 400 metres. He was one of the favourites, since he had won the Sussex Schools title in 51.6 seconds, a county record. In Solihull, he won his heat, placed third in the semi-final, easily qualifying for the final, which he won in 51.8 seconds. He still recalls it as one of the highlights of his career. 'The first English Schools victory at 400 metres was a marvellous feeling, with the family there, me turning back, looking back in the home straight, and they were literally screaming and shouting. That was probably the most emotional race of my life, because, as a child, you've done something. And you never get that again; you get a bit blasé.'

Apart from his family in Solihull that July afternoon, there was another spectator who had made a special trip from almost as far south to see the young Ovett. Dave Cocksedge is an athletics enthusiast, and a member of an organisation called the National

Union of Track Statisticians.' No body ever rejoiced in a better acronym – NUTS. Back in 1970, Cocksedge wrote a regular column for *Athletics Weekly* called 'Spotlight on Youth'. Now in his mid-fifties, Cocksedge lives in semi-retirement in the coastal town of Pattaya in Thailand. One of his other preoccupations is crime, and he does occasional historical pieces for a couple of the English-language newspapers in Thailand. He recalls Solihull, he says, 'Vividly. Barry Tilbury had been writing to me about this kid who had run 53.1 seconds at the age of thirteen, which was pretty extraordinary and I was putting him in my column. I'd only seen his times and read what Barry had sent me, but Barry had said, "Watch this kid. He is going to be something special." He won the 400 final in a championship record. It was considered pretty good then. I went up to meet this kid, interview him. He was gangling and he had long hair down to his shoulders, but I was amazed by his maturity. He was saying, "Yes this is OK, but I want to run the 800 and 1500 in years to come." He was talking like an eighteen-year-old or something. I've never met a fourteen-year-old with so much self-assurance. He had this long hair and buck-teeth. He looked quite weird. But I had feelings that he obviously was a real future star.'

Although Cocksedge was several years older than Ovett, he would get to know the youngster quite well over the next half a dozen years, often going to stay with the Ovett family in Brighton, partying with the increasingly mature and seemingly self-confident youngster. Ovett, similarly, would visit Cocksedge and his mother at their home in south London, not far from Crystal Palace, which was to become a happy hunting ground for the talented teenager.

The Crystal Palace area of south London is the very antithesis of its title. It was named after the glass construction that was originally erected in London's Hyde Park for the Great Exhibition of 1851. The crystal palace was dismantled and moved to Sydenham Hill in 1854, where it became part of a Victorian theme park, which was dedicated to the greater glory of the British Empire. But the palace burned down in 1936, and the rest of the area gradually followed its demise. Some neighbouring parts are quite elegant, and Dulwich just down the hill has its famous college, where P. G. Wodehouse and Raymond Chandler, among many others, were schooled. A couple of their creations – Bertie Wooster and Philip Marlowe – could be said, at a stretch, to prefigure Coe and Ovett. As for the attractions of Crystal Palace, the look on the face of Alain Billouin, the chief Olympic correspondent for the French sports daily *L'Equipe*, when he landed there for the first time in the late seventies told the tale. With the admiration that *L'Equipe* writers somehow retain for all things English – on the basis, I believe, that 'we' had created sport single-handedly – Billouin thought that such places only existed either in North Africa or immediately on the other side of the Paris *périphérique*.

On a personal note, it was a poor performance at Crystal Palace in early 1972 which persuaded me that I was never going to make it to the international level on the track. I'd won a medal at the national indoor championships that year, and harboured a belief that I might even qualify for the Munich Olympics in the steeple-chase. I ran like a hack, and after a listless warm-down I decided to catch a bus back to north London, rather than the train. My depression was heightened by the meandering trip through the dingy south-east London suburbs, with drably dressed people going about their business oblivious to my demise. Two teenage girls got on and chatted away animatedly just in front of me. They didn't have a care in the world, whereas I felt like the Leonard Cohen songbook.

Two years earlier, Ovett would have a very different experience at Crystal Palace. He had already run there a couple of times in early 1970, but the winter meeting in mid-December, a couple of months after his fifteenth birthday, was to be a preview of many such races there over the next decade. Cocksedge was primed and on hand to report on the race. It wasn't Ovett's first attempt over the metric mile – that had been earlier in Crawley when he had recorded an unspectacular 4 minutes 43 seconds. That wasn't unusual. Here he was, at best an 800 metres runner, but essentially a 400 metres man. On 16 December 1970, he ran his second race at the distance at which he would become a master. Dave Cocksedge recorded the event for *Athletics Weekly:*

> The form horse was Southern Boys champion, Paul Williams, who had run 4.12.2 for the distance. They set off quickly in the still conditions, with a lap of 61.2 before slowing to 2.12.6 for 800m. Now was the time for Williams to run away from them, and he did so on cue, with shouts of encouragement from his father Ray and coach Frank Horwill. But Ovett, supported by parents Mick and Gay and coach Barry Tilbury, moved into Williams' slipstream and followed easily. Ovett was racing over his known distance, but seemed quite untroubled by the pace.
>
> Williams floored the gas pedal approaching the bell and drew well away from all but the Brighton youngster. Then he raised the pace still more into the final backstraight, but was powerless to respond when Ovett suddenly exploded into an all-out sprint with roughly 150m left. Williams chased gamely but could not close the sudden gap Ovett had opened. The winner sped through the finish line in 4.10.7 – a personal best by almost 33 seconds!

A rare apposite example of the overused exclamation mark delineates a crucial stage in Ovett's development. And this capacity to run over a wide range of distances would remain a feature of Ovett's career. A 400 metres champion running one of the fastest times of the year for 1500 metres in his age group is extraordinary enough. This is the sort of thing that can happen in speed-skating, but not in athletics. It would be like Michael Johnson winning his speciality, the 400 metres flat, then turning out the next day and beating Hicham El Guerrouj in the mile. Yet, half a dozen years after that race in Crystal Palace, a week after winning the European Cup 1500 metres, and just a couple of weeks before the most decisive victory of his early career, demolishing Olympic champion John Walker and winning the World Cup 1500 metres, Ovett would decide on an impulse to run – and win against international specialists – a half marathon in 65 minutes. Thus, sandwiched between two 1500 metres races, he ran and won an international-class half-marathon – 13.1 miles – and he did it in a pair of shoes he'd borrowed from his training partner!

The ground was being laid for such a feat by that Youth's 1500 metres, which concluded a wonderful year, in which Ovett had started getting noticed beyond the confines of Varndean Grammar, Preston Park, Withdean Stadium and Crystal Palace. Everything was on course. He was receiving some sensitive direction from Tilbury, who would travel as often as he could to watch his charge race. Ovett was back living with his parents, who supported his fledgling career to a fault. Mick ferried him around, and Gay provided the rest of the back-up, which would later develop into a lifestyle – meals when he wanted them, as much sleep as he needed without interruption, laundry retrieved from where it had been dropped, and returned in pristine condition. In short, it was something that any proud, attentive mum would provide. But it was already becoming clear to outsiders that there was an edge to Gay's involvement.

Tilbury recalls that if anything needed to be discussed, it was always with 'the mother. She was very, very strong.'

Reg Hook, meanwhile, says, 'His mother was very supportive. Sometimes it seemed that she was more supportive to him than to her husband, because Steve became the focus of her life. She was the driving force, because she devoted so much time to him. She was very protective of him, and she certainly wore the trousers. It was always easier to talk to Mick than to Gay.' Whatever, it was working.

Despite Dave Cocksedge's evaluation of Ovett's maturity, and what others would see as matiness among his peers, there was a private side to the youngster, on which eventually everyone would remark. As Hook says, 'He wasn't a great mixer, a little aloof. I think basically he was shy, and he's always been this way. He's not the easiest person to speak to; he would talk to you sometimes, but he's not with it, he's not thinking, he's miles away. He wasn't really an approachable athlete. I think he had this attitude that, I like running, I'm good at running, but that's it.'

'Good' is hardly the word for it. Tilbury evaluated the young talent which he had been offered to mould as 'brilliant'. And the progress he made the following year, 1971, was equally rewarding for athlete, coach, parents and an increasing band of admirers. Reg Hook suggests, 'People in athletics don't get the same sort of publicity as second-rate footballers. But I was writing for the *Argus* from the time he started, so I would have been highlighting his exploits from the time he started winning things. He would have been getting reasonably good publicity in the Under-15s.'

A year later, the publicity was becoming even more deserved. In only his third race of the season, on 1 May 1971, his 800 metres personal best tumbled to 1 min 56.8 seconds. In the ensuing months, he also improved his 400 metres time, eventually running 50.4 seconds twice in that summer's English Schools. (However, as if to confirm that he was mortal after all, he finished only third against boys a year older.)

Extraordinarily, he was still competing in the occasional field event. One afternoon at Withdean, he set three personal bests: 200 metres in 23.5 sec; a 5 feet 5 inches high jump; and the aforementioned record-breaking long jump. This was just a prelude to a magnificent finale to his 1971 season. Inside a month, he brought his 400 metres best down first to 50 seconds flat, then won the AAA, the national clubs' Youths title in Wolverhampton, in 49.8 seconds; then, in what Barry Tilbury termed 'perfect conditions' at Crystal Palace, he ran a national record for 800 metres as a fifteen-year-old, 1 minute 55.3 seconds.

This was all happening with what seems ridiculous ease. Ovett himself cannot recall a time when the competition was ever hard. Yes, the training was hard, eventually. It had to be. But normally there comes a time in the career of every young, successful athlete when the 'natural' talent no longer suffices. Peers, late developers, start maturing, shooting up in size and seriousness. They begin to challenge. Some young champions resist, recognise the symptoms, and begin to train harder in order to stay ahead. Others wilt, succumb to outside temptations, or have simply trained too hard as youngsters, and become discouraged when former pushovers suddenly appear on their shoulders at decisive moments like avenging angels. This never happened to Ovett.

To a large degree, he had been getting by on his relative physical maturity as a youth. He was big for his age, already taller than his parents, which, in tandem with their own youthfulness, caused many people to take him for a younger brother rather than their son. But the transition from youth to junior to senior seemed seamless. Reg Hook was a witness. 'If there was a moment when he realised he'd have to train harder it came at the National [English] Schools Championships in 1971, when he didn't even get a medal after winning the previous year.' In fact, Hook misremembers, as Ovett won the bronze medal. But elsewhere Hook admits, 'Steve never encountered the problems of stepping from junior to senior athletics. When he became a junior, he was better than the top athletes in Britain, and even as a youth, he was in effect a mature senior athlete.'

Mick Ovett gradually became more involved in team management at the Brighton club, which included the sort of rudimentary advice to youngsters that he had originally given solely to his son. Having been around the club for a couple of years, he would have picked up coaching tips from others, but no one ever viewed him as a coach, as Reg Hook confirmed. Nevertheless, he was becoming increasingly involved in his son's training schedules, which led to a couple of 'discussions' between Gay and Mick (in that order) and Tilbury.

Things came to a head at the end of the 1971 track season, when the club athletes embarked on their regular short relay season, which usually takes place on the roads, as a precursor to winter cross-country. The same thing happens in springtime, between cross-country and track. Prior to the marathon boom, which began a decade later, the relays were an integral part of the athletics year. Tilbury rang Ovett one Monday evening in late September to discover that Mick had arranged for Steve to race at Camberley the next weekend, whereas Tilbury had no plans for him to race there or anywhere else.

Tilbury wrote to Mick, outlining his grievances. The letter, reproduced below, illustrates Tilbury's concern and training philosophy in terms which do him justice, but also highlights the recurrent problem of parental meddling in promising sporting careers.

> Your increased involvement at club level has brought about a set of circumstances that apparently prevents you from divorcing Steve's training and racing programme from your club loyalty.
>
> Your probable reaction to this is, 'What difference does a $1\frac{1}{4}$ mile race make?' and the answer is, treated in isolation, none. But this could easily escalate into running more regular races at up to two miles. I think I am in the best position to judge what races he needs, but I am sufficiently club-oriented to make sure that all his races this winter are major events of a team nature. The boy is only 16, and needs a careful, progressive build-up each winter, particularly this year, as he will be undertaking weight training as well.
>
> Perhaps the most annoying aspect in this case is one of 'principle'. I do not consider myself unapproachable, and have always been prepared to listen to a helpful suggestion in regard to his coaching. I rarely ever take a major decision without first consulting the athlete, and I expect this to be reciprocal . . .
>
> Being a team manager myself, I can fully understand the problems of getting out a strong weekly team, but as I have stressed many times before (with your agreement), we must not allow this to interfere with Steve's prospects for international status.

Perhaps the most revealing comment in Tilbury's letter comes at the end. The prospect of Ovett becoming an international athlete and an Olympian had been an article of faith throughout the Tilbury years. His parents were telling him that, his coach was telling him that, he was telling himself that, all the time, day after day, session after session, such that it was taken for granted: 'You shall be an international athlete.' It is a crucial part of the young athlete's development. And it would happen with his great rival too. It would make an indelible impression on both of them. When, as so often happens, so much else in a youngster's life is criticism and condemnation, no matter how self-assured the child, assurance from outside, from responsible adults is invaluable, and formative.

Tilbury concludes with an apology for writing rather than speaking face-to-face, but suggests that he did so to avoid a potential argument. The relationship would last only a few more weeks. Behind the scenes, it seems that Gay had been as instrumental in the break with Tilbury as Mick, if not more so. The coach had been sanguine about the great leap forward that Ovett had made with his 800 metres record just before they stopped, or were stopped from, working together. 'That wasn't a great surprise to me. I knew he could do that from his 49.8 second 400 metres. There was no doubt in my mind that eventually he could also be a 1500 metres runner, because anybody who does 800 metres can usually do 1500 no trouble. [But] the mother got involved, she said, "No, he won't be a 1500 metres runner." ' Thirty years later, Tilbury says with a wistful smile, 'He ended up breaking the world record, didn't he?'

Ultimately, there are no great secrets in athletics training. Yes, of course you need a modicum of talent, and Ovett had enough of that to fill the Brighton Pavilion. But 'will' is probably the most important element in the make-up of a champion: the will to work hard, coupled with the sort of bloody-mindedness that comes from self-belief. All you need after that is a bit of common sense.

Ovett's dyslexia meant he was never going to shine academically; he admits his scholastic work was poor at Varndean. But school is not only for academic work. He'd found something he was good at, he was smart enough to recognise that he had a special talent, and that if he persevered, he could become a champion. He had been good enough at football to be considered for Brighton Schools, but he astounded and angered his teachers at Varndean by turning down the opportunity, even refusing to play further at school. The more perceptive masters understood when they saw him run.

Now that his mother is dead, and he hasn't lived close to his father for twenty years, his wife Rachel is the person who knows him best. 'Steve has this steely determination. If he decides to do something, he does have the ability in whatever he chooses to see it through; he is very good at finishing things. He can be totally and utterly focused. And he will just get on with it, he doesn't make a fuss or a noise, he just does it.'

Tilbury's best advice had been caution, and Ovett and his family were smart enough to know that what Tilbury had been advising had worked, and was still working. He had given them the blue-print, so Steve and Mick followed the instructions themselves for the next few months, with the occasional aberration. Ovett himself had started reading about athletics, not just in *Athletics Weekly*, the British bible of the sport, but in biographies of the stars. He was particularly attracted to the *Jim Ryun Story*, which described how a gangling Kansas schoolboy became the world mile record-holder through assiduous training. One of the drawbacks about impressionable youngsters is that they are likely to go out and try to emulate their heroes. Accordingly, since Ryun would run 440 yards 40 times – that's to say, 40 fast laps of the track, with an interval jog between each lap – the sixteen-year-old Ovett would do the same. Well, he'd try. It is testimony to his talent – he would also do impromptu 10-mile runs on his own – that these 'experiments' did not ruin him. Nor did they deter him. An excellent run in a national schools cross-country race in early 1972 under-lined that. But that race was crucial for another reason. Unbeknown to him, he would, for the first time, cross paths with someone who would ultimately become the most important person in his whole career, and from whose name his own would become inseparable – Sebastian Coe.

4

The Toff

In anyone's estimation, Sebastian Newbold Coe was one of the greatest athletes of the twentieth or indeed any other century. He combined the classic competitive tendencies of being able to win from the front when things were going well with, more importantly, the grit to overcome almost unbearable setbacks, and return to greater glory. Yet he had been a timid youngster, a late developer, and was as cautious in public as he was later to be in politics. He was perceived, in the words of *L'Equipe*, as a *fils à Papa* – Daddy's boy. It was intended as a slight, but they were right on the money. Coe's father Percy, known universally as Peter, was to be the seminal influence in his career.

There was an element of gentry in Coe's background: the Newbold from whom both he and Peter took their middle name was the son of Yorkshire landowners. But Harry Newbold was something of an eccentric, later getting involved in the theatre, where he worked with Charlie Chaplin. Coe's half-Indian mother Angela was an actress; her mother had danced with Pavlova; and an uncle was a Royal Academician. Coe's sister Miranda would dance with the Royal Ballet and Ballet Rambert. His father Peter had been a cyclist, but he was going to give far more than his sporting genes to his son. He was going to give him hell.

An executive at one of the Sheffield steel companies, Peter Coe was a martinet. One of Seb Coe's contemporaries in the Sheffield schools system was Kim McDonald. Prior to his untimely death aged forty-five, on several occasions he told me of seeing his tiny early teenage competitor in tears after races, having been given a dressing-down by his father after a poor run.

But it was all to an end. Coe must have had a talent equal to Ovett's otherwise he could not have achieved what he did, but his gifts were not so immediately obvious. They had to be drawn out, nurtured, unlike the immediate dazzling explosion of Ovett's natural talent. And there was another crucial difference. There had always been two distinct strains in British sport, probably best exemplified by the 'Gentlemen versus Players' cricket matches, which persisted through to the 1960s. There was a similar distinction in athletics. If Ovett typically brought to mind the 'chancers', the pro athletes from the nineteenth century, the hard men who lived on their wits and rough talent, then Coe was the late twentieth-century equivalent of the patrician Oxbridge athlete, who lived in sheltered academe and wafted rather than battled his way round a track.

Seb Coe was born in Chiswick, west London on 29 September 1956, almost a year after Steve Ovett. The Coes moved first, through Peter's work to Stratford, where Coe competed in school sports, just like Ovett in the sprints and long jump, but with nothing like the early results of his later rival. But Peter Coe had already recognised that his son more than made up for his slightness of frame with a burgeoning competitive nature: 'He was the most bloody competitive thing you ever met. He never went to the shops and back unless you would time him, and was he quicker than last time? Losing was not in his game. In games of seaside cricket, he was never out. There was one day when he was thirteen or so, he lost a game of tennis to his mother and it was a disaster.'

By then the family had moved to Sheffield, and Seb had joined the local athletics club, Hallamshire Harriers. For almost a year, the youngster relied on the club coaches for guidance, but again in a remarkably similar experience to that of the Ovett family, Peter realised that relying on the club was not the best way to further his son's vocation. 'I listened to a lot of people at the club, and I thought it was all tales, nothing seemed coherent, there was no pattern to it. I thought, Well this is no good, none of this seems to make any sense. I wanted to support Seb, because he enjoyed running, he liked the club. I just sort of gently eased him out, and took it over, and then started really thinking about it.'

This wasn't just a shot in the dark, because, allied to that competitive streak, Peter Coe says, 'I noticed in the way he moved and ran and did things.' But even family friends like Bob Hague were impressed by Peter's prescience. 'It's extraordinary how Peter recognised his talent in the first place,' says Hague. 'I don't know how he did that and how he learned without any background knowledge of athletics to nurture it and develop it and to be able to tailor the training to Seb's physical peculiarities and requirements. How he recognised exactly what Seb had to do to reach a certain performance was almost uncanny.'

The one thing that Peter Coe had going for him was his engineer's training, which, when combined with his managerial experience, would prove invaluable. 'I always had a science-based education,' he says now. 'It's the difference between certainty, which doesn't exist, and dealing with what is a high degree of probability or none at all. All the probabilities indicated that I was dealing with somebody with talent and if you are doing that, don't play about. Put your mind to it. And it was total concentration. Nobody knows better than a parent who is willing to think about it and be objective, and that's what I can be. I can be very objective, get inside their head. So as far as it's possible to know any human being, even your own kid, I figured out what made Seb tick, what was his nature, what he would respond to.

'I had had enough management experience to know how people work and things get done in the factory, preferably by persuasion, but there are times when you just simply say this is what we are going to do, this is the way we are going to do it. This is no way really to get the best out of an athlete, so we devised a trick that I was Dad at home, that was one hat, and I was the coach at the track.'

Steve Mitchell, a contemporary during Seb's time at Loughborough, was just one of the many people who were surprised by the relationship between father and son. 'Seb never called him Dad; he always called him Peter which I found strange. I couldn't work this out. How can you call your dad by his first name?'

But, says Peter, 'That was the rule. It was necessary, because I know it's a natural thing with all kids to test their parameters, they want to see how far they can push parents, they want to push the controls, how much they can get away with, and it can't intrude into athletics, because I'm there to call the shots. I say what is being done, when it's being done and the way it's being done, so on and so forth. The only thing I said was, "If you can do it, I can be there," because there were some rotten nights [when] it was really bitterly cold and miserable. He said to me sometimes, "I can get on with it, I can do it, you can trust me, you don't have to be there." And I'd say, "If you can do it, I can watch." So that was the division and that saved any conflict at all on the coaching front. At home, different: if he wanted to do something else I would advise against it or not.'

There seems to have been more stick than carrot in the early days, but Peter was getting results, and not just on the track. 'He was a very nervous young boy, he suffered from nervous eczema and pollen asthma. He was incredibly sensitive. He was deeply shocked when he failed his 11-plus, but as always I gave it to him straight, saying, "You can either be a secondary modern drop-out or get down to it and get your O levels." He grafted and grafted, and got eight O levels.'

Coe was also taking his first steps up the athletics ladder, although with the occasional snake down. Most of his schoolboy contemporaries would have been just going out for a run and trusting to luck, or maundering along with club coaches relying on the sort of natural talent that an Ovett manifested to get them through and bring early results. But, though frail, Coe at least had the benefit of a 'system', thanks to his dad. In the winter of 1971, he was finishing in the top three of all his schools cross-country races, and eventually won both the Yorkshire Clubs' Colts title and the Yorkshire Schools' Boys title. But he wasn't quite ready for the national championships yet, and could finish only twenty-fourth in the English Schools race in Luton. There was further embarrassment, because his school had laid on two coach-loads of his classmates to watch him run.

But the first substantial success, and recognition beyond the immediate confines of Sheffield schools, was not long coming. Granville Beckett was the *Yorkshire Post*'s athletics writer, and his reports from Huddersfield would be used by the Sheffield newspapers, who were in the same group. Beckett had been a club miler at Longwood Harriers, a colleague of Derek Ibbotson who had broken the world record for the mile in 1957. Beckett recalls his first encounter with the Coes, in May 1971. 'They used to do this meeting on the Saturday evening after the Cup Final. Derek, when he set the world record, gave a trophy to the club, the Ibbotson Trophy. We used to have this schoolboys' mile and the phone rang and it was Peter Coe. He said, "What is the exact time of this boys' mile?" I said it will be somewhere about seven or quarter-past. He was so thorough, he wanted to know the exact time when this race would be run. I said what name is it, and he said Sebastian Coe, and of course Sebastian is an unusual name, and I said, "That fellow is keen, it's only the schoolboys' mile." I said, "I'll have a look for this lad when he comes." Of course, he came and won, and he looked a thoroughbred. Right from those days, he looked a winner.'

Peter Coe's thoroughness would become a byword. Malcolm Grace was a Hallamshire club coach who would give Peter advice, but Grace was to get a closer view of the Coe development than most, since he also worked for Peter at one of the local cutlery factories. 'At work sometimes he would talk to me for hours. He said to me one day, "I'm thinking of getting a bike, Malcolm. When I ride a bike behind Seb it will get me fit and I'll be able to follow him." About a month later I asked what happened to the bike. "Well," he said, "I abandoned that idea because I realised if he pulled a muscle five or six miles from home, he would have to walk back, so I followed in the car." So he had really got his head screwed on, had Peter. He thought of every aspect.'

Bob Hague got to know the Coe family through his brother Ian, a club 400 metres runner (and a big Ovett fan). Ian Hague was one of the young Sebastian's teachers. Bob recalls, 'One day Ian said that he'd got this extraordinary little boy in his cross-country team at school who he thought would be a great runner one day. Ian was always very level headed about making judgements on how good people are going to be, so when he said this boy is going to be amazing, I pricked my ears up.'

Through their membership of the Hallamshire club, both the Hagues became family friends. Bob saw that the young Sebastian was being nurtured not just in running but in a broad range of interests. 'They were an intelligent family that discussed things openly and so he'd know where he was in so many areas from the fact that things had been discussed at home. They were very lively, their interests were not solely athletics, it was only part and parcel of the scene. It was a very full and interesting family life.'

Janet Prictoe, an international 800 metres runner and Coe's first girlfriend at Loughborough, came from a more traditional working-class family, and saw the differences immediately when she began to visit a few years later. 'I think he had greater backing from his family. If you asked my father even now he wouldn't know what event I ran. My mother tried her best. I think he had terrific backing. They prided themselves on being a bit intellectual and clever. They used to listen to the cricket on Radio 3, his mother had been to RADA, and they knew all the actresses' names in old films. It was very stimulating.'

Although their backgrounds were very different, there were some remarkable similarities in the developing characters of Sebastian Coe and Steve Ovett. Despite what many perceived as Ovett's shyness, his exposure to the various characters who inhabited the organised mayhem of Brighton's market place lent him a maturity beyond his years, as Dave Cocksedge remarked when he first interviewed him. Bob Hague would discover a similar trait in young Seb Coe. After a training session one evening in the early seventies, Hague, then about thirty, fell into conversation with the fourteen-year-old Coe.

'It must have been ten years before the first Olympic event, and he said to me, "You know, my dad says that if I keep on developing in this way, I can win the Olympics in 1980." He said it in sort of a detached way. It wasn't as if he was trying to impress; it was just an observation of what he firmly believed. I was impressed by that.'

Again the similarity with the Ovett development is striking. Barry Tilbury had told the Ovett parents that their son could and would be an Olympian. Almost concurrently, Peter Coe was making one of his biggest contributions to his son's progression. 'It was at the corner of our road, going down to the track' recalls Peter. 'I said, "You are going to the 1980 Olympics. Get that firmly fixed in your mind, just accept it that you will be there, this is what we are going to do." '

Just saying it wasn't going to get Coe to Moscow; there was going to be a lot of hard work along the way. Warm-weather training abroad for young hopefuls was also a long way in the future, and the English winters are hardly the best environment for a 10-mile run. Initially, Angela Coe had her doubts about her husband's strictures. 'Angela always said, there were times when I was very cruel to Seb,' says Peter. 'Because, at Christmastime, there was snow on the road. I said, "Seb, now is the time for your distance run." It was hard work going up those roads, it was slippery underneath, plodding away. "I know you've got geography homework, but you've got to fit it in, it's got to be done. You can't allow yourself to be put off things you've got to do." '

Seb himself saw the gradual acceptance of this regime by his mother. 'My mum came from a household where the arts were quite important. There was a stage early on in my career when she suddenly had a child that was training twice a day, coming back mud-splattered and racing at weekends, and clearly obsessive. There were a couple of years when she got quite nervous about just how serious this was beginning to get. Then, of course, she got into it. She became more competitive on some occasions than both myself and my dad. He'd be the one saying, "OK, the season is going all right," and she'd be the one ringing me up and saying, "You know Ovett ran 3.31 in Milan last night." '

But the early hard lessons would be well learned. Malcolm Grace says the difference in application between the young Coe and his contemporaries was painfully evident. 'He came down one day and there was a group of athletes sat on the grass by the side of the track, trying to decide what they were going to do. Seb warmed up and he did a speed session on a terribly maintained track. He ran three 200s in 22 seconds with ten minutes between, warmed down and went home. He knew exactly what he was doing, he knew exactly what effect he got. It was a speed session, out, see it off, long rest in between because it was speed, off home. He had been down and done his bit while all the others were making their mind up what to do.'

In later years, some rival athletes and coaches and some sections of the media would be scornful of the Peter–Seb Coe axis. But those closest to them saw only the positive side of it, both in terms of athletics success, and in forging the sort of relationship that few fathers and sons enjoy. Bob Hague says, 'I always thought that they had an excellent relationship, it was unique, and I did see more of it than anybody else. I saw them at home, in their family life. Seb has a tremendous affection for his father and respect, and it just worked. They talked things through. I think it was a relationship that brought them closer together.'

More than that, the hothouse family atmosphere produced a well-rounded son who, as well as a broad appreciation of athletics, football and boxing, would develop an abiding interest in jazz and opera. He was also being nurtured in the good manners that the media in particular would highlight in contrast with what they saw as a recalcitrant and 'awkward' Ovett. Granville Beckett, the journalist who first started circulating Coe's name around Fleet Street, says, 'I always had a soft spot for him. People always said to me, "He seems so goody goody, is he like that?" I said you can only take people how you find them, and I find him well mannered, well spoken, always willing to talk to you and if you saw him at a press conference he would always acknowledge you.' Malcolm Grace concurs: 'He always treated me with respect, and I would say even as a man of forty he treated me with the same respect. I met him at the Hallamshire centenary dinner, and he treated me with the same deference as he did as a boy of fifteen.'

Later, there would be the occasional divergence from that image. There seems to be an element in Coe's character that wants to be laddish, even caddish. Maybe all those years of toeing the line have nurtured a desire to break out a bit. Given some of the more manic elements in their support, his affiliation with Chelsea Football Club has always mystified people. Dave Warren, the third Brit in the Moscow Olympic 800 metres, says, 'If you wanted to find Seb on a Saturday afternoon in the winter, most of the time, you'd find him down at the Shed at Chelsea, and I think he was really happy being a Chelsea supporter on the terraces, which goes a little bit against the image other people had of him. I think he wasn't quite as goody two-shoes as we were led to believe.'

Janet Prictoe saw a definite early scratch in the veneer, too. She recalls being at the Coe family home when the children were being presented to a guest. Coe was in his early twenties by then. 'I can remember saying to Seb, "Oh, isn't it lovely that she obviously thinks so well of you?" There was slightly that within his family, presenting this lovely picture, which I'm sure wasn't anywhere near as rosy, as nobody's is. I can remember him saying, "It's a bloody pain having to be polite to all these people." So there was even then within the family this thing of creating an image and Seb is very much that: he created an image, or he lived up to the image that was created for him.'

Both Coe and Ovett would have illnesses or injuries during their junior years, which would necessitate lengthy periods off training and out of competition. Coe would miss most of the 1974 season with stress fractures – hairline breaks, usually in the shinbones, which come from training on hard surfaces. Ovett missed the winter of 1973/4, with glandular fever. But, like Ovett, once Coe began his rise, there was never really a time when it seemed that he wasn't going to be successful. There wasn't that difficult transition period when a career can be in the balance. As Peter Coe says, 'No, because we won so much. In terms of age records, he didn't rank. But he won. This is the greatest gift that the coach can be given – consistency.'

In 1971, Coe was still a long way behind Ovett in his development, a reasonable situation, given that he was nearly a year younger. In contrast to Ovett's times for 800 and 1500 metres – 1 minute 55.3 seconds and 4 minutes 10.7 seconds – Coe's bests were 2 minutes 8.4 seconds and 4 minutes 18 seconds. But, unlike Ovett, who was still concentrating on the 400 and 800 metres, Coe was already regularly competing at the distance at which he would make Olympic history. His first national competition at that distance, however, would prove dismal. He finished last in his heat of the English Schools Junior 1500 metres. If he had been watching the Intermediate 400 metres final, he might have spotted the strapping Steve Ovett taking third place.

The next English Schools Championships, the cross-country events in 1972, would be the first time they would meet in competition. Coe trailed in the older boy's wake. But he had plenty of time. They both did. Right now, apart from a small coterie of family and friends who could see their potential, they were virtually anonymous. But when their time came, almost everybody in the world would know their names.

5

Mum and Dad

'They fuck you up, your mum and dad,' the poet Philip Larkin memorably wrote. Well, they do and they don't. Most people who met Peter Coe thought him a disciplinarian with political views somewhere between those of Margaret Thatcher and Genghis Khan. Those who knew Gay Ovett lived in fear of her 'market mouth'. But it is doubtful whether their first-born sons could ever have achieved what they did without their 'driven' parents' considerable input.

So obvious was their influence that well before Moscow 1980 insiders were saying that the rivalry was as much about Gay and Peter as it was about Steve and Seb. Everybody who knew Gay said that she was the driving force, the motor for her son's achievements. And you didn't even need to know Peter: simply seeing him there on the infield, dervishing around with a stopwatch, was enough to convince anybody that he was the puppet-master. Angela Coe and Mick Ovett might have played huge roles in the development of their sons, but their influence was largely offstage, in the wings, while their spouses wore the red coats, and wielded the metaphorical whips.

I spoke to Gay Ovett only once, a few months prior to Moscow 1980. She rebuffed my telephone request for an interview with her son with that exaggerated politeness that can be construed only as contempt. She left me in no doubt that I should not bother to call again. I got off lightly by all accounts.

Gay James was only fifteen when little Steven was conceived. She must have been a solitary child, because on the evidence of Ovett himself, and the testimony of friends and family, she was not awash with social graces. She was blunt and brittle, and her language reflected the street markets where she and her husband worked. While recognising her faults – and they had their own vociferous fallings out – her elder son paints the broader picture, though.

'She was incredibly supportive, and immensely proud,' explains Ovett. 'She was the front that most people got if they wanted Steve Ovett. And it was a very abrupt front. She was a very market person, sort of "take it or leave it". There was no margin for greyness; it was black or white as far as my mother was concerned, and I think that was probably a portrayal that most media people found very hard to accept. I mean, most people would love to get their name in the press. And most mothers would love to see their son's name in the press. My mother adopted the attitude that Steve has got a job to do and if he doesn't want to talk to people, then that is the way things are going to be. And there is no compromise.

'The surface of my mother was very hard, but I think she was a very shy woman, a bit like me really, and socially a bit inept, the same as me. I think we were very working class people, who withdrew into a hard shell when we found ourselves in situations which we couldn't get on with. And I think she just, well, not retreated exactly, but I think she used that. She was a very emotional woman. She was never hard as nails, my mother, and I think she used that "just get on with it and to hell with anyone else" attitude as a methodology for whatever she wanted to do in life. She adopted a very "we do our thing, and if everybody else doesn't like it, well then tough luck"!

'And it was easy for me to follow in that vein – a united front, as it were. I mean, if my mother adopted that attitude and I suddenly broke out of that mould and started deviating from that way of things, then I think it would have caused problems, because then she would have had to cope with everything that I brought into the family. And it would have been very hard for her. My mother wasn't an ogre. She would give as good as she got, simple as that, and if someone was being hard on her, then she must be equally hard back.'

For those people who could take that sort of 'first-degree' personality, it wasn't necessarily a problem. Dave Cocksedge was one of the first 'outsiders' regularly to visit the Ovett household, from the early seventies. He remembers, 'She was prickly, a very prickly woman, she could take offence just like that, but I liked Gay, she was nice. I always got on quite well with her.'

Gay and Steve were very close, possibly because they were so close to each other in age. Cocksedge said that when the teenaged Ovett came to stay with him in south London, 'He would call Gay every day. They'd spend hours on the phone; they were real pals.'

Whether the early years that Ovett had spent with his grandparents had instilled some sense of guilt in Gay, that she thought she had not taken as much care of her infant son as she should have done, no one can know, and in any case Ovett says he saw her virtually every day when he lived with Pop. But when he was back living with his parents, Gay made sure everything was right, to a degree that outsiders saw as almost suffocating.

Neil Wilson was one of the few journalists ever to get past the front door of the Ovett household. It was in 1973, before the press boycott, and Wilson had recently travelled back from Germany with Ovett, after the seventeen-year-old had won the European Junior 800 metres title. That performance had earned Ovett the British Athletics Writers' Association Junior Athlete award, and Wilson, who lived in Brighton, was going to give Ovett a lift to the annual dinner and presentation in London. Wilson had children not much younger than Ovett, but detected a very different atmosphere to his own household when he went to the Ovetts' home in Harrington Villas. 'We went in and Steve came down and he was suited and booted, and Mum was all over him, dust off the shoulder and checking his tie was straight and all this sort of thing. It was probably the biggest occasion he had been to at that stage as far as any presentation was concerned, and she was a very solicitous mum and he was clearly the apple of her eye. You could see that.

'But there was a slightly strange atmosphere. The guy who was driving us, a friend of mine, picked up on it straight away. There was something odd about the atmosphere at that house. It was the fact that he was so beholden to his mum. She was the presence in the house and it was, you know, "What time are you going to be back?", and he was slightly too old for those sorts of questions, even in those days. She was overbearing almost.'

Mick Ovett was a very different character, and life on the market – exchanging banter with the customers and repartee with his peers, forays down to the bookies' and the pub, and a ciggy over a cuppa at the caff – was sufficient distraction. When he came home he just wanted to have a meal and crash into a chair in front of the telly. Gay, on the other hand, allowed herself to be drawn completely into the phenomenon which her son became.

Ovett says that his mother was a stabilising presence in his life, rather than a motivator, but long-time training partner Matt Paterson felt that she had a more formative role in the early days. 'I would say Gay was very influential on Steve's younger mental build-up, psyching himself up for races,' says Paterson. 'She was a hard taskmaster, really very aggressive, "never take second best". She always wanted Steve to be a winner and there was quite an atmosphere in the house. And driving up to the Crystal Palace when he started getting involved in a lot of the competitions, you could cut the atmosphere with a knife at times, especially as the races became progressively more important.

'I remember once we were driving up and I think it might have been the AAAs or the Olympic trials, and Steve was a little bit worried about someone, I think it was Tony Settle, an 800 metres runner. And Gay just turned round and said, "For fuck's sake, don't worry about him, you know he's no good. You can beat them all." And I'm sitting there thinking, Christ! And she was like, "What do you think, Matt?" And I'm going, "Yeah, yeah, I agree." Because every second word was "fuck" this and "fuck" that. But I do think she had a major part to play in Steve's athletic experience and upbringing.'

Paterson, like Cocksedge, is several years older than Ovett and is a forthright character, with a reputation for speaking his mind. But he admits to being cowed by Gay. 'Oh, I was like a mouse. I must admit I picked up a few swear words from Gay along the way. And when the press used to phone her up I was sometimes in the house and I used to laugh my head off when I heard some of the bleeps down the phone. She used to rip the shit out of some of these people, big time. Gay was the buffer; she was the one that just tied them in knots. She was good for him. I would just say she was a tremendous part of the Ovett build-up and philosophy, and character building, personality, everything.'

It seems incongruous that a woman like Gay, who worked in a market caff and then managed a bar, should be so ill at ease with people generally. However, several visitors had found themselves welcome at the Ovett household: athletes John Walker, Steve Scott and Craig Masback, as well as regulars like Dave Cocksedge and Matt Paterson. But women were another matter. One of the few girlfriends that Ovett had before Rachel was a training partner, Lesley Kiernan.

Ovett was seventeen at the time, and Kiernan over a year younger. Now Lesley Foley, with a teenage daughter who is Essex County Junior 1500 metres champion, she says she understands Gay better now that she is a mother herself. 'Not many people got on with Gay, in all fairness, but I think her bark was worse than anything else. But she did try to control everything he did. Her [in fact, Mick's] parents had him for quite a while, and I think maybe that was an underlying problem, trying to overcompensate. She didn't mean to be as she was. I didn't think she was really that bad. Her heart was in the right place. She wanted the best for him, and she wanted to do it properly. We all do what we can as parents, we don't know whether it's right or wrong, but you do what you think is best for your child.'

Obviously, Ovett had a much more serious relationship with his future wife Rachel, and his mother's reaction to his new girlfriend was consequently much stronger. He feels that Gay's resentment towards Rachel was exacerbated by the fact that the Moscow Olympics were so close. An Olympic gold had been the family target for many years, and suddenly he had introduced somebody else into the tight-knit group at the eleventh hour. He had started courting Rachel in 1978, but the fact that it took him around a year from meeting her to bringing her home indicates that he knew it would cause problems. He was right to be worried. It was a rancorous argument about Rachel that caused him to leave home soon after the Olympics.

Rachel Ovett is a chatty, sociable woman with a disarming manner. At the Rome Golden League in 2001, Ovett related to me, with as much bewilderment as pride, that his wife had gleaned more in a ten-minute conversation that morning with a former rival than he himself had learned in a twenty-year acquaintanceship. But the Ovett household, dominated by Gay, was too much even for Rachel Waller. 'There was always a lot of noise, a huge amount of noise, but there was quite a lot of avoidance of relationships, I think. I've never met a household like that in all my life. I found it very difficult to be in a situation where I was immediately judged, even disliked. When Gay met me, she shook my hand, but she didn't look at me. And it was very odd. I just knew how hard it was for her.

'She was so young, and it was such an unusual situation. I mean, to be pregnant at fifteen, can you imagine what that must have been like? I think she was probably quite lonely, and didn't have any friends. She made Steve so important, they were great friends, and she really didn't have anything else. I just feel that she should have trusted Steve a little bit more, but she did a brilliant job, an amazing job.'

It is a credit to Ovett that, although the rift with his mother never really healed, despite intervention by Rachel, he was able to add an amusing footnote to the mother–son relationship. Craig Masback, now the head of USA Track & Field, the American federation, had visited the family home in Brighton and trained with Ovett in the late seventies. Masback had obviously been as bemused as everyone else by Ovett's relationship with his mother. And, as Ovett recounts, in the wake of a rare outburst in a tabloid by Gay – despite the press boycott, she would call to complain from time to time – 'Craig saw this headline, "Gay Ovett Speaks Out". And he said to himself, "Oh, that explains a lot: domineering mother, no girlfriend, still living at home . . ." He thought I was gay.'

My first conversation with Peter Coe was worse than that with Gay Ovett. I called him in early 1981 to get some information on an upcoming indoor race. Peter tore me off a strip about ringing him at home, and slammed down the phone. It is perhaps unfortunate that the indoor meeting was a few days later, because, still furious, I launched into him for his bad manners. He stared at me, nonplussed, through his horn-rimmed spectacles, and said he was quite happy to talk to me while at any athletics meeting. Suffice to say, we didn't speak again for several years, despite my occasional approaches. If Seb knew about these exchanges, he never let on, and was almost always accessible and courteous, as he was with all the media. The truth was probably that he knew his old man could fly off the handle at anyone, Seb included.

Most people in athletics find it impossible to understand how a son could be coached by his father well into his mid-twenties, given the sort of problems which inevitably arise between parents and offspring. Steve Cram said it was one of the contributory factors why he never really related to Coe. Dave Warren, who eventually got to know Coe as well as he'd known Ovett, sums up the general mystification: 'An athlete's relationship with his coach is an extraordinary relationship. When your father is your coach, it's even more extraordinary, and it takes a very special athlete even to endure it. My father was always very supportive of me, and very knowledgeable. But the thought of him being my coach as well? It just wouldn't have worked. And the fact that Peter and Seb could have had that relationship speaks volumes for one or the other of them.'

The consensus was that it spoke volumes for Seb, and it certainly puts the term 'endurance training' into a different perspective. Because Peter was not an easy man to get on with, even by his own accounts. While it may be admirable to tell your children that you will help them out in anything they want to do seriously, it hardly seems necessary to add, 'If it's fun you're looking for, don't come to me.' Similarly, his admission that Seb was the only one of his four children who 'learned obedience' is something that would make most parents wince.

'I don't think there was ever a time when it didn't feel natural for him to be coaching me,' says Coe. 'It's not that he suddenly came on the scene when I was twenty or sixteen, I think that might have been complicated. But from the age of twelve he was there and driving me to cross-country races and school races. He has always been incredibly supportive of anything his kids did. My sister showed a big talent for dance very early and he made sure that she got to the Royal Ballet School. My other sister has had interests pushed and promoted and fostered. I think we would all agree that my dad is just a great believer in doing things, it was never that you had to be a runner or an artist. I always remember him talking to my brother because nothing at school excited him. He's now vice-president of Levi Strauss, but I remember Dad turned to my brother with a complete air of desperation and said, "I don't care what you do, I don't care whether you are a dustman, but just for Christ's sake be the best at something." He doesn't suffer fools very gladly, he's always been tough, but he would do anything for you. I've seen the most extraordinary acts of kindness. I mean, if somebody writes a letter to him, even today, with limited sight, he will sit and do an eight-page reply to some seventeen-year-old athlete.'

'My athlete' became a source of fun, derision and disbelief for many years, beginning in 1978, when Coe broke through into the big time. Because 'my athlete' was how Peter invariably referred to his son. Even as late as 1982, the British federation's secretary Nigel Cooper was party to a conversation which sounds like it's taken from an episode of *Fawlty Towers*. Few athletes and coaches get on with their national federation, and 1982 was the cusp of the transition from 'amateur' to professional athletics when there was a legacy of athletes feeling that they were treated like chattels. A few days before the European Championships in Athens, the federation was demanding that athletes compete in an international meeting at Crystal Palace and a row blew up about it. Ironically, as he is now the federation's CEO, Dave Moorcroft was one of the athletes at odds with the administrators. Coe was the other. Cooper relates the exchange between himself and Bill Evans, then the federation's president, and Peter. 'We went to the hotel, and there was Seb sitting with his knees hunched up on the bed, and Peter in the middle of the room, hands behind his back. He very subtly started off saying, "We will not run." I said, "Fine, then you won't go to Athens." That started it off. Peter kept saying, "I will not run." And I kept saying, "But you're not selected, Peter, we're selecting Seb." And from Seb there was a diplomatic silence, because he certainly is not a fool. But I thought it was symptomatic of his relationship with his father.' It's worth noting that Coe and Moorcroft, both world record-holders and strong favourites, substantially underperformed in Athens.

The man who had probably the biggest falling out with Peter Coe was George Gandy, the coach at Loughborough University, Seb Coe's alma mater. Gandy was an expert in biomechanics, or how weights and other resistance training could build the young Coe's body strength until he could compete with naturally powerful athletes like Ovett. Peter Coe was always the first to admit that he knew little or nothing about athletics training when he began coaching, but he was eager to learn and to approach anyone for advice. He could see the sense of using Gandy's expertise, but, as the Gandy–Seb relationship blossomed, a collision with Peter became inevitable.

Gandy recalls his first meeting with Peter. 'He was very forthright: some arrogance in the belief that you can actually get the information you need, and have the personal capability to make things work on that basis, without a great personal background. I would doubt that it's possible, but he actually proved that it was.' To Peter's credit, he sat back, got on with his own job as production manager at the cutlery company, and let his son get on with his job, with gymnasium input from Gandy. As Gandy admits, 'My relationship with Peter and with Seb was growing, and there was increasing confidence. Peter was holding me in growing trust.'

Nevertheless, Gandy felt that Seb was not relating everything back to Peter. 'The first sign that he was a politician was how he handled the situation between his father and myself. In Seb's words, "I know Peter overreacts," he said, two or three times. And I think that if Seb knew there was likely to be an overreaction from Peter on some particular issue, he probably just didn't tell him. I thought he had the courage to take on the whole world, except his father.'

Gandy was also privy to Peter's volatile nature. 'He blew hot and cold, Peter. There were times when he was very warmly acknowledging things. I went and stayed at their house. He came to my house for dinner. My wife thought he was the rudest man she ever met, and she doesn't take offence at people very regularly. But from the moment he came in the door to the moment he left, he didn't acknowledge her.'

Given Peter Coe's inaccessibility at home, when Seb started to gain success in the late seventies, Gandy increasingly became a route to Seb at Loughborough. And Gandy himself started to receive a lot of publicity and no small credit for the gym sessions that had helped strengthen Coe, in the lead up to Moscow. 'Peter was beginning to feel that he didn't like that very much,' remembers Gandy. 'I detected some degree of friction then, and I think that Peter decided it was a good move to take away Seb, to put in some preparation for Moscow, and he went away for a good couple of months. I think it was partially motivated by a wish to have Seb out of this close environment, so he could establish clear ownership. You have to understand the person. When Seb broke the world record in Oslo, with the crowds rapturously applauding, Peter is standing on top of the rostrum with Seb, waving to the crowd.'

Many people felt that Peter deserved the accolades. Dave Moorcroft was a forerunner of Coe, both at Loughborough University, and as a leading British middle-distance runner. He articulates the appraisal of many people in respect of Peter Coe. 'One of the wonderful things about many of the African runners is that they don't have artificial barriers, and neither did Seb. That's the way barrier-breakers tend to be. Look at what Paula [Radcliffe] has done. It *can't* be done. Luckily, someone forgot to tell her, and that's the way it was with Seb. A little guy like that can't run that fast, but he did it. And his dad hadn't read enough books to tell him he couldn't do it, and thank God he didn't, because you need that sort of vision.'

Even visionaries can be a pain in the arse, though; perhaps it even goes with the territory. And nobody says you've got to be a nice guy. I always had the impression Peter Coe didn't waste too much time thinking about such fripperies. He had work to do. And his life's work was his son. Since his son is, at the time of writing, the only man successfully to defend an Olympic 1500 metres title, he didn't do too badly. And his son obviously found ways of dealing with his dominating and opinionated father.

Neil Wilson, who had had an insight into Steve Ovett's home life with his mother, would also get a close-up of the Coe father–son relationship. By the late seventies, Wilson was the athletics correspondent for the *Daily Mail*, which did a deal with the Coes in the months leading up to the 1980 Olympics. He travelled to a race in Italy with Seb and Peter.

'[The race] was going to be in Turin, and we were picked up at Milan airport by the organiser,' remembers Wilson. 'Seb sat in the front and Peter and I in the back, and for the entire hour's drive Peter went on and on and on. Meanwhile, in the front Seb was asleep or appeared to be asleep. He was going on about everything, from how you made cutlery to political stories. He was very, very right wing, Peter. But it was all detailed stuff, and terribly boring. And we get the other end and checked into this hotel and Peter said, "I'm just going up to my room," while Seb said, "I'm just going to have a juice in the bar." So Coe indicated with his eyes that I should come this way and we started an interview there. But right at the start of the interview he sort of smiled and said, "Now you can see why I pretend to be asleep." '

Peter Coe remains unrepentant. Now in his mid-eighties, with a dodgy hip and deteriorating eyesight, he has mellowed a little, but not to the extent that he is going to disavow his former rigidity.

When I visited him in late 2003, my opening sally solicited the response, 'It's a rotten question, because it leads to my natural arrogance.' But there is an element of teasing in his manner. He had greeted me with, 'Where do you live exactly?' On being told, he turned to his wife and said with a frown, 'Do we talk to people from up there?'

Peter has always maintained that he was a soft touch within the family. When I telephoned early in 2004 to do some fact checking, Angela related with glee that when he had gone into hospital in the early 1990s for a hip replacement, and was logged under his original name of Percy, 'Everybody called him Perky, it just killed me.' His old friend Bob Hague says, 'I didn't like Peter at all at first. I thought he was arrogant and big-headed. I didn't realise I would end up almost loving the guy. He is completely loveable. He does overreact sometimes. When we've discussed politics I've had an eruption on my hands. But he is genuinely upset, he's not arguing for arguing's sake; it's because it's something he feels passionately about. And that's the thing about Peter. You think he's a bad-tempered — but he just feels things, he's very sensitive. But I don't think he would like to be known as a sensitive person.'

Steve Mitchell, whose house in Loughborough Coe shared in the early eighties, when they were training and listening to jazz together, has a similarly polarised view of Peter Coe. 'He's a bit dry, Peter, I like him, but I wouldn't like to get on the wrong side of him. I've had lots of discussions with him, [he's a] very articulate and a very knowledgeable man. You can have a discussion on almost any subject you like and he's got an opinion and it's probably backed up by facts. But if you only meet him occasionally, I guess people perhaps thought he was a bit stern, but he's quite a soft old bugger really.'

You can't escape history in England. Angela and Peter Coe now live in Fulham, south-west London, barely a mile from where Walter George and Willie Cummings had their epic race in 1886, when George ran the mile in 4 minutes $12\frac{3}{4}$ seconds, the world record that would last for three decades. Nothing remains of the Lillie Bridge Stadium today. It was burned down the year after

George's feat there, when the two leading sprinters of the day, Harry Gent and Harry Hutchens failed to turn out for a match (their backers couldn't decide which one should lose). The angry mob of punters, who had paid a shilling to get in and staked much more in wagers, tore the place down and set fire to it. Peter Coe, of course, made a telling contribution to the history of the mile himself.

As an engineer, he brought his profession's rigour to his son's training, even to the extent of taking an evening class in statistics, so that he could better map out the future. Malcolm Grace, as Peter's work colleague and a member of Seb's athletics club, clearly had a unique perspective on the father and son. 'They really did have a wonderful relationship. He ran Seb's life like a project. It was almost like switching a light on and off. At any other time he was Seb's father and did what a father should do, and then when we went down the track, down went the switch and there was a change of character, he became coach. The extraordinary thing about it was that he was able to divorce himself from being a father to being a coach. I've seen Peter do things that a parent couldn't do to their child.

'There was a situation where his schedule was six 600s in 84 seconds with three minutes between. Seb had done five and was puking up on the fence, and Peter did his tight "Russian face" thing. He had got three minutes' rest and Peter shouted out two minutes, one minute, thirty seconds and Seb was off. I would suggest that most parents wouldn't do that. He said he wanted six and six he did.

'Another time, we were having a Christmas party and he came across. "Hey Malcolm," he says, "don't get liquored up. I've got a job for you." He and I lifted this enormous metal weight into the back of his car, it was two inches thick, two foot six long and two foot wide, and Peter took it to his home. We got it upstairs into Seb's bedroom and he made a leg press out of it. It must have been at least two hundredweight. That was Seb's Christmas box.'

It is hard for people of my generation and younger, who didn't even have to do national service, to understand what two world wars did to the psyches of successive generations of our pre-decessors. During my chat with Peter Coe, he evoked an experience as a prisoner of war in the early 1940s, the better to illustrate a point. 'During the war, I had to sit down and make a decision. I'd seen how the Nazis had behaved, and I said, "This is no place for me, I'm off." It took me six months to get out of Europe. I was locked up by the French and the bloody Spanish. But I think if you've got the bloody-minded resolution to do something, if it matters enough, you'll do it.'

For all that self-belief, Peter Coe was never closed to the expertise of others. He couldn't afford to be, since he had started from a position of zero understanding of the sport. And he gave credit where it was due. Frank Horwill, another opinionated man who is not slow to voice criticism, explains: 'Peter wrote to me, "I've heard about your five-pace system, could you explain it to me?" To his credit, he had listened to a lot of other coaches. He had a very open mind to that sort of information. A lot of people accuse Peter of being a charlatan. He'd never been a runner, yet if there was such a subject as the physiology of exercise, he could take a doctorate in it, because he was clued up to the eyebrows.' Horwill said that some of the rumours among other coaches of Peter's domineering manner with Seb went to ridiculous levels, such as, 'Peter starts on Seb first thing in the morning and harangues him.'

Although Janet Prictoe didn't like Peter, she saw a different picture on her visits to the family home at Sheffield. 'People say Peter didn't suffer fools gladly, but that is a polite way of saying he was bloody rude, which he was, [but] I think they had a good relationship. It wasn't completely dominant. Seb was his own man, he wasn't totally a puppet of Peter. There was a mutual respect. I don't see him as being particularly controlling. I know people say that, [but] in fact it was his dad's professional attitude to it that made Coe. He was the first in this country to tackle athletics professionally, to do the high-quality training, to research it.'

Peter Coe should have written a book entitled, *Seb and the Art of Monomania Maintenance*, because, like Robert Pirsig's famous book, Peter's training philosophy is based entirely on quality and the understanding and application of it, as he explains: 'Some of the club members never understood, never came to terms with the intensity with which he was training – quality, not volume. They would accuse me, and say, "Seb is only fourteen, you're killing him, he must be doing forty, sixty miles a week at least." I said, "He does twenty, maybe twenty-three, something like that." He got third in the European [Junior] Championships on just under thirty. On quality. Every year, he was going to have to do more: there was going to come a time when he would touch sixty, seventy miles a week, which would be high for a low-mileage runner. But when you are hitting that stuff early on, there is nowhere else to go.'

There is a striking similarity with the Barry Tilbury philosophy of coaching the young Steve Ovett. And these men were instructing young runners in the wake of a generation of British middle-distance runners locked into a 140-plus miles a week training regime. For all the difference in the physiques of their charges, this careful nurturing of young talent, the insistence on quality and the progressive nature of their training regimes would lay the foundations for some of the most memorable performances in athletics history.

Former Olympian and television executive Adrian Metcalfe has an interesting perspective of the Coe father–son relationship. Metcalfe is alone in feeling that it had a strong element of theatre about it. 'A wacko dad, but a very interesting man. "My athlete", he called him, never Seb. It was a kind of game really that they played with each other. It was an extraordinary relationship. They adored each other, and they adored each other's mind, and they adored plotting and scheming.'

Maybe Metcalfe has read Kenny Moore's *Sports Illustrated* feature on the Coes, from a lengthy interview conducted in late 1979. Former Olympic marathoner, Moore stayed at the Coe home in Sheffield over the Christmas following Coe's first three world records, and in the article he describes several instances of Peter's gallows humour in exchanges with his elderly mother, before adding an explanation from Peter himself: 'My father was not a happy man, but dour. One might even say bitter. In reaction, my mother and I developed a certain humour, involving a good deal of fantasy, which I'm afraid my father never understood.' Nor did many other people. But, crucially, Seb would. And the results of their partnership would be unrivalled in the history of track and field athletics.

6

Brief Encounter

It was clear from the way he answered an unsolicited phone call that Kirk Dumpleton has not lost much sleep over the intervening thirty years, wondering whether he should have been an Olympic hero, like the pair he beat in their first ever encounter. My sister had remarked on his 'Dickensian' name, and if Dickens had created a character based on Dumpleton, he would have referred to him as 'the cheery party'. Dumpleton is an uncomplicated man, a middle-aged teacher, head of Humanities at a secondary school north of London. He was marking A-level exam papers when I arrived at the homely, hastily tidied suburban semi-detached in Luton, from which he had despatched his wife and two young children for the morning. 'Otherwise, we wouldn't have got a minute's peace,' he explained.

When I had mentioned this book to a young colleague, he asked if I'd tracked down the 'mysterious' Kirk Dumpleton. That amused Dumpleton, as it did Ovett and Coe, both of whom had got to know him well after his demolition of them in the English Schools Intermediate cross-country in 1972. Dumpleton had gone on to feature highly in domestic races right up to the mid-1990s, when a debilitating illness had ended his competitive career. So there was nothing too mysterious about him. But he was tickled to be considered a cult figure – the only Englishman to beat Ovett and Coe in the same race during their entire careers. That he didn't go on to emulate them once again says something about talented youngsters in athletics, and the thin line that divides those who make it to the top from those who don't.

Dumpleton was bright, smart, amusing, thoughtful, communicative, everything you'd expect a head of Humanities to be. And he was a middle-distance runner, ready to chew the fat. After weeks of interviewing international runners, I was back on home territory. But this wasn't so much an interview, as two old hacks discussing the thing we loved most – running. As a bonus, not only had Dumpleton won that schools race in 1972 – Ovett was second and Coe tenth – but he would later share a coach, Harry Wilson, with Ovett and would spend two years at Loughborough with Coe.

'I suppose I was one of the favourites, but only one, because I hadn't run against the northern boys that much, and it was mainly schools races in the south of England. I couldn't think of many who'd be beating me – I'd have been in the top four, five, six you'd be looking for. I only knew of Coe as a name from the north of England that you'd spot in the results. I'd come across Steve on a couple of British Milers' Club courses. I was only just getting to know Harry Wilson; it was after that I got to know Steve a bit better. They were just names really. At sixteen, I was probably training more, I was totally free of injuries that year, I wasn't doing a big mileage, about thirty-five miles a week, but some of it was absolutely lung-busting. Training-wise, it was a very good year.

'What I remember most is running at the front of the field, in second or third, and thinking, I'm jogging. I do remember Ovett loping alongside me, and thinking at one stage, He looks fairly easy. He had that sort of style where – he was always a big, strong lad – he looked easy. I think I knew from the breathing, although he looked easy, his running style, I could tell the others were breathing harder than myself. But on that particular day I felt great, I just thought, I can step this up, and I was just waiting really until the stage when I thought, I'm not going to wait any longer. You know, when you really are at your fittest, you run races, and you can't believe how easy you feel. I remember about two-thirds of the way through, I thought, I'm going to kick in, and I did, and just went. Obviously I was hurting at the end, but relatively it felt easy. It was just lovely.'

Coe recalls, 'It was boiling hot, I was absolutely sweltering. It was March and it must have risen to something like seventy degrees. I think I finished fourth or fifth in the Yorkshire Schools that year and we all lined up in the positions we finished in the county championships. I remember getting caught up really badly in traffic and for the first half-mile I was way down and I was starting to pull-back slowly. I came through really strongly at the end.'

Ovett says he can't recall anything of the race, and I don't think in this case it is the amnesia that often accompanies defeat. He claims that dyslexics have poor memories, and his close friend Matt Paterson concurs that not only did Ovett not remember many incidents in his career, but that he wasn't given to talking about the past much anyway. That fitted with other people's observations about him: he realised he was good at running, and that was it. He didn't bang on about it then, and he doesn't now. Paterson says they never talked about running when they were training. And when they meet up now, they rarely discuss the past.

For Dumpleton, who beat Ovett by 200 metres, the race would remain a career highlight. 'It was the best race I had in a way, because when I won at Brighton two years later [the Senior School-boys race], I won that in a sprint; it wasn't as easy. Steve was very good, he came up to my dad afterwards and said, "Oh, you've got a good 'un there," very charitable, very good in defeat. It was around that time that I joined up with Harry Wilson. I ended up getting to know Steve, and stayed at his house for three or four days when we were eighteen, and got to know him better.

'I always liked Steve, as an affable sort of runners' runner. He was so talented, [but] the way he talked to you, he was never patronising. He liked to joke, he was a bit of a joker, and we'd have a drink. He was never the guy who was going to knock back a lot, but he wasn't someone saying, "No, I'm only going to have a Coke tonight." He really struck you at that time as being a good bloke.

'Coe [was] quite a different personality to Steve. Seb was a lot more serious, very systematic about what he was attempting to do, [but] he would have a joke at times. But there was an occasion when some of us were running really well at Loughborough, and he did a six-mile cross-country with us. He was very fit, we knew from his track sessions. And we were just starting to be aware that he was going to be very special. Anyway, six of us beat him, but it was a muddy, wet six miles and he trailed in a bit disconsolate. Later, we were at a club do and we had a big university relay in London coming up, and one of us jokingly said, "You know, Seb, you might scrape in the team." He didn't see the funny side of it at all. He said, "Well, you know, I can see the point of a three-mile road relay, as opposed to slopping around a six-mile cross-country," and we had to say to him, "There's no doubt you're running, Seb." So he was very serious in some ways. He wasn't without humour, but it wasn't as natural as most people's.'

Coe improved steadily throughout the summer of 1972, but there was still a huge gap between the slight fifteen-year-old and the burly sixteen-year-old Ovett. That was best demonstrated when Coe was comprehensively beaten in a 1500 metres at Crystal Palace by Paul Williams, whom Ovett had slaughtered in his first 1500 metres at the venue two years earlier. Coe had the consolation of a personal best of 4 minutes 5.9 seconds, and was now regularly running in British Milers' Club races in the south. It was all part of Peter's master plan.

'There was always this feeling in Yorkshire that you had to be so much better than anybody else in the south of England to get selected,' says Seb. 'There was part truth in that because the BAAB [federation] used to say it would cost them thirty quid assembling costs to get somebody down from Yorkshire, but cost only six quid to get them to Heathrow from Hertfordshire. That was often the selection criterion. I remember my old man saying, "I don't know if this is true or not, but what we'll do is we'll just make sure there is no doubt about that."

'When I was about fourteen we went down to a huge cross-country race in Luton. We went specifically down there to turn over anybody and everybody who was in the south of England. His view was, "I'm not experienced enough in the politics of this sport, but if there is any doubt about this, we'll make a mark early." So we used to go down regularly and compete in the British Milers' Club things on Saturday nights at Barnet Copthall. We did a big cross-country race in Luton, which I won by about a minute. My old man was always slightly more aware than people in the north about what was going on elsewhere.'

Frank Horwill recalls in his inimitable fashion the first time that Coe came to Barnet. 'I first met Coe when I put on a boys 800 at Copthall. I always remember he wore a little pink cap. I remember getting 'em all together before the race. I said, "Look here, boys, the BMC hasn't paid your fares to come down here and fuck about, so get stuck in." Seb must have been a bit nervous. I forgot about this, but Seb reminded me: I looked at my watch, and I thought, Dreadful first lap, so apparently I stepped onto the outside lane, and yelled out, "If you can't do better than this, get off the track," and he said, "We ran the next lap as if we'd had a shot up our arses." He broke two minutes, he came second, and I don't think his father was very pleased at his performance, because I saw him looking at him. He wasn't shouting, but more or less saying, "What were you doing?" '

Horwill also met the young Ovett early in his career, during a weekend which demonstrated the youngster's talent and personality. 'I first met Steve at a Southern Counties Easter training event. Tom McNab was the coach in charge. Our first meeting wasn't too friendly. Tom had a habit of introducing a thing called a Funtathlon, which was having to do things like sitting down and throwing a medicine ball over your head, or doing a standing Fosbury flop. Tom was in the habit of addressing the middle-distance people as the "spastics of athletics", 'cause all they could do was run. Ovett had to do this standing Fosbury flop, and he did a higher jump than the high jumpers.

'Anyway I was in the middle of explaining some exercise, and I remember saying, "Listen carefully, because we've got to get this down," and I turned my back and I heard a raspberry. So I said, "Who did that? No need for the culprit to own up, I can see who it is. It's you! You'll never make a champion, you haven't got the right attitude." ' Ovett disputes it was him, but, as Horwill says, 'He was the one who went bright red,' and Ovett's pal Dave Cocksedge agrees that it fits perfectly the young Ovett's joky demeanour, as typified by Ovett referring to a young rival by the name of Tony Dyke as 'Tony Lesbian'. Years after the raspberry, Horwill, as founder of the BMC, presented Ovett with a world-record plaque. 'I handed it to him, and he said, "You know, this is strange, because I was told by Frank ten years ago that I'll never make a champion, and those words stung me into action." '

Despite not having a coach, Ovett continued his impressive improvement that summer. His range of ability – from 5-mile cross-country to sprints – was still much in evidence. He won the Sussex Senior Men's 800 metres title in 1 minute 53.6 seconds, then won the County Schoolboy title in a personal best of 1 minute 52.5 seconds. He won the English Schools Intermediate 800 metres, while Coe was finishing thirteenth in the 3000 metres. Ovett then won the AAA Youths 400 metres title, secured a 400/800 metres double against international opposition at a meeting in Southend, then set a national Youths record of 48.4 seconds for 400 metres. He ended his season with another 400 metres victory at Crystal Palace, then added a 200 metres race for good measure, recording another best of 23 seconds dead at a Southern Counties meeting.

But joy and satisfaction at his progress were tempered by the first tragedy of Ovett's young life. At the Sussex Schools event at the Withdean Stadium, Pop collapsed. 'No one told me until after the race. I don't know why, but they didn't,' Ovett recalls. 'He had a heart-attack at the stadium and they took him down to his flat that was just a quarter of a mile away, and he died there while I was running. He was a lovely man, my grandfather, a very gentle man. I think perhaps as a child he subconsciously moulded me a lot more than I realised at the time. I was very close to him, and it was numbing. I always thought that he would be there when I was running, and there he was dying at quite a young age. I never said goodbye to him, but he always loved watching me run, so maybe that was the way he wanted to go.'

7

Genius

What is most intriguing about Coe's career at this point was that he and Peter were firmly convinced that he was eventually going to be a 5000 metres runner. The 1500s were simply stepping-stones, and despite that personal best of 1 minute 59.9 seconds in north London, the 800 metres barely came into the equation. Coe and Ovett would surely have met at 1500 metres and the mile, but the 800 metres races and all the double debate of Moscow would not have ensued. That English Schools cross-country in Hillingdon in March 1972 could have been the only time that they would ever meet, and their great rivalry might never have happened. It would still be a few years before Coe discovered his 'true' distance.

In another of those remarkable parallels in their careers, the same thing would happen to Ovett, but from the opposite end of the racing spectrum, and a little sooner. He was the leading young 400 metres runner in the country. But a fortuitous meeting with Harry Wilson at a Southern Counties training weekend in early 1973 would turn him into a serious 800 metres runner sooner than he might have envisaged. It was a move which would eventually lead to the Moscow gold medal. Ovett arrived late at Crystal Palace to find the sprint group oversubscribed. He was sent to the middle-distance group. Ovett recalls, 'Harry said, "You shouldn't be here," and I said, "Well, what am I supposed to do?" He said, "OK, join in, and then next time you can go back to the sprint group." And that was my introduction to middle-distance running. I went from doing sprint drills back at Brighton to running 1000s with Julian Goater and Barry Smith. I came back absolutely exhausted. I remember my dad had to carry me up the stairs.'

Goater and Smith were on their way to becoming world-class 10,000 metres runners, and in his book *Running Dialogue*, Harry Wilson describes his amazement at the young sprinter's ability to emulate the distance men in his first attempt at a more strenuous training regime: 'To my astonishment he not only did the repetitions, but led on practically all of them . . . matching Julian without any apparent discomfort.' Wilson continued, 'I never dreamt I'd coach a genius, or the greatest runner in the world, yet I came to regard Steve Ovett as both of those.'

The meeting with Wilson was to prove the most crucial of Ovett's career. During the next two years, the 'dogmatic, brash extrovert', as Ovett once described the coach, would give the teenager the benefit of his broad experience. As a runner, Wilson had been a Welsh cross-country international; as organiser, he was involved with the British Milers' Club; as a coach, he had guided a generation of club runners. What Peter Coe was picking up from others and piecing together himself as quickly as possible, Harry Wilson had assimilated from years on the front line of what had seemed a losing battle against an indifferent administration and limited talent.

Lesley Kiernan, Ovett's girlfriend, was also coached by Wilson, and saw how the pair hit it off. 'Harry was such a good motivator. If Harry had told me I could climb a mountain, I would have done it. I believed whatever he told me, and I think that Steve was the same in the early days. Steve felt if Harry said you can do it, you could do it. With Harry, there was something extra, that's why he was such a good coach. For Steve, in those early days, he was the best thing that could ever have happened. They had their disagreements, but Harry idolised him, and I don't think it was because he was successful; it was because they just got on really well.'

Ovett says, 'There was a certain confidence in Harry's coaching. He'd learned by working with people with not much talent, and I think a lot of coaches did prior to the so-called golden era of the seventies and eighties. A lot of hard work went on with coaching, the [Geoff] Dyson era and people like that, very technically minded guys, public schoolboys who had gone to university and they loved their sport, become Blues at Oxford and Cambridge and God knows what else. They came out, joined the clubs, became very good track middle-distance runners or coaches and worked with a lot of club athletes who hadn't got much talent and weren't very good. They formed the British Milers' Club, people like Harry and Frank [Horwill] and Ron Holman and a few others all keen for something to happen. It was like the tinder was there, the firewood was there, they just needed a few sparks. And the bright sparks came along at the right time and *whoosh*, the combination just suddenly took off. And that heady mixture of experience, understanding and talent was what I believe produced that great era that we had.'

And the brightest spark, of course, was Steve Ovett. Almost immediately, Wilson's guidance was going to accelerate Ovett's development as a middle-distance runner. Within four months of increasing his workload with Wilson, Ovett won the Sussex Senior 1500 metres title, taking 8 seconds off his personal best, in 3 minutes 53.4 seconds. The next three months were going to see another great leap forward, as the seventeen-year-old Ovett consolidated his status as a leading junior international while making considerable inroads in the senior ranks.

In contrast to Ovett's charge into the world rankings, Coe continued his steady but unspectacular progress. The most significant improvement in his results was that he was winning more races; what's more, they were important ones. After another second place, but with another personal best of 1 minute 56 seconds, in a BMC 800 metres at Crystal Palace in mid-May, Coe won the Northern Counties Youths 1500 metres in 3 minutes 59.5 seconds, his first time under 4 minutes for the metric mile. Of those behind him, Malcolm Prince and Sean Butler would become close friends and training partners at Loughborough two years later, and Kim McDonald would go on to be the first serious athletics agent when the sport went professional a decade later.

Coe then scored two of his most significant wins to date. Coming from behind on the final bend, he won the English Schools Intermediate 3000 metres title by over 10 metres in 8 minutes 40.2 seconds. A month later, in early August, he won the AAA Youths 1500 metres title in 3 minutes 55 seconds, the championships record for his age group. Coe's achievements were enormously satisfying for both himself and his father, who realised that he was on the right track with his self-taught coaching methods.

But those accomplishments were not so much put in the shade as almost buried out of sight by the superlative performances of Ovett. Because, despite Coe's improvement, the gap between the pair was becoming a chasm, as was demonstrated in three races inside ten days in early July. While Coe was still competing in the National Youths Championships, Ovett, although still a 'junior', had graduated directly to the senior championships. The highlight of the two-day meeting at Crystal Palace was Dave Bedford's runaway victory in the 10,000 metres, setting a world record of 27 minutes 30.8 seconds. But Ovett would make a mark of his own. He finished a close second in his heat of the 800 metres in 1 minute 47.5 seconds, surprising himself and his family, who had to change their plans and stay in London because he had got to the following day's final. There, he ran even faster, 1 min 47.3 seconds, the best ever in the world by a seventeen-year-old.

A week later, he ran a mile race at Motspur Park in Surrey, where Sydney Wooderson had set his world record of 4 min 06.4 sec in 1937. Ovett chased seasoned international Nick Rose all the way to the line, and, with Rose clocking 3 minutes 58.4 seconds, and Ovett just a few strides behind, Harry Wilson confidently told his charge that he had broken the magical 4-minute barrier, less than twenty years after Roger Bannister had done it for the first time. But, in a repetition of the scenario of three years earlier when officials had denied him his 2-minute 800 metres, the clock-watchers gave Ovett 4 minutes dead!

It would be a year before Ovett finally realised the dream of every schoolboy miler and went sub-4, but, given the 109-metre difference between the 1500 metres and the mile, and their comparative times, Coe would have just been coming round the final bend as Ovett was crossing the line. That was the difference in mid-1973. And the rest of Ovett's season more than made up for the minor disappointment. He earned his first international vest in a match against France in Sotteville, where he acquitted himself satisfactorily by placing third. He then went to his first major event as a favourite, the European Junior Championships in Duisburg, West Germany.

Neil Wilson was one of just two British journalists who covered the championships. He says Ovett simply 'played with the field' before winning the 800 metres by an ace. Ovett looks back on it very differently. 'Oh no, not at all, it was my first championship. I don't think you'd ever be that confident, when you consider the field that was there – van Damme, Wülbeck, [Erwin] Gohlke – that was a fairly tough field. It was probably the toughest race of those championships. That race produced more people that went on to become champions, Olympic medallists and world champions or whatever. Lesley Kiernan was running in the women's 800 metres just the race before mine. She ran the race of her life and finished second, and literally fell into my arms as she came through the line. I remember thinking, God, you know I've got to win this one now, otherwise I'm going to have to take second place to my girlfriend, which is a bit of a hard job for any bloke to swallow.

'I came off the bend just behind Wülbeck, and van Damme was just behind me. We ran literally inch-by-inch to the line and we crossed the line all together. I mean, it was not an easy race. I just won it by a breadth of a vest, and everybody thought, Oh, you ran that one well, but really I couldn't have done much more about it. I was actually flat out and the fact that Wülbeck, the [1983] world champion and van Damme, the [1976] Olympic silver medallist, were just behind me just shows you the calibre of field in that particular race.'

Lesley Kiernan was not in the least surprised by her boyfriend's achievement. She had seen enough of Ovett to recognise the qual-ities that he brought to his racing. 'Many times, he wasn't neces-sarily the favourite, but he always managed to pull through. And if he didn't, he was so disappointed. That real want of succeeding was always there, always evident, and it was obvious that was going to happen. He trained really hard, he never shirked, and I never knew him not finish a session. That's just how he was, and, to be a good athlete, that's how you've got to be.'

Neil Wilson saw another side of Ovett as they travelled back from Duisburg together. 'We came across on a boat from the Hook of Holland to Harwich and then train all the way home to Brighton together. So I got to know him reasonably well; not that anybody ever got to know Steve terribly well. At that stage he was very questioning, he wanted to know everything you knew, and he had questions he was going to ask. Even though he was pretty raw, inexperienced internationally, it was obvious he was a man of fairly strong opinions. You could give him your opinion on something, but he didn't just take it without questioning.'

So everything was progressing well for Ovett; except, that is, for school. He has said he enjoyed his time at Varndean, but his dyslexia prevented him from shining academically. Since the school prided itself on its academic achievement, it is perhaps not surprising that Ovett's athletic successes were not highly regarded. Audrey and Ray Spinks, who organised the Brighton & Hove AC junior teams, had a son, Corin, who was also at Varndean. Audrey says, 'I don't think they were very geared to athletics. I don't think they realised just what he'd achieved. Corin and three other little boys got full colours for winning their Sussex Schools cross-country and Steve got half colours when he won the European Junior Championship.'

But there was one local headmaster who realised just how good Steve Ovett was, and he was going to become another crucial addition to 'Team Ovett'. Matt Paterson was also a member of Brighton & Hove AC, and was not going to be put off by what many club members perceived as Ovett's 'arrogance'. As head of a local school, he invited Ovett to come and talk to the kids about winning his European title. 'I didn't find him in the least bit arrogant. I think he was quite wary of people, and there was a certain amount of jealousy as well, as there often is when you get someone like

Steve with so much talent at such an early age. We just got chatting, and it was like speaking to someone of my age. He seemed to be ten years older than he actually was. We started training together, and I thought I was training pretty hard then. I had a good idea what I was doing, and then you get this young kid coming along who you thought had done no kind of background in any aerobic training. He comes along and just absolutely screws you.'

Ovett returns the compliment with interest, saying, 'Matt was probably the most significant factor, apart from Harry, in my success. He was the perfect training partner. He literally lived across the road from me. He used to get me up in the morning, not me going across getting him up. He would bust his gut to keep up with me most days, whereas I was just cruising. People said, "Why doesn't he run very well?" And I used to say, "He's always too bloody knackered after training with me to run anything like as well as he should." And to this day I don't know why he trained as hard as me and for as long as he did, because there was no apparent reason. But thank God that he did, because without that I definitely wouldn't have carried on. He was consistent; he was always there; he never failed.'

Poor Paterson. He won ten Sussex County titles during his career, but at one point he was only the third-best 5000 metres runner in his *street*. Ovett lived across the road, while Brendan Foster – who was at university in Brighton – would come and stay with his girlfriend, now wife, who lived a few doors away. But Paterson does not agree that his career suffered. 'No, I loved just running with Steve and looked forward to every session, and I mean I was just absolutely jumping out my skin sometimes. We were just like brothers and we've still got that very close relationship. All I wanted to do was to make sure that someone like him could get to the very, very top.

'I was a reasonable athlete, a club athlete, but you know when you are eighteen, nineteen, you are never going to become a world-class athlete. So all I was wanting to do was to get the best out of myself, which I think I did, and also help Steve, because there's nothing more satisfying than seeing someone you know achieve all the things that you would dream about when you were younger. I wasn't living my life through him, I wasn't looking for any adulation or any praise. I got that from Steve. He would go out of his way to thank us for what we did. Sometimes I would say, "I think I'm holding you back," and I really thought that he had to find someone else to do some training with. And eventually Bob Benn came along and did some speed work, but the distance stuff he said was fine. When I had a good day and Steve had a bad day, that was when we were probably together.'

Paterson was privy to an interior force that would help Ovett just as much as his physical prowess: his ability to switch-off, which his wife Rachel says exists to this day. Dave Cocksedge noticed it, too, saying, 'He would sit for an hour and say nothing.' Matt Paterson recalls Ovett coming to his house and sitting watching TV with his kids. 'I'd say to him, "Steve do you want a cup of tea?" and you'd get no answer. Then you'd ask him again, and still no answer. I'm thinking, What's wrong with him? He'd just be switched off, you know, completely and utterly in a trance. He could do that before races as well. It didn't matter what: you could have bombs going off around about him, he would be just utterly in his own little world. I know myself, my best races were the races where I was completely focused. I think Steve was able to do that every time he raced, whereas the rest of us, you might do it once in your lifetime.'

All the pieces had come together for Ovett. After two decades in the doldrums for British middle-distance running, Mel Watman, the editor of *Athletics Weekly*, was already enthusing about his medal potential on the biggest athletics stage in the world three years later. After Ovett's world age best for the 800 metres in the AAA Championships, Watman wrote, 'One wonders what he will be achieving in this event and the 1500m by the time of the Montreal Olympics.'

The Commonwealth Games in New Zealand in early 1974 might have provided Ovett with the invaluable experience of a major, yet low-key championship, to ready him for the Olympic maelstrom that was going to be Montreal. But in the trials for Christchurch, held at the end of the 1973 season, Ovett finished third, and was not selected. A 'lively' debate ensued, with both Mick Ovett and Harry Wilson writing to *Athletics Weekly*, which provided a forum in the absence of any public accountability from the federations and selectors.

There were to be many such selection debates during the Ovett and Coe years, generating acrimony, antagonism and reprisals. For the most part, Ovett and Coe were so good that there was no question of them not being selected. But what was ignored in 1974, even though it was clear to Mick Ovett and Harry Wilson, and to Mel Watman, was that Ovett was a young winner who would benefit greatly from the experience. The lesson that Ovett drew from his disappointment was that he would become so good that he could not be ignored in the future.

8

Burn-Up

Even in adversity, the careers of Sebastian Coe and Steve Ovett seemed to steer parallel courses. After missing out on Commonwealth selection, Ovett contracted glandular fever, and couldn't train for three months during the winter, which would have jeopardised Christchurch anyway. But the setback was only temporary, and he would charge through 1974, maintaining his assault on the world rankings.

Coe would not be so fortunate. After an 800 metres time trial in April, he sustained stress fractures (hairline breaks) in his growing legs, ammunition for some of those club members and coaches who felt Peter was pushing him too hard. Coe would miss the whole of the summer season, but there would be a beacon amid that gloom to sustain him. Running alone in the time trial, he had recorded a new personal best for the 800 metres – 1 min 55.1 seconds.

Ovett went back to junior competition at the start of the summer season, but even there he did something startling. Having run the Southern Junior 1500 metres the previous season, he dropped back down to his original record distance of 400 metres, and beat two of his 4×400 metres relay colleagues from Duisburg, setting a personal best of 47.5 seconds. If anything, the enforced rest had done him good. The results for the rest of the season suggest so, and give the lie to athletes' obsession with training. After an enforced rest, an athlete often runs much better, yet the lesson is rarely learned.

One of the men he beat in the Junior 400 metres was Bob Benn, who would later become a training partner and a pacemaker in the Ovett record-chasing years. Benn must be the only man who has ever joined an athletics club on crutches, as he relates: 'I spent my formative years doing all sports and passionately wanted to be a soccer star. Actually, I was a far better sprinter and my parents always encouraged me to do running. Eventually I was taken by my mum to Croydon Harriers. I got some forms to sign up, it was Sunday morning and in the time I was down at the track, the football club I played for rang up to say they had arranged a friendly that afternoon and would I mind playing? I agreed to play, and promptly broke my leg! I never heard anything from the football club again. They never contacted me or found out how I was at all.

'I got a two-page letter from Mike Fleet [former international and Croydon secretary] saying how disappointed he was, and that I should come down and meet everyone and get involved. That was an illustration of the difference between the two sports at that time. I was pretty green at athletics at that stage and I didn't know much about this chap Ovett. He seemed to be the life and soul of the party [in Duisburg], always laughing and joking, and it turned out that he was a pretty good athlete, too. He was very aware of what everyone was doing even at that age. He definitely lightened the atmosphere because not only was he very accomplished in his own field; he was a good man to have on the team.'

Still a junior internationally, Ovett was firmly ensconced not just among the seniors but ahead of them, most of the time. Inside a month in midsummer, he won 800 metres races in the Southern Championships at Crystal Palace and in an international match in Warsaw, took the national title back at Crystal Palace, then rectified that little mishap of his 4-minute mile by clocking 3 min 59.4 seconds, the same as Bannister had done nineteen years before, in winning at Haringey (later to be the London home track of his great rival, the currently indisposed Seb Coe).

While Coe was languishing at home in Sheffield, Ovett was packing his bags again and setting out for the Eternal City. One year after winning the European Junior 800 metres, he was going to have a crack at the senior title in the European Championships. Rome's Olympic Stadium had been the venue for one of the greatest 1500 metres races in history, Herb Elliott's victory in the Games of 1960, when he set a world record of 3 min 35.6 seconds to win Olympic gold. It doesn't get any better than that. To my generation of club runners, the one immediately prior to that of Ovett and Coe, Elliott was untouchable, a god, the only man never to lose a 1500 metres or a mile as a senior. When I finally met and interviewed him in 1985, I was not disappointed. The strength of character was as obvious as the impression that Elliott would have been successful whatever pursuit he had chosen. Ovett and Coe would eventually be mentioned in the same breath as Elliott, but not quite yet.

The 800 metres world record-holder at the time, with 1 min 43.7 seconds was Marcello Fiasconaro, a South African rugby player who had started running 400 then 800 metres, and had been persuaded by the Italian federation to swap nationalities to race for the country of his father, who had been an Axis airman, shot down by the British over Sudan during the Second World War. He had been sent to a prisoner-of-war camp in South Africa, and liked the country so much that he returned there after the war. South Africa was excluded from the Olympics and international athletics during the apartheid period, and although 'Fiasco' did not suffer anything like the treatment that Zola Budd received in Britain a decade later, he says, 'One Afrikaans newspaper had a headline, "Fiasconaro the Traitor". But most of them were really happy, because in those days I was known as a South African. It was such a pity. With Dickie Broberg, Danie Malan and myself in 1973, we would have had three in the top five in the world.'

Fiasconaro eventually returned to South Africa after his athletics career finished, but with one of his sons now a rugby player in Italy, he is a regular visitor to Rome. Fiasco is a big, jolly extrovert, and at Rome's Golden League meeting in 2003 he recalled with some amusement how the young Ovett had brashly predicted his (Fiasconaro's) demise at those European Championships in 1974. 'I became quite friendly with a lot of the British guys. There used to be a hotel, it had a swimming pool on top, and we used to meet there regularly. They couldn't believe that I was actually training for a major championship because what I used to do was train in the morning and go and lie in the sun, which was probably not the ideal build-up for a major championship. But I read an article and Ovett had said, "While Fiasconaro fiddles in Rome, I'll be burning up the track." But you know he was right. He was good, I met him once or twice, a hell of a character and also very happy-go-lucky in those days.'

In fact, Fiasconaro had been injured and unable to prepare sufficiently for the championships, but, having had some success front running, he gave it a go in the final. He delighted the crowd for 700 metres, but then, as Ovett had suggested, he went down in flames. Ovett might have been good, but he was not nearly good enough to defeat Luciano Susanj, a Slovene running for Yugoslavia. Ovett has always said that he ran a poor race tactically, which was true, but there was little more he could have done that evening. He was boxed in when Susanj kicked for home, but the Slovene won by almost fifteen metres, an incredible margin in a two-lap championship race. His time was impressive – 1 min 44.1 seconds – well beyond anything Ovett could have achieved at the time. But the young Briton fought his way to the silver medal in 1 min 45.8 seconds, a personal best and a European junior record.

Nevertheless, there is a photo of Ovett coming off the track looking disgusted with himself, and thirty years later the experience still rankles. 'That was bloody annoying. I was tactically outwitted. I don't think I would have got any better; Susanj on the day was better than I was. But I got so boxed in, I didn't really break for the silver until fifty metres from home. And I think I could have probably run a little bit faster. I was annoyed, because I did run badly that night.'

Ovett in turn was going to do some annoying – of a man who would turn out to be a close ally during his final push into the top stratum of world athletics. Andy Norman was the administrator of the Southern Counties AAA, which organised the training weekends, such as the one when Ovett had met Harry Wilson. Norman was also in charge of recruiting for the end-of season Coke Meeting, Britain's biggest TV athletics spectacular. At the end of the European Championships, he asked Ovett to run at Crystal Palace the following week, but Ovett had already arranged to tour around Europe with a new girlfriend. When Ovett refused the offer, he got the gimlet-eyed treatment from Norman, who threatened to block his entry to the following year's meeting. That would soon be forgotten, when Norman started arranging trips for Ovett, but for the time being Ovett went off on his own trip, which was in part a way to celebrate leaving school. Even to the end, Varndean schoolmasters had been oblivious to his talent. In a season when he broke 4 minutes for the mile and won a European senior silver medal, his school report for sport read, 'Continues to improve'.

Following his European junior victory the previous year, Ovett had been approached by over two dozen US universities, and offered athletic scholarships. For Irish juniors this had long been a way of getting an education while furthering their athletics careers. Track luminaries like Ron Delany – who won the Olympic 1500 metres in Melbourne 1956 – Noel Carroll and Tom O'Riordan in the sixties, and Eamonn Coghlan and Ray Flynn later all benefited from transatlantic scholarships.

British athletes had started to follow suit in the sixties. Nick Rose was one of the most successful transplants, coping with college demands while continuing his career as a British international. But many promising athletes suffered in the US collegiate system, which often stipulated several races each weekend, in order to satisfy team and coaching commitments. Ovett had discussed various further-education options with his parents. He had been to see George Gandy and the art school in Loughborough. But he would ultimately stay at home and opt for Brighton Art College. He got swiftly into character by growing a goatee beard.

His wife Rachel says that if he hadn't pursued a career in running, Ovett would have made a good architect, such is his spacial awareness and design capabilities. But he also put his practical ability to good use in his hobby of collecting cars. The next year cannot have been so arduous, because, even with training for the Olympics and pursuing the art foundation course, he found time to rebuild a sports car from scratch. In the end Mick had to beg him to sell one of the other three jalopies cluttering the pavement in front of the family home. The goatee lasted longer than the college career, because he dropped out when he failed his exams and was asked to repeat his first year.

His parents were far from wealthy, although good and plentiful food was never going to be a problem with the Ovett market stall, and they offered to underwrite his athletics career. 'I think I took the easy option,' Ovett recalls. 'I mean, if you can get your washing done for you and your cooking done for you and someone giving you pocket money each week, as opposed to doing all your bloody washing at university and all your cooking or whatever ... I took the easy way out. If it hadn't have been offered, I don't think I would have taken advantage. I was a successful athlete, I was always winning, so they had a great deal in return for what they were doing in a sense. They had a great deal of pride in their son, and it went on. It started at the English Schools and it went right the way through to the Olympics. So they had the perfect, non-stop climb up the ladder. I think it was difficult for them, but I think it would have been harder if that success hadn't come along. If they had put all that work in and didn't have any success, then it would have been terrible.'

9

Boycott

The highlight of the 1974 season had been a performance that still stands out in the 150-year history of organised athletics – Filbert Bayi winning the Commonwealth Games 1500 metres title in Christchurch from the front, and setting a world record of 3 min 32.2 seconds. It provided a lesson that would not be lost on Peter Coe. When his son, now eighteen, and having his first race in around eighteen months, returned to the track in early March 1975, he won the National Junior Indoor 1500 metres title with a tactic that earned him the highest praise from *Athletics Weekly*: 'Coe leading every step of the way in a manner Filbert Bayi would have been proud of.'

Three years later, Coe would be widely criticised, accused of being naïve for using a similar tactic in the European Championships 800 metres in Prague. He is still annoyed by those jibes. 'A point that very few people make in track and field is that front running is actually a tactic in itself. It isn't a negation, it is actually utilising a strength. Now you may choose to do it because, like [Dave] Bedford, there is not much else you *can* do when people start kicking in with 52-, 53-[second] laps at the end of a 10,000 metres. But it *is* a tactic. Nobody would say that Ron Clarke was clueless tactically. He ran from the front, and there is a perfectly good reason for that.

'My old man sent me out regardless of the fact that John Walker, Dave Moorcroft and Eamonn Coghlan were in a mile race, but to run to schedule. His view was "I don't care if you finish sixth, seventh or eighth, but one of these days you have to learn, you've got to understand what it's like to really commit and hurt." '

This was the next stage in the Coe apprenticeship, and it was a tactic that he would use widely and frequently, and to good effect, over the next two years. In his first race after injury had blanked his 1974 season, he had won another title with another personal best, 3 min 54.4 seconds.

Coe was back in from the cold, while Ovett was back out in it, creating another bit of history when winning the National Junior cross-country by over 200 metres. He was still running the occasional 400 metres on the track, but here he was, defying the odds again, and winning a 10,000-metre cross-country race, and by a street. A further measure of the progress he had made in the previous two years was that Kirk Dumpleton and Kevin Steere, youngsters who had beaten him into second place in the English Schools cross-country championship races in 1972 and 1973 were now finishing over a minute behind him.

Coe continued his front-running tactics with equal success in his first outdoor race of the season, another personal best in the 1500 metres, 3 min 49.7 seconds in Spenborough near his Sheffield home. He carried on in a similar vein, occasionally varying the tactics by taking up the running from halfway in a series of races across the north of England. But the results were invariably the same. He won the Northern Junior 1500 and 3000 metres on successive weekends, then the AAA Junior 1500 metres a month later, in another personal best of 3 min 47.1 seconds. A future international rival, Ray Flynn of Ireland, finished third.

'That was the first time I had seen him,' says Flynn. 'He was still very boyish. I had heard a lot about him, and I saw his dad outside the stadium holding his spikes. It was very, well, I wouldn't say odd . . . I mean, sometimes when you see what is perceived to be a very overbearing father, who was always with his son and they were almost only seen together and he was the prodigy runner. I think there was intrigue.'

It would only add to the Coe mystique. And that was going to be introduced onto a larger stage. That victory in the AAA Championships secured Coe his first international race, a 1500 metres in a junior match against Spain and France, at Warley in the West Midlands. There he would meet another man who would spend a long career chasing Coe's and Ovett's shadows, José-Manuel Abascal. Coe won, with Abascal five metres behind.

Although Ovett was on a bigger stage, it was to be a season of mixed fortunes. He had a poor start to his outdoor campaign. Filbert Bayi made his British debut in late May, two weeks after breaking the world mile record (3 min 51 seconds in Jamaica). The Tanzanian now held both the 1500 metres and mile records, but what looked in the early laps of the Emsley Carr Mile at Crystal Palace like an opportunity for Ovett to measure himself against the very best disintegrated as he dropped from being a close second to Bayi at halfway to finishing sixth. Bayi ran impressively from the front to victory. Ovett looked sluggish and thought he might be suffering a recurrence of glandular fever.

The next month would prove to be the worst of his career, as he was beaten in successive races in East Germany and Stockholm, the latter being another hammering in the mile, this time by John Walker of New Zealand, whose potential match against Bayi for the Olympic title the following year was eagerly awaited. Even though Ovett then started to win again, in both the European Cup semi-final and the AAA Championships 800 metres at Crystal Palace, he was perplexed by what he perceived to be his poor form.

His dissatisfaction may have contributed to two incidents which were later seen to be supremely indicative of the Ovett persona. In winning the AAA title, he admitted that he had badly jostled old perennial Pete Brown, who had been a sort of guardian to him in his first senior international race two years earlier. Ovett said, 'I hit him a couple of times, which is a bit unfair. I could have been disqualified, and I would not have argued.' But it was a spat off the track following his European Cup semi-final race a fortnight earlier that became a cause célèbre. The British team had won through to the European Cup final a month later in Nice, and Ovett was asked as a matter of course about his chances. He surprised everyone by saying that he wasn't going, that he had already arranged to travel to Athens to watch Lesley Kiernan race in the European Junior Championships. Terry O'Connor, who was the athletics correspondent for the *Daily Mail*, was incensed and accused Ovett of being unpatriotic.

O'Connor is a bluff character, whose erect bearing, clipped diction and military manner betray his wartime service in the Royal Air Force. But he knows his athletics. He has followed the sport since the forties. He saw Gunder Hägg and Arne Andersson run; he saw Sydney Wooderson win the European title in Oslo in 1946; and when his paper, the *Evening News*, sponsored athletics in the fifties, he was the meeting promoter. He covered every Olympics from 1948 to 1988, and also wrote Derek Ibbotson's biography. But he is old school. Thirty years later, O'Connor is still slightly abashed by the incident. 'I recall him saying that, although he had been invited to run for Britain, "It depends if it suits my circumstances." Now, I'm not a loyalist, I wouldn't say I'm overly patriotic, but I had served in the air crew in the war and it just seemed astonishing to me that anyone could turn down their country. I said to him, "You can't do that! It's an honour," and he dismissed it.'

Neil Wilson, who would eventually take over from O'Connor at the *Mail*, recalls, 'It was embarrassing. Those of us who were young and not working on national papers at the time were sheltering in the back, keeping our heads down. It was in that little back room that exists at Crystal Palace, very small and the athletes sat on a chair and everybody grouped around, standing up above. It must have been quite intimidating for young athletes. I'm not saying that Ovett was intimidated. He certainly decided from that moment that he would never come back.'

Ovett says he had already begun to be annoyed by some of the inane questions he was being asked at previous meetings, which contributed to his reaction. 'I genuinely felt that I wasn't really doing much by going up to the press box. It was a bit like a royal command, you had to ascend the steps, sit down and be grilled, and I thought, Hang on a minute, what am I getting out of this?

I'm running, I'm not getting paid for it, these guys are sitting there, they don't know much about the sport, they haven't really done their homework, they haven't found out, sometimes, even what my name was. Because they'd say, "Could you spell your name, and where were you in the race?" And I thought, Well, why bother with this? There were a couple of occasions where people said pretty ridiculous things, got a bit on their high horse and I thought, That's enough, and I just stopped. Of course, that created even more problems because they couldn't comprehend that. They had never had anybody who didn't want to speak to the press. It went on and the bad-boy Ovett image obviously ensued from that, which was fine by me.'

As chairman of the British Athletics Writers' Association later, it fell to O'Connor to try to mend fences, in order to get Ovett to the annual dinner. 'I wrote him a letter and said I might have gone over the top or something like that, and he eventually turned up. I actually got on with him quite well. But he was right. Some of that stuff that comes out is such drivel. There is terrifying ignorance. The majority of people who covered athletics, eighty per cent of them, knew nothing about it. I was taught that you can't write about track and field, or rugby, football or any particular game, well unless you know the history of the sport.'

The 'O'Connor incident' has grown over the years to include Ovett taking a chair, plonking it in front of the assembly, and telling them to interview that. But, as O'Connor admits, and Dave Cocksedge concurs, it was O'Connor who stalked out, unable to contain his patriotic rage. Ovett followed, never to return. He would always be asked by a press attaché on the infield for a comment following his numerous successes at Crystal Palace over the next decade, and he would occasionally proffer a reply. The one everybody remembers is 'Happy Christmas'. It was the middle of August.

One repercussion for O'Connor was a brief conversation that Dave Cocksedge recalls from being in the Ovett household when the *Mail* journalist phoned to ask about Ovett's racing programme. Gay replied, 'I don't know, but you'll be the last to find out.'

But after all the controversy, Ovett did in fact run in the European

Cup final in Nice, and duly won impressively. However, this season ended as indifferently as it had begun, with two comprehensive defeats in the mile, both to John Walker. On the latter occasion at Crystal Palace, the meeting was held up due to an IRA bomb threat.

Coe was having a calmer and more upbeat finale in his first international championship. He didn't win the European Junior 1500 metres in Athens, but he did get a bronze medal behind the statuesque Finn Ari Paunonen, whose feats had resulted in him being touted as a talent to equal Ovett. Like so many others, Paunonen did not ultimately live up to his promise, but he was too good for Coe in Athens. Coe again showed his aggression by leading in the early stages, and although he couldn't contend with Paunonen's final lap of 55 seconds, he was rewarded with yet another personal best, 3 min 45.2 seconds.

There was still a substantial gap between Coe and the senior ranks in which Ovett – despite the minor setbacks – was now operating with such distinction and character. But that gap was inexorably closing.

10

Blown Away

Coe began to blossom at an accelerated rate both socially and athletically after he left home to go to Loughborough University in autumn 1975. Resident coach George Gandy would not initially have a great deal to do with Coe, but his input, as was mentioned earlier, was eventually crucial. I have known Gandy for over thirty years, since a fortuitous combination of a little talent, a lot of training, competitive fortune and the wholesale incompetence of rivals resulted in your scribe winning the first British Milers' Club race organised by Gandy, when he was a teacher in the West Midlands, prior to going to Loughborough in the early seventies. The race was at Warley Stadium, where Coe had his first international race and victory. This minor footnote to British athletics history is intended to convey in terms other than Olympic gold medals just how good Coe and Ovett would become. When I won that race in Warley, I knew that I was fitter than 99.9 per cent of the population could ever conceive of being in terms of running. But Ovett and Coe at their best would have beaten me in a mile by the length of the finishing straight.

With his usual thoroughness, Peter Coe had consulted Gandy about the biomechanics aspect of his training programme at Loughborough, which in those early days of his tenure was more geared to sprinters. 'Peter had some concerns about Seb's running action in those days,' recalls Gandy. 'We had another guy who had a similar sort of arm action and his nickname was "Coat Hanger".

Seb's was a little bit like that. It was shoulders up a bit, elbows up a bit, which was mainly the upper-body response to the fact that he had relatively long and quite strong legs.

'He started joining in the gym conditioning work. I wasn't a hundred per cent sure at that time of the extent of the relevance for 1500 metres runners, but Seb wanted some connection with 400 metres-type runners. I remember a little bit of a problem with one of the exercises we did back then: hanging from wall bars and raising the legs straight to horizontal position. The first time Seb came he overdid it, and actually missed a session. I had a slight concern because I thought maybe I'd lost this guy after one session, but sure enough he came back.'

Gandy has always been an easygoing and amiable character who would readily join in with his students on social occasions. He was well placed to see just what sort of character had joined his training group. 'At that stage I don't think he was particularly used to the rough and tumble of intermingling with the kind of people he initially came into contact with. And the thing was, he was small, slight and appeared to be not overly socially confident.

'Seb was never a big socialiser or drinker, but he did grow to like the student scene. It was somewhere he felt comfortable; he wasn't treated like a star. And people respected him because he did just mix in and behave as normal. On one very early occasion, there was a typical student thing where the demand was that certain people downed a pint in one go. I had to do mine, then Seb got the same demand, and being a very protective kind of person, I said, "I'll down it for you, Seb." But he said no and took it, and it is not a major thing, but he did it.'

Something else that would emerge at Loughborough was the aforementioned caddish element. Although they had a two-year relationship, Janet Prictoe still wonders whether she and Coe were actually the 'item' that she thought at the time. Several people who knew the couple confirm that they were, but Prictoe still has her doubts. She remembers how the relationship began, at one of the first warm-weather training camps that federation sponsors organised for promising juniors in early 1976.

'The first trip that they took us on was to Gibraltar. Seb was there and neither of us was that impressed with the set-up. We just hit it off, we got on because we had a similar sort of humour, and it went from there. I had actually applied to go to Birmingham University to do English and I ended up applying for Loughborough. Seb contacted George Gandy, and I think he helped me on my way because my A levels weren't brilliant. So Seb actually smoothed the path a little bit and I started that September.

'He had a very good sense of humour. He was very witty, very funny, he's very slick really and I was a young, naïve seventeen-year-old. When I look back I realise he won me over. He's very charming, he's the perfect boy next door, take home to mum and all that sort of thing. I see things differently now. I think if he was interested in somebody he could just charm the pants off anybody.

'I considered us very much an item. Over time Seb got more and more famous, and although I was running internationally I wasn't making a mark like he was. There was a children's programme on TV, Seb went to present an award and whilst he was there he met this producer. I didn't know anything about this; I don't think he mentioned it to me. One weekend shortly after, he said he was going back to Sheffield to do some training. I never thought anything of it and I was swotting for my exams. That same weekend Loughborough were playing at Twickenham in a big rugby match, and a couple of coach-loads of supporters went down. On the Monday morning I was at gymnastics, and one of my fellow gymnasts said, "Oh, we saw your boyfriend this weekend jogging round Richmond Park." So he had been rumbled in a big way. Somehow I put two and two together with this producer. I remember him coming into my room, and I said, "Did you have a good time in London this weekend?" And he went, "Oh, I was in Sheffield," and I said, "I never want to see you again," and that was it. That was the end of our relationship, as dramatic as that. In the end, I actually took a year off university because I couldn't cope with seeing him.'

Despite her disappointment, Prictoe had always recognised the talent and application of her former boyfriend. And she had an offbeat example of his strength, despite the slight frame. 'I always thought he was like poetry in motion, exceptionally talented. I can remember the first week I went to Loughborough, I was living in a converted garage, which was part of somebody's posh house, and I had to cycle into Loughborough. For some reason, I accompanied Seb, who was going on a run, and he went up a really steep hill, but I couldn't get up it with the bike, and I was fit in those days. I remember him running up the hill, pushing me and the bike and I was thinking, Gosh, I thought I was fit, but he must be phenomenally fit to be able to push me and this bike up this whacking great hill and then just carry on. He was exceptional and he was focused.'

All those attributes were combining to push Coe closer to his goal. Between races for Loughborough and his commitments back in Yorkshire, where he continued to support the county championships, he opened the summer season with personal bests at 800 (1 min 52 seconds) and 1500 metres (3 min 43.3 seconds). This was the first year that Coe and Ovett began to appear regularly at the same meetings. When Ovett won the Inter-Counties 800 metres at Crystal Palace in 1 min 47.3 seconds, Coe was being taught an interesting lesson in miling tactics by Glen Grant, who put in a hard third lap to get away from him, then continued with another fast last lap, to leave Coe twenty-five metres back, albeit with another personal best, of 4 minutes 2.4 seconds. Ovett won the Olympic 800 metres selection race at Crystal Palace the following week in part one of the trials for Montreal. In part two a week later, only the vagaries of qualifying-heat draws prevented another historic Coe–Ovett confrontation in the 1500 metres trials. Coe was in the first heat and Ovett in the second. There is little doubt who would have come out on top, since Ovett won the final the following day in a personal best of 3 min 39.9 seconds, while, despite taking a sliver off his own best with 3 min 43.2 seconds, Coe finished seventh in his heat and didn't even qualify for the final. But he did run faster than Ovett in those heats, as the latter recorded only 3 min 44.4 seconds to reach the final.

That final was significant for the unveiling of the Ovett wave.

Matt Paterson was watching in the stands with Gay Ovett. 'He ran down the straight and there was no gap and he ran between David Moorcroft and someone else [Frank Clement], and he turned round and waved to myself and his mother in the stand. And I just thought, What is going on here? It was one of the most exciting races I've ever seen. And he wasn't doing it to be arrogant at all. It was just his excitement; he loved it. It was the first time he waved to the crowd. He did it so many times [after that] and people would say, "What's he waving to the crowd for? He'll miss out on a world record?" Steve didn't worry about that. He just loved to wave to his mum, to say he was OK. It was an entertainment.'

Ovett maintains that it was exuberance, 'a bit of fun'. But the Ovett wave would come in for much criticism over the years, including from his greatest rival, who recalls being told in no uncertain terms by one of his elder training partners in Sheffield, 'Don't ever let us fucking catch you doing that in the finishing straight, son.'

While Ovett was gearing up for his Olympic debut, with much expectation from himself, his growing legion of fans and commentators, Coe was quietly reducing his 800 metres best to 1 min 50.7 seconds in a match that would become as much a staple of his athletics year as the county championships, the Loughborough versus AAA fixture. Ovett was only marginally faster in an 800 metres in Finland, but that race was significant for two reasons. It was the first international race that Andy Norman fixed up for him independently of the federation, thus earning him a couple of hundred dollars. And he put down a competitive marker for the following year, because he beat John Walker of New Zealand for the first time.

The 1976 Olympic Games would result in personal bests for Ovett at both 800 and 1500 metres, and provide him with an experience that would prove invaluable in Moscow four years later. But Montreal was a huge disappointment for him. The Crystal Palace public and the national television audience were seeing a performer confident and competitive enough to nudge opponents out of the way if necessary, then waving to them as he won. The national press was seeing an arrogant and bombastic yob who wouldn't talk to them. But in Montreal, Ovett was a twenty-year-old whose demeanour was largely a front for his own uncertainty. He was out of his depth.

He acquitted himself well enough at first in the 800 metres, winning his first round, and placing third in the semi. But in the final, he was drawn in lane eight in a year when the international federation was experimenting with running three-quarters of the first lap in lanes, in an attempt to prevent the collisions that are part of the 800 metres game (as the delicate Coe would discover). Ovett ran the first lap far too slowly, and his race was over. He finished fifth in 1 min 45.4 seconds, a time which would win him gold four years later.

'I felt as if I'd been hard done by, because I was a fairly young athlete and I really did want to run well and thought I could have run a lot better than I did. I never saw anybody for half the race. It's a bit like having a 5000-metre run and you are running for 2500 and then they suddenly bring everybody else in. I was an inexperienced young lad out in lane eight, there was the greatest 400 metres runner of all time [Juantorena] on the inside running a very fast 400 metres, which I suppose I would have expected, but you don't know. You don't go off and run 49 [seconds] from lane eight because you could find yourself ten yards in front of the rest of them and you blow up. So it was a very unfortunate situation for me and I felt disappointed. I felt a bit let down by my sport because after that they changed it back again, and it [the experiment of running in lanes] never got repeated.

'I felt very down and my dad must have sensed that when I phoned him up. He flew across and took time off work to console me. My dad was always a bit like that. He never said much but whenever I needed him he was always there. It was good to see him. He was laughing because he was totally out of his depth: fine hotels and whatnot to eat. He'd never done it before. He had only probably travelled away once before in his life.

'It came to the 1500 metres and I thought, I've got another shot at it. And, I don't know if it was in the heat or the semis, but I was

The Mighty Atom – Coe at 13 is only a year younger than the clubmate behind him

'Did he win? Those little pair of legs went . . . and he was away. He won easy' – Ovett at 13

Seb at 16: the Sheffield schoolboy with visions of bringing the world mile record – once held by Derek Ibbotson – back to Yorkshire

Nature Boy – Ovett at 19

A rare shot of Ovett (aged 17) with sister Susie

Family debate – Angela Coe and Seb, aged 21

Ovett's first international title, 1973. 'He wasn't necessarily the favourite, but he always managed to pull through'

Running dialogue – coach Harry Wilson and Ovett, aged 22

The future Olympic 1500 metres champion takes on the current title holder, John Walker, in an 800 metres at Crystal Palace in 1977

Student in form – 1977

Above 'Olaf who?' Prague 1978, after the European 800 metres final

Left Zurich 1979 – Coe's third world record in 41 days

Opposite page The Moscow 800 metres – a work of art for Ovett and Italian painter Angelo Titonel

'. . . treading in his footprints
before the dust could settle
there' – a Homeric rivalry

Ecstasy!

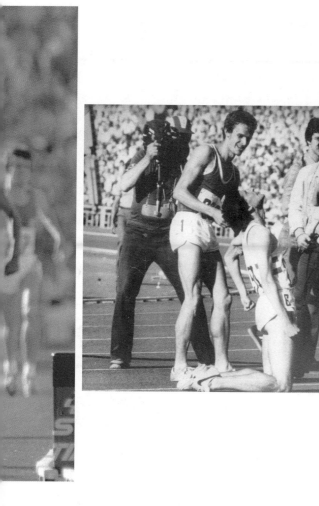

Peter Coe and Seb

1981. Brussels. Another record falls . . . and another, Zurich

Ovett blooms late in 1983 with the world 1500 metres record in Rieti

Coe begins 1983 with an 800 metres indoor world record (*above*), before the season falls apart. A year later he climbs Richmond Hill on the way to scaling another Olympic peak

Don't look back – Ovett's only win in LA, in his
1500 metres heat

Opposite page The finest, maybe the final flowering of the Great Tradition. Ovett, Cram and
Coe in LA

After the Olympic 800 metres, Los Angeles – 'We're too old to be playing with fire'

1989 – 'Didn't you used to be . . . ?'

in the same race as Dave Moorcroft, and I was running well, and with about a hundred and fifty to go Dave Hill [of Canada] tripped in front of me and fell. I literally hurdled him, and as I hurdled him the others just went round the outside and qualified for the final. And I thought, Ah, the Olympics and me are not destined to come together. I saw my dad and again it was great. He said, "Well there was nothing you could have done there, it was just bad luck." The next year in Düsseldorf, I proved that I could run 1500 and I knew that I was virtually in the same shape going into that race in Montreal, but I just didn't get the chance in the final. That's not to say I would have done anything, but I would have loved to be in the final.'

Ovett was just one of many British disappointments in Montreal. There were some good performances, but they were obscured by the inevitable bottom-line assessment: how many medals did the British win? The answer was one, a solitary bronze for Brendan Foster in the 10,000 metres. And even that was a disappointment, because Foster had emerged as a long-distance runner of world-record class. Furthermore, given that his competitive record against Lasse Viren, double-gold winner from Munich 1972, was 10–2, there was hope, even expectation, that Foster would beat the flying Finn. But Viren triumphed again, at both 5000 and 10,000 metres.

Back at home, out of the limelight, but in a season of significant development across the board for Coe, the most important event happened in the downbeat location of Stretford in the suburbs of Manchester. Coe had run there several times, in Northern Championships and British Milers' Club races. It was in one of the latter events that the seismic shift occurred. Coe front-ran his way to a startlingly improved 800 metres personal best of 1 min 47.7 seconds, three seconds faster than he'd ever run before.

There had already been a change of emphasis that year: Coe's desire to be a miler had resulted in Peter beginning to abandon plans for the 5000 metres. But this was of a different order altogether, as Coe recalls. 'It was a big chunk. I remember driving home with Peter in the car in complete bloody silence across the

Snake Pass and we got to the other side of Glossop, and he turned to me and said, "I think we might have found your distance." '

On that night, 8 August 1976, the Coe–Ovett rivalry was really forged. Henceforth, Coe would be concentrating on the classic combination of 800 and 1500 metres, the same as Ovett. Their paths were marked out, and it was only going to be a matter of time before they crossed. But Coe still had a lot of work to do before he'd be ready for that encounter. 'I was physically less mature,' he confirms. 'I was not as strong as he was, I didn't start off with his advantages. I could run quickly, but I really had to work on the weights and the circuits and I had to work on upper-body strength and hamstring strength to have a very good kick. If I hadn't done that, I would not have been a kicker. If I hadn't lifted tons of bloody weights every year, you know, I would not have done what I did in LA, I would not have done what I did in Moscow, I wouldn't have done what I did in Brussels. And I don't think Steve, because Steve was so physically gifted, I don't think he actually had to go through a lot of those things. Steve got away with running mileage, doing track work – but not always on the track, doing it on grass.'

Coe was already well into Gandy's gymnasium conditioning, and he also set about reducing the gap on the track with a will. While Ovett was restoring some self-esteem by beating newly crowned Olympic 1500 metres champion John Walker in an 800 metres in the AAA Championships, Coe was improving his 1500 metres best behind another New Zealander, Rod Dixon, who won the title in 3 min 41.4 seconds. Coe was fourth in 3 min 42.7 seconds. The time was roughly equivalent to a 4-minute mile, and in his last race of the season Coe would go sub-4 for the first time, in the Emsley Carr Mile at Crystal Palace on 30 August. His colleague at Lough-borough, Dave Moorcroft, who had finished seventh in the Olympic 1500 metres, won the race in a personal best 3 min 57.1 seconds from Filbert Bayi (who had raced the day before in Italy). Eight men broke 4 minutes. Coe was seventh in 3 min 58.4 seconds.

But it was a mile in Gateshead the week before that had made everybody sit up and take notice of the slight nineteen-year-old.

Brendan Foster was now working for the local council and promoting the meeting. 'I was doing the two miles and John Walker, the Olympic champion, came and ran the mile,' remembers Foster. 'And there was this young kid from Sheffield who set off like he was trying to win it, to beat the Olympic champion. And Seb was clear of John Walker with a lap to go. It was like "Whoops, hang on a minute, who is this and what is he doing?"'

Nearly half the finishing straight behind, with just one lap left to run, Walker was asking himself the same question. 'It was a windy, horrible day and Coe took off, about thirty, forty metres in front the whole way, and he stayed there right until the last fifty metres and I ran him down in the straight and won the race. Thank Christ it was really windy that day, and the wind blew him backwards and I managed to catch him, because I wasn't going anywhere. I wrote to my coach and said, "I've just run against a little guy and if it hadn't been windy, then he would have beaten me. I don't know who he is, but it's unbelievable." I couldn't understand how somebody could even do what he did. And that was Coe.'

The Fatman

I always knew when Andy Norman wasn't being truthful. He would append a plaintive 'Honestly!' to even the most minor fabrication, almost as if he was trying to convince himself at the same time. We haven't spoken in around fifteen years, due initially to various newspaper exposés I'd done on his antics, such as manipulating dope tests. But the bullying tactics, both private and public, that he was to use on a profoundly disturbed Cliff Temple, which contributed to the suicide of that fine *Sunday Times* athletics correspondent in 1994, have put Norman beyond the pale of most civilised company in Britain.

But he was a seminal figure, probably the most important person – Coe and Ovett themselves apart – in the development of British athletics over the last thirty years, transmuting it from a backwater, occasional Olympic pastime to a frontline, highly mediatised professional sport. At the same time, he was an invaluable ally to the emerging Steve Ovett, and he would ultimately have a significant role to play in the career of Sebastian Coe, too.

Norman comes from Ipswich and joined the police force straight from school in the late fifties. An early measure of his capabilities was his promotion at twenty-three to become the youngest sergeant in the Metropolitan Police Force in London. He was a good runner, sub-50 seconds for 400 metres and 1 min 54 seconds for 800 metres, but an injury truncated his competitive career, and it was as an administrator for the Metropolitan Police Athletics Club that his true qualities – for organisation – came to the fore. His successful running of the police team made him some powerful contacts, notably Gilbert Kelland, who became Assistant Chief Commissioner of the Met (which made Kelland's nomination on the tribunal to judge Norman's subsequent involvement in manipulating drug tests highly questionable, but that's another story).

By the mid-seventies, when Ovett was emerging as a potential world-class talent, Norman was ideally placed to team up with the talented youngster bandwagon. The good work that he was doing for the Met Police AC had resulted in him taking over as administrator for the Southern Counties AAA, which organised the training weekends that had introduced Ovett to a wider athletics community. The Southern Counties' administrative area covered Brighton and Hove, home to Ovett and his club. Athlete and administrator would have been aware of each other very early, since Norman was also the guiding force in the graded meetings promoted by the SCAAA. These events were extremely popular and very successful. The rationale was the same as that of the British Milers' Club, with a wider remit: to unite athletes of similar capability in peer events; for example, milers who could run between 4 minutes 20 seconds and 4 minutes 30 seconds would run together, and those who were ten seconds slower would run in a different race. The idea was to improve standards, bring the 4-minute-40 guys and gals down to 4 minutes 30, and so on. The meetings were so successful that athletes would even come from outside the SCAAA area to compete. Dave Moorcroft recalls coming down from the Midlands to race, and Coe came from Sheffield. Ovett set a couple of early personal bests in the meetings.

Norman quickly acquired a reputation for organisation and hard work, allied to a capability to think on his feet and take decisions. His agile and compendious mind was also apparent. Part of later Norman lore was his capacity to organise an international meeting 'on the back of an envelope'. But he was also a bit of a bully, the caricature of the suburban copper: bluff, narrow-eyed, foul-mouthed. None of these 'qualities' was necessarily a disadvantage. For the best part of a century the sport had been run with patrician indifference by public schoolboys, intoxicated with Corinthianism and the specious Olympic imprimatur of amateurism. They were as remote from working-class kids like Ovett as London's West End theatre was from the Punch & Judy show on Brighton beach.

One man impressed with Norman's organisational abilities was Mike Farrell, an Olympic 800 metres finalist in 1956, who was Norman's equivalent at the Midlands AAA. 'Norman was doing enormous good for the sport at the time,' recalls Farrell. Another grass-roots administrator, Doug Goodman, remembers him in a more equivocal light. 'The way he shouted and talked to people sometimes was disgraceful, but, on the other hand, he was really helpful to a lot of athletes.' Farrell's ultimate summation was 'an honest rogue'.

The graded meetings involved mostly locals and junior, upcoming athletes like Ovett, Moorcroft and Coe. But Norman's application would soon be noticed elsewhere, and allowed him to establish a foothold on the international stage.

The social changes of post-war Britain, the collapse of class barriers, were slow to percolate into amateur sport, but even university athletes were fed up with being treated disdainfully. And a British athletes' association called the International Athletes' Club had grown in the years following the Tokyo Olympics.

Two- or three-nation matches were still the norm for international competition through to the 1970s, and still exist today at junior level. The Golden League and Grand Prix circuit were yet to come, although Zurich had put on its Weltklasse meeting, often described as the one-day Olympics, since the late 1950s. Scandinavia, energised by the Hägg–Andersson matches in the 1940s, also had an 'independent' circuit.

Adrian Metcalfe, a voluble 400 metres runner from Yorkshire with an Oxford classics degree, was instrumental in setting up the first athletics 'extravaganza' in Britain. He had retired at twenty-two, as was the norm in the sixties, and gone to work first as a print journalist before moving into Independent Television. Until then, athletics on television had been strictly the preserve of the BBC, but the combination of an executive from Coca-Cola looking for a new advertising vehicle, Metcalfe's boss John Bromley and Metcalfe himself as the general secretary of the International Athletes' Club resulted in the birth of the Coke Meeting in the late 1960s.

Metcalfe still works as a freelance TV adviser to several international sports bodies, including the IAAF. He recalls the genesis of the Coke Meeting: 'The IAC applied for a permit for a meeting at Crystal Palace, and somebody signed it, a bit cautiously, because they didn't like the idea of athletes running anything. Athletes were dirt. Then, suddenly, we've got Ron Clarke, Kip Keino and a whole raft of top names.

'The BBC went mad, they tried to stop it, but they couldn't because it was a five-year agreement. It was good for British sport, it was good for British athletics, an enormous number of British athletes wouldn't have been able to run in their own country against competition of a standard they hoped to attain. So it lifted the general standard. And ITV was giving it tremendous exposure. Andy [Norman] was basically so useful that after three or four years, we put him in as the meet director.'

Brendan Foster, Britain's leading runner by then, epitomised the 'new' British athlete: bright, working class, dedicated, enormously successful, a media hero who could draw thousands of paying customers into Crystal Palace or any stadium near his home in the north-east of England. But, despite his professional approach to the sport, with the long hours of training and planning that entailed, the 'Pied Piper of Gateshead', as one newspaper styled him, was still condemned to being an amateur.

'The sport was in a mess,' he says now. 'You had a billionaire [Avery Brundage], who was the boss of the International Olympic Committee, saying this sport should remain as an amateur sport, which was bloody nonsense, and it collapsed, but the turn to professionalism was a slow, messy business. In 1973, I was a schoolteacher, and I had to run in the Europa Cup in Edinburgh. I came back from Edinburgh on the last train on a Sunday night, to be in the classroom by nine on Monday morning. The following Friday night, there was the Coca-Cola Meeting.

'It was being run by David Hemery [Britain's Olympic 400 metres hurdles champion in 1968]. He had John Walker and Rod Dixon and Dick Quax, and maybe Jim Ryun as well, all running at Crystal Palace. I'd won the Europa Cup, and I was getting all the headlines, and I was supposed to run at Crystal Palace against these guys. Hemery told me, "We can't pay you what we pay all the others," so I said, "OK, I'll tell you what I'll do, I won't take Friday off school and lose my day's wages. I'll run home from work on Friday, and I'll watch the Coca-Cola Meeting on telly." And I did.

'Next year, I was getting ready to run in the Commonwealth Games. We had met in London and we went to Crystal Palace to do a training session. Andy [Norman] appeared, because he heard I was at the track. He said to me, "I'm organising the Coca-Cola Meeting." I said, "Well, I'm not running." He said, "Ill pay you to run. In fact, I'll pay you more than anybody else." I then won the European Championships on the Sunday, and the Coca-Cola Meeting was the following Friday night. There were so many people there, they'd pushed the fence over, round the back straight at Crystal Palace. I ran the two miles against Viren and Steve Prefontaine. It was the last event of the day, and I won. Andy said to me, "There's your money," and I said, "This is more than you offered me." He said, "Yes, I had to pay Viren and Prefontaine a bit more, and I told you I'd pay you more than anybody else." So that was the beginning.'

The sums at the time were probably not much more than a couple of thousand dollars, but at last the athletes had found someone on home territory who was talking their language. Norman was not the only person doing this; he just became one of the most successful. Amateurism was clearly now untenable, but with a world-wide membership of over 150 countries in the international federation, with the USA and the Soviet Union still playing their Cold War games, engineering change across the board was not easy. 'No one was breaking the law, just the rules of the sport,' said Norman later. Nevertheless, it made many people uneasy, because they felt they were doing something wrong. Coe summed it up well in the first volume of his autobiography: 'It made honest men dishonest.'

In contrast to the other honorary officials who, in Norman's accurately acid estimation, were 'more interested in which table they'll be sitting on at the banquet afterwards', he was prepared to undertake an enormous workload, thus making himself indispensable not only to the national administration and the international athletes, but to television and sponsors. Even better, he could keep all the details in his head.

This was the beginning for Steve Ovett, too, and he recalls the early days of his relationship with Norman in the mid-seventies. 'It was getting Andy the first foothold in learning what athletics was all about. That was definitely a learning curve for both of us, because we were coming through a sport that was turning from amateur to professional, literally within the space of a few years. And with the likes of myself and Seb, and media and TV who wanted a bit more of the action, it needed organising. And it wasn't coming from the sport [i.e. the national administration].

'Andy was a very, very good administrator. He would have been a great chartered accountant, merchant banker, that type of guy. Facts and figures meant a lot to Andy, you know. Profit meant a lot to Andy, which is not a bad thing in the right context. But it's not my be-all and end-all, and I think that is probably why we got on so well. He took care of that sort of thing and I just took care of the other side of things.'

'When it all started, it was just a bit of fun, two hundred dollars a race, and an air ticket or two,' says Ovett. Over the next decade, he and Norman became virtually inseparable, working their way together up through the echelons of the athletics rankings (and clandestine earning power) and administrative hierarchy. It was, recalls Ovett, the perfect symbiosis. 'Andy didn't say to me, "Right, I want you to do this, do this, do that." I would say to him, "Look, if I'm going to run this, I need this and I need that," and I used to get it from him.

'He wasn't an exciting ideas man, Andy, no way. Sometimes he used to say to me, "What about this?" And I'd say, "No, I think that's a bad idea, because that would happen. And if you did that, this would change this," and he'd say, "Yes, I think you are right. So what shall we do at this meet?" And I'd say, "Perhaps you should put this on and that on, and maybe the people will come," and he'd say, "All right well do that then." I'm not boosting up my own side of things but I don't think it was a one-way situation. Andy Norman did not have control over where I raced; vice versa, really. I think he used me as a tool sometimes to get other people races because, if you put up a good trump card, you can use that to your best effect, and I think he was learning the ropes administrative-wise as much as I was.'

The strength of the Met Police Athletics Club – due largely to Norman's administration and management – reflected well on the force, and Norman was soon given a virtual sinecure in a sub-station near his home in Bromley, the south London borough which includes Crystal Palace National Sports Centre. He was already expanding his horizons through his Coke contacts. Even before he moved out to Bromley, coach Frank Horwill, an early associate of Norman, recalls regular visits to his central London base in Chelsea. 'I used to call in and see him on a Friday,' says Horwill. 'He'd say hello, then a policeman would appear and say, "Andy, call from Norway," then, "Andy, call from Sweden." And it went on and on like this. He was virtually running an agency from there.' The amount of police work that Norman did at Bromley after that must have been even less, judging from the experience on myself and others, who would phone him there and have our calls answered with 'Three As [Amateur Athletic Association]'. It was another measure of his commitments elsewhere that when he retired, in the mid-eighties, he was still just a sergeant.

With his increasing portfolio of contacts, Norman became as instrumental in the organisation of meetings in Oslo, Brussels, even North America as he was in Britain. Yet he was still a desk sergeant in a south London cop-shop. He was a pivotal character to the athletes who wanted to race in Britain or at those meetings abroad that he helped organise and the vast majority of international athletes and meeting organisers I've interviewed for this book won't have a word said against him. Adrian Metcalfe goes even further: 'Andy Norman should be president of world athletics.' Although he has always denied it, Norman was suspected, in the early seventies, of being involved with 'old mucker' Frank Horwill in the distribution of *Athletics Truth*, a scurrilous mimeographed magazine which attacked the leading lights in the amateur administration at the time, Arthur Gold and Marea Hartman. Horwill was the principal author, and hardly a model of self-restraint. His abrasive style was apparent in a public meeting during the same period to discuss selection policy. He accused a national coach of favouring a female athlete for Olympic selection, 'because he is fucking her'. The magazine articles were written in a similar vein, and it ceased publication only under threat of legal action. But no one pressed charges, fearing adverse publicity. That lesson would not be lost on Norman.

By the time of Ovett's breakthrough to world class in 1977, Norman was assuming a dominant position in the organisation of athletics in Europe, albeit from an ostensibly minor role officially. The AAA invitation meetings, with stars like Foster, Ovett and, soon, Coe, were the envy of Europe. And Norman's other major asset was the huge pool of US athletes he could invite to the first meeting of the season, in Britain, paying their expenses. They then headed out to the Continent for the summer, on the proviso that they would return for the season finale, the Coke Meeting. With increasing television coverage of star-studded meetings, sponsorship money started to pour in.

With his gift for making things happen, and his single-minded devotion to the cause of athletics success, he was a man with whom increasing numbers of elite athletes were happy to do business. He was effectively becoming both agent and promoter, an obvious potential conflict of interest, but, since British athletics was beginning to boom as never before, he still had more supporters than critics.

The latter group comprised mainly the enraged 'old school', who were shocked by some of his stunts, as when he sold television rights for a meeting to one US network but coverage of the highlight event, the mile, to another. But New Zealander John Walker, the 1976 Olympic 1500 metres champion, who was one of the first to benefit from Norman's largesse, summed up the athletes' attitude: 'Andy justified his whole means by the number of gold medals he won for Britain.'

Other critics were summarily dismissed. David Bedford, the former 10,000 metres world record-holder (and now an elite-race organiser for the London Marathon) was a rival promoter to Norman at the time, having taken up the running of the International Athletes' Club. Bedford began touting a file of photocopies from Companies' House, trying to prove that Norman was profiting personally from his *de facto* agency. Nobody in the press was much interested, myself included. We still felt that Norman was the lesser of two evils – the other being the incompetent, old-style national administrators.

Norman had another coup in 1982, at the IAAF Congress, which preceded the European Championships that year. In a speech written for him by Ovett's biographer, John Rodda of the *Guardian*, Norman called for the end of amateurism, warning that if under-the-table payments were not formalised, the sport would fall into the hands of the increasingly powerful agencies, such as Mark McCormack's International Management Group. The possibility was immanent: IMG was already managing Coe by then – he was the first track and field athlete on their books. The company had also arranged a three-race series between Ovett and Coe, which should have taken place six months earlier. That hadn't come off but IMG was also promoting the idea of a Grand Prix athletics circuit, which was of great interest to the independent promoters of the 'spectaculars' like Zurich, Brussels and Oslo.

A result of Norman's speech, which was widely applauded, although not by the communist bloc, was the setting up of trust funds for athletes. This was a halfway house to professionalism, but essentially a sop to the Eastern Europeans, whose athletes were either 'students' or 'military personnel', and thus strictly amateur, or so it was claimed. They were actually about as amateur as the US college 'students' who had trouble reading and writing, but this was international politics, played out on the sports field. Anyone doubting it has only to recall the Olympic boycotts of Moscow 1980 and Los Angeles 1984.

Despite his acumen, the street-fighter side of Norman would ultimately lead to his downfall. It would take a while, until the mid-nineties, but the bad seeds were already being sown. As organiser of the Crystal Palace meetings, Norman was responsible for ensuring the collection and delivery of urine samples to the dope-testing laboratory at King's College, Chelsea. Dr David Cowan, then assistant director of the Drug Testing Centre at King's, has revealed that, in the early eighties, his staff had doubts about the samples that Norman was delivering personally.

'We were very surprised', Cowan told me, 'that we didn't find any positives from the samples, given the positives we were getting from other branches of athletics. We weren't even getting ephedrine traces – that's to say, from accidental, over-the-counter cold remedies – showing up. Either Norman was being super-careful, to make sure none of the athletes were taking drugs, or we were not getting genuine samples.' Mike Farrell, the 1956 Olympian who retired as AAA general secretary in the early nineties, confirmed that, as a result of Cowan's concerns, Norman was relieved of his dope-testing duties.

But that wasn't the only issue of suspect ethics involving Norman. US hurdler James King has admitted to myself and several other journalists that Norman paid him to lose to Alan Pascoe in the Briton's farewell race at Crystal Palace in 1978. Pascoe, now head of Fast Track, the company which markets UK Athletics, was unaware of the arrangement at the time, and displayed huge satisfaction when he pipped King on the finish line. King subsequently told a British television interviewer, 'Andy wanted to make sure that I would at least give Alan a great race – you know, make it close. He wanted Alan to go out on a really good note, and make it look good for the public.'

In contrast, anyone deemed to have crossed Norman, like the ever-popular Kriss Akabusi, got no such favours. Akabusi took over from David Hemery as British 400 metres hurdles record-holder.

But he had several spats with Norman over appearance money in meetings that the latter organised. Following one argument, Akabusi reported that Norman told him, 'You'll never race in Europe again.' Fortunately, although Norman's power was widespread at that point (in the early nineties), Akabusi was good enough to command respect both at home and abroad for his achievements. But, in his retirement race, also at Crystal Palace, Norman lined up the Olympic champion and world record-holder, Kevin Young, who duly despatched Akabusi to a long and losing goodbye.

In his autobiography, Steve Ovett describes Norman fulsomely: 'advisor, coach, financial assistant, bag carrier, minder, airline ticket supplier, best man (at his wedding), counsellor. But above all he has been one of my very best friends.' That friendship began to wilt less than a year after the publication of *Ovett* in late 1984. Initially, Ovett felt that Norman's interest in him waned along with the athlete's career. Then Norman took up with Fatima Whitbread, the javelin world record-holder, now his wife. The relationship made Ovett uncomfortable, since he knew Norman's first wife, Gerd, and their children very well. Their paths diverged.

Ultimately, in the middle of the 1989 season, not having communicated for several years, Norman phoned Ovett out of the blue and offered him £20,000 to compete in the AAA Championships against Coe, their first meeting in Britain since their schoolboy race in 1972. It was unauthorised to pay money for a championship event back then, and the story leaked out. Ovett performed poorly, while Coe won the race. There was another inquiry instituted by the AAA. The report came to the intriguing conclusion that, although Ovett had obviously been telephoned and offered money to compete, it could not be proven that the caller was Norman. Ovett put the seal on their fifteen-year relationship with, 'I think Andy's lost touch with reality.' Espousing a conclusion like that, the AAA wasn't far behind. Ovett and Norman have not spoken since.

The following year, Norman was involved in another dispute over money. He said that a plastic bag containing $40,000 in athletes' appearance fees had been stolen from his Crystal Palace hotel room. Norman admitted 'gross negligence', but again the federation did nothing. Later, he would tell a journalist, 'They just didn't have the balls.'

Since Norman's fall from grace, Coe insists, 'I'm not ashamed to say it, I have maintained a close friendship with Andy. I wouldn't say anything to you that I wouldn't say to him, and I have in the past to his face been critical about some of the things that he's said and done, and his attitudes. But I think the one reason that I stayed friendly with him is that I never had a commercial relationship with him. He brought an air of professionalism to it. He was street-smart. Some of his pre-race instructions to the field when I was racing used to be very funny. They'd be all lined up and he'd wait until I was at the very end of the warm-up room just before we went down to the track, and he'd grab them all together and say, "You've only got one instruction tonight. For fuck's sake, keep out of his way, and don't hit him. The public don't like it!" '

There are still those who think that Norman's dismissal from the British federation for his hounding of Cliff Temple was harsh, and, has been mentioned, Norman still has many friends on the international athletics circuit. It is probable that his previous record was taken into account when he was sacked in 1994. The head of the British federation at the time was Peter Radford, an arch anti-drugs campaigner who is also a conservative and moral man.

Cliff Temple was one of the best athletics journalists that Britain has ever had, but he was never a confident man. His marriage had broken down, and he felt that he was in financial difficulties. Everyone in the athletics world knew that he was suffering from grave psychological problems. When Neil Wilson told Norman that Temple was 'on the edge', Norman's response was, 'Anything I can do to push him over, I will.' Peter Radford might have had more support for his draconian stance towards Norman had others been privy to another remark that Norman made to a colleague of his. During the inquiry that led to his dismissal, Norman confided, 'It only needs some other arsehole to commit suicide, and I'll really be in the shit.'

Monster

New Year 1977 began in a sober fashion for the world-wide athletics community, with the news of Ivo van Damme's death in a car crash on 29 December 1976. The Belgian, who had finished fourth behind Ovett in the European Junior 800 metres three years earlier, had gone on to do what Ovett had signally failed to do – star in the Montreal Olympics. Van Damme had won silver medals behind two of the greatest athletes in history, Alberto Juantorena of Cuba in the 800 metres, and John Walker of New Zealand in the 1500 metres. Ovett, now aged twenty-one, wrote to *Athletics Weekly* with a mature judgement about the nature of fame and perceived destiny.

> Athletes are a strange breed who tend to have a certain disrespect of fate, believing that it plays little or no part in their lives or those of their fellow athletes. Only when something of this nature happens are we all shaken, and we take it hard. To win two silver medals in any Olympics is a fabulous performance; to win them in only your first Games, and at the age of 22, marks the greatness of the man, who surely must have gone on to greater honours.

Reflecting on British domination of middle-distances between 1978 and 1986, Dave Moorcroft said in 2003, 'The one person who could have got in the way of that was Ivo van Damme.' John Walker, who beat the Belgian by less than a stride in Montreal, elaborates:

'If van Damme had survived, the enigma of Coe and Ovett may not have been there, because he might have been better. He may not have been better, [too,] but he would have been a force to consider. He ran 1 minute 43 seconds for 800, he was tall and strong, and he could only get better. He might have knocked us all off our pedestals.' The Belgian is remembered every summer in the Memorial Ivo van Damme, the athletics spectacular in Brussels which began in the summer of 1977 and is now a Golden League meeting.

But it was Ovett who would knock Walker off his pedestal later that year, while Coe was making quieter progress in the wings, building on his breakthrough at 800 metres the previous summer.

Ovett amazed the cross-country fraternity by finishing second in the Inter-Counties Championships in mid-January. One week later, Coe had his most impressive senior victory thus far. He won the National Indoor 800 metres title by fifteen metres, in the third-fastest British time. Then, within eight days in mid-February, he made his first substantial moves into world class. In his first international match, an indoor 800 metres in Dortmund, Germany, he ran away from Paul-Heinz Wellmann, the Olympic 1500 metres bronze medallist and reigning European indoor champion. Coe broke the British record by half a second, with 1 minute 47.6 seconds, which was also faster than his best outdoor time. A successful summer beckoned, since the 200-metre indoor tracks militated against really fast times. Coe was making a name for himself in the national press now. He followed up his Dortmund victory a week later with another international win, against France, lowering his best by a tenth of a second. But the best was yet to come.

After the depressing result in Montreal – that single bronze medal for Brendan Foster – the small British team at the European Indoor Championships in San Sebastian, on the Spanish Basque coast, came back with three gold and two silver medals. Given the respective opposition, Coe's gold was the pick of the bunch. Winning his heat and semi-final on the same day, he ran away again in the following day's final, setting another UK record by knocking a full second off his recent best. However, his delight was tempered ten days later, when he strained an Achilles tendon, and had to take three months off racing. But this was not necessarily a drawback. He had finished his indoor season with a massive improvement, and had plenty of time to return for the outdoor track season, which would not begin in earnest until June. A short rest never did any athlete any harm, and George Gandy said that one of the most impressive things about Coe was that, unlike obsessive trainers who do themselves more harm than good, 'If Seb wasn't well, he'd just disappear for a few days.'

Meanwhile, Ovett made news of a different, but no less important, kind. The sand dunes of Merthyr Mawr on the south Wales coast had long been a training ground for his coach Harry Wilson, a devotee of the celebrated Australian Percy Cerutty, who had guided Herb Elliott to a 1500 metres gold and world record in the 1960 Olympics in Rome. Cerutty had a training camp at Portsea, on the south-east Australian coast near Melbourne, and the dunes that Elliott trained on became famous through Cerutty's books, particularly *How to Become a Champion*, which was highly influential on the sixties and seventies generation of club runners. At a seminar conducted at Merthyr Mawr, Ovett roundly criticised the lack of back-up for young athletes or newcomers at major games. Ovett described the boredom of Olympic village life, the training tracks overcrowded with poseurs, and the lack of any management guidance. This was an old saw among athletes – the fact that management seemed to think they were more important than the athletes – and was why Andy Norman would find so many allies among the new breed of athlete, like Ovett and Foster, who hated the 'amateur' ethic and all who supported it.

Foster retains an indelible memory from the Montreal Olympics. 'The federation was an obstacle, but the Olympic people were a bigger obstacle. After the 1976 Olympic opening ceremony, we were called together to a meeting, and castigated by the British Olympic people, because they'd had reports back from London saying that this was the most disgraceful marching performance [in the opening ceremony] by a British team ever. Seriously, this is true. I said, "You know why? Because this is the first British team that hasn't been in the bloody army. The medals aren't for marching; the medals are for running." '

Shortly after the Merthyr Mawr training weekend, Ovett flew to Jamaica for a mile race at a festival in Kingston. His principal opponents would be Filbert Bayi and Suleiman Nyambui of Tanzania, and Steve Scott, a young newcomer from the USA who was having his first international race. Scott got to know Ovett quite well over the following years. He is now an assistant university coach in southern California, north of San Diego. In his late forties, he looks in great shape, and instructed me to be sure to tell all his old rivals that he still trains every day with his students, and had recently run a mile in 4 minutes 26 seconds. Runners, eh?

Kingston would provide Scott with the best possible introduction to his international career. 'It was a big thing for me because I was still in college. I was able to take my girlfriend with me, so that was interesting. It was a great trip because that was really the first time for me to travel out of the country, my first real international exposure. I had never heard of Ovett before. I mean, I was pretty raw as far as who the top international people were. It was just a thrill for me.

'So, to win the race was like icing on the cake and it was such an exciting race. They had a rabbit for the first couple of laps and then Filbert Bayi took over the lead, but the pace wasn't, you know, by relative standards, that fast; I think we ran 3.39. It all happened in the last lap, it was one of those big last-lap kicker races. And it was me and Ovett going past Bayi down the home stretch, so there was basically the three of us all the way down the last hundred metres, and I was just able to inch by Ovett at the line. It was a hundredth of a second between the three of us and no one really knew until they checked the photo who had run the race. I thought, Oh wow, that's great to beat Filbert Bayi, not realising how good Steve Ovett was until later that year. I think I was lucky because it was very early in his season. I was in mid-season shape and I'm sure I surprised him because he didn't know who the heck I was at that point, some upstart long-haired American [who] would nip him at the tape.'

This race became a milestone in Ovett's career, since it was to be his last defeat at a mile or its metric equivalent, the 1500 metres, for over three years, forty-five races, during which time he became the most feared middle-distance runner in the world. The cross-country training, combined with the hard interval sessions he was doing with Matt Paterson, and the searing acceleration he had nurtured since his early teens with those 100, 200 and 400 metres races, had made him the perfect middle-distance machine.

As for Steve Scott, he soon realised that he had had a victory to savour. He had beaten the already legendary Filbert Bayi and someone who would become possibly even more revered. During our interview, he reflected that he never beat Ovett again. That shows the dominance the Ovett exerted over his rivals, because Scott *did* beat him again, in the inaugural World Championships in Helsinki in 1983, when he won the silver medal. But, as he reflects, 'Ovett beat me so many times he owned me. You know when I get to the [start] line, I want to beat Ovett, [but] do I really believe I'm going to beat him? No, because he owns me. And that is the way that racing is until you beat them: they own you.

'I don't know if you would call it a rivalry because he kicked my arse every time we raced. I had a tremendous amount of respect for his ability and it's like I couldn't have a break. Because, indoors, I'd be racing Eamonn Coghlan, and I'd try all different types of tactics to beat him. You know, I'd take it from the start, I'd take it from the middle, I'd try to jump him with a lap to go, try to jump him with two laps to go. It just seemed like there was nothing I could do to beat Eamonn except get him when he was tired. And Ovett, he was always real intelligent in his racing and I never got him when he was tired, or he would kind of evade me when I was at my very best and make sure that I wasn't in the same race. But I tried all different types of ways to try to beat Steve as well, without any success.'

Ovett was narrowly defeated the following week, Filbert Bayi returning the compliment of Kingston. But that was over 3000 metres – Ovett's first serious foray into the distance – so there was no dishonour to lose to a man like Bayi. Two months later Ovett had a crack at 5000 metres, and lost to another all-time great, Miruts Yifter 'the Shifter' of Ethiopia. For a man who was essentially an 800/1500 metres runner, these performances were wonderful. Between the longer races, Ovett had come within a tenth of a second of Frank Clement's UK 1500 metres record, with 3 minutes 37.5 seconds. Various correspondents pointed out that, had he not started waving to the crowd at Cwmbran, south Wales, he would have broken it.

Ovett's next two trips would serve to encapsulate the very different faces of the man: the mediated and moody, and the private and the personable. The first race was just up the (London) road at Crystal Palace, on 26 June. Alberto Juantorena and Mike Boit had been lined up to race in the 800 metres, a much-anticipated match that had been missing in Montreal the previous summer, when Boit's Kenya had joined the boycott by African countries protesting over the New Zealand rugby team touring apartheid South Africa. For the same reason Filbert Bayi of Tanzania had not been able to race John Walker in the 1500 metres. That was to be regretted even more, given that Bayi had run away from Walker in the Commonwealth Games two years earlier, setting a world record from the front – a rebuke to every middle-distance runner since who thought he or she couldn't achieve such a feat without a pacemaker. Walker was to meet Ovett at Crystal Palace in the mile.

But a row erupted when the Cuban delegation refused to let Juantorena race against Boit. Andy Norman proposed moving the Kenyan into the mile. According to Ovett's autobiography, 'It was obvious they used Juantorena as a political tool, which would be blunted if he were defeated by the man he did not face in Montreal ... Less than an hour before the race was due to start, I told Andy that I did not want Boit in my race, and that he should go back to the 800 metres. If the Cubans pulled out ... then let them.'

Ovett was starting to use the muscle of his own celebrity, but that forced a compromise with Juantorena and Boit, who were put in separate 800 metres races, which they won, the Cuban in

1 minute 45.5 seconds, the Kenyan two tenths slower. Everyone who regrets that Ovett and Coe did not race each other more frequently – and never in Britain apart from their schoolboy race and the 1989 AAA Championships – need look no further than the bad example set by this compromise.

Mel Watman, the perceptive and indefatigable editor of *Athletics Weekly*, put Ovett's mile victory over Walker into perspective:

> It was a passionate race, one of the finest at this distance since Derek Ibbotson's world record 3.57.2 20 years ago ... 250 metres from home, Walker burst ahead. With 200 to run it was the Olympic champion by 3m from [Ari] Paunonen, with Ovett and the year's fastest miler [3.53.8] Wilson Waigwa in close touch. Ovett moved into second place around the turn and mounted his attack on Walker coming off the bend. With the crowd delirious, Steve edged past Walker 70m from the finish and sped to a well-taken victory. The time was a bonus – three tenths inside Frank Clement's UK record of 3.55.0.

As Watman recorded, the 20,000 full house at Crystal Palace loved it, but the rest of the press took a more austere view. The headlines the following day included, 'Ovett Coward', 'Boit Boycott', 'Ovett Shies Away From Boit', and the considered opinion, 'I Blame Selfish Ovett'. Some of Ovett's peers took a similar view. Dick Quax said, 'I have not been impressed with his attitude to racing at all. You run against everybody, I think.' Since Quax was an Olympic silver medallist, world 5000 metres record-holder, and one of the trio of Kiwis – with Walker and Rod Dixon – who had virtually created the European circuit, with a bit of help from Andy Norman, his opinion held weight. But it is a measure of tabloid news values contrasting hugely with appreciation of competitive excellence. Ovett had beaten Walker at 800 metres before, but never over the New Zealander's Olympic title distance. On the other hand, Walker was not on top form, and he had only just arrived in the UK. He put Quax's criticism into perspective, but had his own reasons to be displeased with Ovett. 'Ovett was getting rubbished by Quax, saying he was never going to make it, but he'd said that about me. You've got your mantle, and you don't like anybody coming along and knocking you off your pedestal. I had four years of number one in the world, it was probably longer than most. I was still the world record-holder for the mile, and you don't like these young, fresh kids coming up and beating you, [but] I couldn't believe what I saw. Ovett won the race, he ran out in lane five and he waved to the crowd coming down the straight. He just treated us with contempt. I mean, we were flat out going nowhere, he made it look so easy, and I thought, Well, this is a one-off, we are not going to do this again, but he treated us with total arrogance, and I thought, You asshole.'

Ovett then took off on one of those whimsical trips that said so much of the character that few people really knew. Throughout his career, the 'down-home' Ovett preferred to run in small-town venues, but he outdid himself now, even to the extent of falling off the map, when he went to the centre of Ireland on the Cork/Limerick border. His support for the eccentric organiser of a meeting there, and his refusal to accept payment for competing, is one of the reasons why the Irish athletics community adores him.

There is a small coterie of Irish athletics fans who travel the world to watch the major events. They are voluble, good-natured, great company, and manage to get into places where even journalists fear to tread. One of them got himself a seat in the lead car at the Boston Marathon one year. This is the car that precedes the runners, and it virtually requires a papal dispensation to clean it, let alone ride in it. On another occasion when the World Cross-Country Championships were held at the Auckland Racetrack in New Zealand, the media was not permitted on the course. We watched on closed-circuit TV in the stands. As the cameras panned down the back straight on the first lap, waiting for the race leaders, a lone figure came into view, preparing his Brownie camera for a close-up. It was, inevitably, one of the lads.

They do not travel alone, but with a man who might be described as their spiritual adviser. Well, he says the mass for them on Sundays at a preordained hotel when they're on the road. And they put a stopwatch on him, because he doesn't want to waste time when there is a world-class athletics to be watched. When he's not wearing his priest's dog collar, which is most of the time, he is carrying a camera and a notebook, because he has an athletics magazine to get out. His name is Fr Liam Kelleher, and he is a legend.

Fr Liam, as he is universally known, has been the bane of his bishop's life for over thirty years. Since his ordination as a priest, he has organised athletics meetings and trips to championships from every parish where he has worked. After moving him several times, in attempts to short-circuit his enthusiasm for his extra-curricular activities, it seems the church authorities have given up, and Fr Liam now has his own parish, in County Cork. His greatest achievement, apart from getting the likes of Ovett, John Walker, Thomas Wessinghage, Eamonn Coghlan, Ray Flynn and John Treacy to run at his meetings, has been to build a track in the middle of nowhere, Tullylease, put on an athletics meeting, with Steve Ovett as the star, and get any vehicle coming within a mile of the track to pay an entry fee, even if they weren't staying to watch the races. It's a mixture of Don Camillo and the building of the international airport at Knock.

In the words of Eamonn Coghlan, 'Tullylease is an asshole backfield in a little tiny village in Cork. Fr Liam Kelleher had this ability to force his friendship on runners, through the power of the white collar, and through his persuasive and intrusive personality we got to love the guy. Steve was hooked in . . . more than anybody else.'

While Ovett had been in Jamaica losing to Steve Scott, Fr Liam had been at a college reunion in England, where he discovered that one of his colleagues was a priest in a Brighton presbytery just two doors down from the Ovett household. Fr Liam invited himself to Brighton. Gay Ovett might have been a better guard than Cerberus to the gates of the Ovett perceptions, but not even she was a match for Fr Liam. 'I knocked on the door and said I want to see Steve, and his mother took my phone number, and, fair play, as soon as he came back he rang me, and said he would like to come to Ireland. From that day on, we had a great relationship.'

In 1977, Ovett combined a run at a regular fixture on the athletics calendar, the Cork City Sports, where he beat Eamonn Coghlan in the mile, with a 5000 metres debut race on grass for Fr Liam in Midleton – home to Powers and Paddy whiskey distilleries. He beat John Treacy, who would go on to win two World Cross-Country titles. While he was there, Ovett did a seminar for the local youngsters. But it was an event two years later which would become part of local folklore, and even make it into the pages of *Sports Illustrated*, through an interview with John Walker, who claimed he had never run in a stranger place in his life.

Fr Liam had always had it in mind to build a running track at one of the communities where he worked, and Tullylease seemed the ideal place. 'There were about four, five houses in the village, right up at the top on a kind of a hill, and no facilities whatever, no playing pitches, nothing,' says the priest. 'The Land Commission were dividing up the farm and we went up to Dublin and we bought five acres. I know exactly the amount, 3,502 Irish pounds. Then I was up at Cork City visiting a friend in hospital, and I looked at these huge machines that were taking away soil – they were building a shopping complex. Fine machines, built like kangaroos, and I said to the guy in charge, "Are they expensive?" "Oh yes," he says, "very expensive." So I said, "When you have finished here I have a job for you," and he came and had a look at the field the following night. There was a thirty-three-foot drop in the field. And I said, "How much would it be to level that, and build a track around it?" "Well," he said, "about eight and a half to nine thousand pounds." I said, "Fine".'

All that remained was the little matter of raising the money. Fr Liam organised a concert featuring several groups, including the celebrated show band the Wolf-Tones. That raised around half the money, and after a session of head scratching with Brendan Mooney of the Cork *Examiner*, Fr Liam hit on the idea of a sponsored run. 'I said, "Look, I'll do a hundred and fifty laps of the track," not knowing what the distance was. And there was this banner headline in the *Examiner* the next day that I was to do it on St Patrick's Day, of all days. That St Patrick's Day turned out to be a really savage day, but I still did the hundred and fifty laps, which was thirty-seven miles without stopping, and it nearly killed me, but we raised four thousand punts. Every child that sponsored me for the full distance got a free ticket to the World Cross-Country in Limerick.' The kids' pennies were well spent, because John Treacy successfully defended his title on the Limerick mudheap a week later.

When Ovett arrived in Tullylease another two months after that, the bulldozers were still at work. 'It was in the middle of nowhere, and he'd got all the local contractors levelling this damn thing, and it was just unbelievable,' says Ovett. 'He took me to his mother's farm, he took me to Blarney Castle, and they were just closing, so he whipped out his dog collar, and says, "Mr Ovett's here," and the guy said, "Right, Father," and opened up again. We did Blarney Castle, and kissed the stone, and when we got back, the rest of the boys had arrived. I'm staying at Fr Liam's, and I went into his study, and he's got a picture of the Pope, then he's got a picture of me, and a picture of John Walker, and he's got John Treacy's vest next to that, and a crucifix underneath. It's a mixture of the Bible and a *Who's Who* of world athletics.'

There were still a few problems to overcome before the meeting the next day. Overnight rain had reduced the greenstone track to porridge. After one of his sprint-masses, Fr Liam led everyone in a prayer for the rain to stop. According to Ovett, 'As they walked out of the door of the church, the sun broke through. It did literally stop raining. I remember it was bright sunshine from about ten o'clock onwards.'

But the track was still in a terrible state, so Fr Liam changed the race distances – 800 to 1000 metres, the mile to 2000 metres – so that the expected poor times wouldn't reflect on the world-class line-up he'd tempted into the wilderness of the Cork/Limerick hinterlands. Ovett beat Coghlan in the 2000 metres, and all that remained was to pay the runners with money collected at the gate and from the unwitting car-drivers.

Ray Flynn recalls the set-up: 'He had almost a cult following from the people who helped him. I had to go into a little college to get the money that Fr Liam had agreed. One of the things I always remember was this old man saying, "You're an awful man, taking the money off the priest" – working on our guilt. One of the strangest places I ever ran in my life.' 'Here's Steve,' says Coghlan, 'the greatest runner in the world, coming to run in Ireland, and doing it for nothing, while we guys, we were saying, "Bullshit, we're taking the money." And he was taking dirty, old, scruffy pound notes that were handed in by farmers, they were bagged and handed to Walker, Coghlan, Wessinghage and Scott, as everybody else. But Steve, I believe, did it for nothing.'

He did indeed. As Ovett says, 'He was quite an entrepreneur on the quiet, because he charged people to come and watch. It wasn't done for generosity. But the money that Liam makes gets filtered back to the magazine, or to him travelling round the world to watch the sport or whatever. There are a few people I would definitely take money off, but I don't think I'd take it off Liam.'

Fr Liam was transferred again in 1981, and the Tullylease track is no longer there: it was taken up and covered over in 2002, and the field is now a Gaelic football and hurling pitch, used by a local Gaelic Athletic Association club. It is, as Fr Liam says, 'Just a memory.' But it is one that no one who visited there – athlete or spectator – will ever forget.

Fr Liam still travels the circuit, he was in Paris in the summer of 2003, maintaining his record of never missing a World Athletics Championships. He and Ovett – who was commentating for Canadian television – spent a while reliving old times. A couple of days later, Fr Liam confided, 'Of all the athletes I have ever been involved with in Ireland, I suppose Moses Kiptanui and Ovett would be the top two, both character-wise, and as friends, people you could talk to. Very, very human people, and yet so thoughtful; I suppose Christian. It's a great thing to be able to say.'

By June 1977, Coe was back in action, and surprising himself in his first race back with an outdoor 800 metres personal best of

1 minute 46.8 seconds, finishing second in the AAA Championships to Milovan Savic of Yugoslavia. That earned him selection for the European Cup in Helsinki. At that event, while Ovett underlined that he could run at any pace and still win – the 1500 metres was a stroll until he kicked in with a 52.6-second last lap – the inexperienced Coe would get a lesson in rough-house 800 metres running. This may have contributed to his competitive uncertainty over two-lap championship races in the coming years, for after being bundled out of the way and defeated by Willi Wülbeck – Coe ultimately finished fourth – he admitted to 'the lingering doubt at the back of my mind that I was vulnerable to the hand-off'.

If Coe was manifesting signs of frailty, Ovett was demonstrating that he was some sort of superman. A week later, he had one of those runs which defied belief. Unable to get to Edinburgh for a 1000 metres against John Walker, he offered to drive his training partner Matt Paterson the fifty miles or so to Dartford, where the Scot was going to run a half-marathon. As they were driving, Ovett realised that after a hard 13.1 miles, Paterson would be unable to accompany him on their traditional Sunday-morning long run the day after. So Ovett decided to race, too, and asked to borrow shoes and kit from Paterson. 'I was saying, "Don't be stupid," ' recalls Paterson, 'and the bloke said, "You can't win the first prize." He said, "I'm not interested, I just want to run." Barry Watson and a few other international marathon runners [were] in there and Steve was just jogging with me and he says, "I feel all right." I said, "Well, just go, bloody go," and he shot off after five miles and won it in about sixty-five minutes. He was laughing his head off at the end, it just felt so easy.'

This was three weeks after beating the Olympic champion at 1500 metres for the first time, two weeks after chasing home double Olympic champion-to-be Miruts Yifter over 5000 metres, and two weeks before a race that would place him firmly at the top of the athletics tree. Ovett's extraordinary talent was now undeniable. The Dartford course was not easy, he entered on a whim, and he ran 65 minutes 38 seconds, beating Olympic marathon men. No wonder his rivals despaired.

Coe, though, would get an opportunity to show his talents just a week later. He ran in a club 400 metres race and clocked a personal best 48.9 seconds, still a long way from Ovett's best, but the strength training he was doing at Loughborough was starting to enable him to put together two laps like that back to back. The following day at Crystal Palace, in a match against West Germany, he won the 800 metres with another solo front run. As a result of which, he was asked to run the Emsley Carr Mile the following day, Bank Holiday Monday.

The race is named after the then proprietor of the *News of the World*, who put up the pot in the early fifties as an enticement to British milers to run sub-4 minutes. Ironically, Roger Bannister achieved the feat the next year, 1954, in a completely different race, but Derek Ibbotson's world mile record of 1957 came in the Emsley Carr, and the event has had a long and distinguished history of victors. None more so than Sebastian Coe.

The previous year, Coe had essayed his usual front-running tactics and been swamped in the last lap, finishing seventh. But this was a stronger, more mature and, after the rumble in Helsinki, *smarter* Coe. He was more cautious in this, his third race in three days, the more so since Bayi was running – although the Tanzanian had arrived directly from Italy, where he had won a 1500 metres the previous day. Bayi took up the running at halfway, and Coe attacked off the bottom bend, with a hundred metres to go, and won by a metre in a personal best of 3 minute 57.7 seconds. He was now firmly situated in the hierarchy of the world's top milers, and the *Daily Mirror* underlined that with his first back-page headline the following day, 'BOLD KING COE'.

The sub-editors were going to be stretched to find superlatives to describe Ovett's next run, in the World Cup 1500 metres in Düsseldorf – just two weeks after his impromptu half-marathon. The ever-astute Mel Watman called it the 'Perfect Race'. Coe terms it 'one of the four great 1500 metres performances I've ever witnessed'. Another young miler, soon to join Ovett and Coe on the British team, Tim Hutchings, was holidaying with friends in Germany. 'We went down to the World Cup,' he says, 'and I can remember being high up in the stands in the back straight. It was great: Juantorena beat Boit in a staggering 800 – 1.43. And I remember the 4×100 relay. We were in Row 57, and I can remember hearing the slap of the baton in the guy's hand at the first change-over. And Ovett blowing away Walker in the 1500.

'I did expect Ovett to win. Walker hadn't got any significant European challengers then, because [Ivo] van Damme had been killed. Steve was like the new European knight in shining armour, and it was probably a bit of a shock to Walker to have somebody just tear away from him like that with two hundred to go. And it was impressive, the fact that they were actually in line with each other when they came into the back straight, then Steve had got fifteen to twenty metres, and at that point Walker stepped off the track.

'John had a very robust mental approach, he was renowned for his consistency, but look at the actual circumstances of that race. He must have just gone, "Jesus, what the hell is that?" when Steve kicked, because he was operating at a different level. That must have been a huge shock for Walker. I don't know if it was any kind of a watershed in his career, but you know from then on, he wasn't going to beat those two again.'

Athletes hate to admit defeat, and Walker still has difficulty in coming to terms with what happened in Düsseldorf. 'It was a funny race. I got accused of quitting, but I lost many races in my life, and I never walked off a track or quit. I can take a defeat like anyone. But on the last lap, I remember it vividly, this German guy pushed me, and I took three or four steps off the track, and normally you would just walk back on the track, and start again, but because we were coming round the bend, I lost my momentum, and that was it. So I just quit. If I hadn't been pushed, I would have been third. Before the race, 55,000 people applauded me; and 55,000 people booed me after the race.'

After his first English Schools victory, with his family in attendance, Ovett admits that Düsseldorf is his next favourite memory, but he's very low-key, to the point of dismissiveness, about his racing history. Perhaps those who make history can afford to ignore it, but no one else who saw that race can ever forget it. In fourth place, and an occasional supporting actor at 1500 metres over the next couple of years, was Abderahmane Morceli, the elder brother of Nourredhine. The latter would ultimately follow Walker, Bayi, Coe, Ovett, Steve Cram and Saïd Aouita as the world's leading middle-distance runner, only to be surpassed himself by Hicham El Guerrouj. And so it goes on.

Probably the most impressed by Ovett's run in Düsseldorf was a clean-cut young man sitting with friends and training companions in his living room in Sheffield, watching the race on television. It put his own fine year in perspective. 'For me, that was probably the single most definitive run he ever produced,' says Coe. 'Walker was the Olympic champion, Wessinghage was effectively the European record-holder, Eamonn Coghlan as well. Walker? I mean the guy [Ovett] completely destroyed him. Even if I had allowed myself the luxury of thinking I had won the [European] Indoor title, which was a good progress at twenty, you were soon brought back down to earth by this monstrous performance.'

And the 'monster' wasn't finished yet. But nor was the mini-monster, his admirer. At the traditional season finale at Crystal Palace, Coe chased Mike Boit to the line of the 800 metres, losing by just a couple of strides, but breaking Andy Carter's British record by two tenths, in 1 minute 45 seconds. It was his first senior national record, underlining the promise of those years of hard thinking and training by himself and his father, and his brave front running against all-comers.

But Ovett was on hand to remind him how hard the future would be, winning the mile in 3 minutes 56.6 seconds from Wessinghage on the same evening. Ovett went on to impress further, both by his astonishing range (again), and by demolishing Henry Rono, as he had John Walker. The following year, 'Sir' Henry, as L'Equipe dubbed him, was to break four world records. One of them would be at 3000 metres. But at that very distance in Wattenscheid, Germany, on 23 September 1977, the Kenyan had a six-metre lead on Ovett with two hundred metres to run. Ovett beat him by four metres in 7 minutes 41.3 seconds, a time that had been beaten in

Britain only by Brendan Foster, when he ran the world record of 7 minutes 35.2 seconds.

If Coe was the King, it was over some lowly earthly domain. Ovett was in a stratosphere where minor royalty like his putative rival was cowed and bowed. Olympus, perhaps? He had the wit and countenance, and the obtuseness, of a Greek god. And his nemesis was still a long way off.

13

Eastern Block

The Ovett–Coe rivalry began in earnest in 1978, as did the media obsession which would last the best part of a decade. They could have met at that year's Commonwealth Games (something that ultimately never happened at all), but both decided to give Edmonton a miss. Apart from a misjudged experiment in the late sixties and early seventies, when the European Championships were shifted to odd years, the Commonwealths and Europeans are always held in the even years between the Olympics. Usually it is possible for middle- and long-distance runners to do both. But in 1978, Edmonton in western Canada was only a month before Prague, in central Europe. The distances and time differences probably militated against doing both well, and the comparison between the two championships was beginning to reflect the political situation – Europe and the European Championships were far more important to Britons with ambition.

'I honestly thought I wasn't capable of running both,' says Ovett. 'I have always been cautious. Rather than spread myself too thin, it is probably better to concentrate on winning the ones that you want to win, and as a European, the European Championships, I suppose, hold more kudos, (but) I remember I was quite upset when the Commonwealths were going on, thinking I wasn't there, and that I would like to give it a go. And Dave [Moorcroft] won. I think I had flu in between the two, so I was lucky I didn't go in the end.' For Coe, 'Europe was where it was at,' and a further justification for him was that, of all the people who did both, 'only Daley Thompson and Dave Moorcroft got a medal'.

Ovett began the year as he had left off the previous September. As if to rub in the lesson of his final race of 1977, his first big outing in 1978 was over-distance again, in the Inter-Counties Cross-Country Championships. This was second in importance only to the National Cross-Country. Yet Ovett won in thick snow – hardly the track runner's medium – by eighty metres from Steve Jones, the Welsh hard man who would become one of the world's leading marathoners half a dozen years later. It was further evidence of Ovett's catholic talents. Here was a man who could run 400 metres in 47.5 seconds winning one of the world's biggest cross-country races by a street. If Coe was impressed by Düsseldorf, he had every right to be completely overawed by this performance. Ovett then went even further, finishing fourth in the National beaten only by Bernie Ford, Ian Stewart and Tony Simmons, all Olympic 5000/10,000 metres finalists, and men who over their careers either won the World Cross-Country title (Stewart) or finished in the top three. Ovett did make one concession to sporting mortality by passing up on the World Cross-Country Championships, saying it would encroach on his track season. Long-distance runners across the world slept easier.

But then Coe made another leap forward himself, and rivalling Ovett no longer seemed such an Olympian task. After a tentative training period, due to a badly sprained ankle, when the track season began in late April Coe reduced his 400 metres best to 47.7 seconds. It was still not quite as fast as Ovett had run four years earlier, but Coe's next race at 800 metres was altogether in a different register. Ovett's cross-country feats had come at Allestree Park in Derby and Roundhay Park in Leeds, neither very far from Coe's stamping grounds. It was an equally mundane setting, Cleckheaton, in the Yorkshire County Championships, that Coe ran 800 metres in 1 minute 45.6 seconds, easily a personal best, and the world's fastest for 1978 at that point. Everything was coming together over two laps. Peter Coe could sit in his factory office in Sheffield looking at all sorts of flow-charts, but the one where the graph was heading relentlessly upwards was that which sketched out his son's destiny in the Lenin Stadium two years hence.

In contrast, Ovett seemed to be in full 1500 metres mode. He barely raced 800 metres, and was just as likely to run 3000 metres, as he'd done at the end of the previous track season, or 2000 metres, which he did on 3 June at Crystal Palace, becoming the third-fastest man in history, with 4 minutes 57.8 seconds. His range of competitive distances continued to startle. Nevertheless, Ovett had a qualifying time for the Prague 800 metres, and had been given the option of running in the event. Characteristically, he left it until the eleventh hour to declare. Coe admits he was irked by Ovett's gamesmanship, but says he would probably have done the same, had he had the opportunity.

While Ovett concentrated on the mile and 1500 metres, Coe increasingly put himself in pole position for the only race he would run in Prague, the 800 metres. In just about the only big foreign meeting he ran regularly, he set a UK record of 1 minute 44.3 seconds at the second Ivo van Damme Memorial in Brussels. The emphatic nature of his win – by fifteen metres – and the time, just 0.9 seconds off Juantorena's world record, made him the Prague favourite in virtually everyone's estimation, including Ovett's. But not in his own: 'I was beginning to inch closer to him, but we [father and son] were both realistic enough to know at that stage I was not the finished product. I was not closing the gap at 1500, but I knew the gap was really beginning to close at 800.'

Ovett was still winning the occasional 800 metres race impressively enough, even if his times were nowhere near as fast as Coe's national record. Accordingly, everyone across Europe expected the 800 metres to be a two-horse race in Prague. Coe says, 'I never thought of anybody else. I thought basically it would be between the two of us.' Ovett concedes that this was the year he began to see Coe as a rival. 'Yes, he ran very fast that year, faster than I'd ever done. Everybody thought that it was going to be a very fast race.' No one was prepared for quite how fast, nor for the identity of the eventual winner. But Ovett, though he hadn't realised it at the time, had had a preview of another potential rival.

The 'spectaculars' like the Coke Meeting, with athletes drawn from across the globe to ensure good competition in every event, were making the traditional two- and three-nation matches, with empty lanes and disparate results, increasingly redundant. But in mid-June, six weeks prior to Prague, there had been a UK–East Germany match at Crystal Palace. Ovett ran in the 1500 metres, and demolished another man who would be a party-pooper in the future – Jürgen Straub. The former steeplechaser had become a very good 1500 metres runner, and had already beaten Thomas Wessinghage earlier in the season. But, virtually ignored, winning the 800 metres very easily (Coe was not competing) was Olaf Beyer.

He recalls the London prelude to his day of days. 'I had certainly expected them [Coe and Ovett] to run [at Crystal Palace]. So, I was pleased they didn't, since that gave me a chance to win. I would never have expected to beat such great runners. Looking ahead, I would have thought, Where can I finish? First and second are already booked, so I might take third or fourth. When they weren't there, we could raise our estimates a bit.' It was a valuable lesson, but only for Beyer.

In Prague, life went on as normal, despite the change of scenery. Coe was available to the press, Ovett wasn't ... with the very occasional exception. He'd always said the press boycott was not 100 per cent, and one man who could testify to that was Alain Billouin from *L'Equipe*. But Billouin had to work hard for his interview. 'I found out where Ovett was staying in Prague, and I went to his hotel, and got David Jenkins to go in and talk to Ovett for me. Jenkins came out and said, "Sorry, but he won't talk." But I decided to stay anyway, and three hours later Ovett came out. He saw me and said, "Look, I've got to go somewhere, but I'm happy to talk to you as we walk." So that's what I did, and he was perfectly good, and answered everything I asked.'

Ovett vaguely remembers the incident. 'I was never totally averse to talking to the press and I think the foreign press were a little bit different. I suppose you treat them with a certain amount of respect, whereas I had very little respect for what was going on domestically. *L'Equipe* was always the magazine that I used to respect as an adolescent. It was proper, a bit like the *Financial Times* for financial information. And Alain was a persistent guy. I remember talking and he was happy, it was an exclusive interview. I didn't give him the in-depth Steve Ovett, but I think he was more than happy with it.'

Which is more than most could say for Prague. But many Western Europeans visiting the East for the first time and labelling it dour were being signally unfair. Had Prague been part of Western Europe after the Second World War, it might even have rivalled Paris. The German annexation of Czechoslovakia meant that the city had not been destroyed, like Warsaw, or scarred, like Budapest. And the medieval buildings, narrow cobbled streets and avant-garde theatre, opera and puppet-shows, for those who sought them out, made an intriguing adjunct to the championships. Added to which, the lively bars and restaurants, serving the best beer in the world, and the Czech *joie de vivre*, personified by the ebullient Emil Zátopek, one of the greatest distance runners in history, meant that it was a cut above most cities in Eastern Europe, and many in the West.

But it was two West Europeans who were setting the pace in the stadium. The British pair dominated their heats, with the other two qualifying races being won by Beyer and Andreas Busse. The East Germans underlined their heat wins by finishing second to the Brits in the semi-finals. Even so, no one saw them as threats to Coe and Ovett.

Coe and his father had their plan, as usual, and they decided to go through with it even though Coe was feeling the after-effects of a stomach bug, which had caused him to lose a couple of valuable pounds in weight. 'We sat down before the race, and we analysed it honestly, and said never go into a race without believing in yourself. But this is an opportunity to learn a lot about these guys. I remember my old man saying to me, "I want to know at the end of this race what these bastards are made of. And it's probably not enough to win, but it will get you onto the rostrum." So I said, "You just want me to go out and run as quickly as I can in the first lap?" He said, "Yes, and hang on for as long as you can. I want to find out how much it's going to hurt." '

And that's what he did. Coe ran the first lap in an unprecedented 49.3 seconds, with television commentators screaming that it was an insane pace, while even experts looked on in astonishment. Yet there was still somebody with him, and it wasn't Ovett. 'I knew I was going quick, but when I got to two hundred metres, I'm fighting this guy off for pole position,' says Coe. 'And I was thinking, This is not supposed to be happening. Now, if I'd been a bit more experienced, I would have said, "Thank you, you take it," and I've got a very nice pacemaker, which would have made the first six hundred metres marginally easier. I wouldn't have won it, but it would have got me to seven hundred metres in better shape, because by that time I was caving in.'

Coe's first lap was just one and a half seconds slower than his best in a 400 metres race. That is a recipe for what is called 'oxygen debt', where the body's ability to run at speed is eroded by the build-up of lactic acid in the blood and muscles. It is a form of blood poisoning, the result of which is that the muscles and the mind begin to seize up, the result characterised by the graphic phrase 'treading water'.

Ovett had been waiting his moment, and it had arrived. 'I'd realised I was in terrific shape, and Seb went off very fast. I remember thinking, I don't feel tired. It was disconcerting. I was clicking my heels behind him, and I kept thinking down the back straight, When is he going to "go"? It took me two hundred metres before I realised he wasn't going to go; he was flat out.'

Coe got to 620 metres still in the lead. 'He came alongside, he was taller, and there was a white vest, and I thought, I've gone, there is nothing I can do, I've shot my bolt. He was off, not pulling away dramatically quickly, but he was away. The next thing I know, this blue vest came from absolutely nowhere.'

Dave Moorcroft, waiting to do battle with Ovett at 1500 metres, was an entranced spectator. 'With two hundred to go, I was convinced Seb was going to win. With one hundred to go, I was convinced Steve was going to win. With probably fifty to go, I was even more convinced that Steve was going to win it.' Ovett thought the same thing during the race, briefly: 'I swung around him [Coe] and kicked for home. Then Beyer, who had been accelerating from two hundred metres out, came past both of us, and pipped us at the post.'

Beyer had run 1 minute 43.8 seconds, exactly two seconds or a dozen metres faster than he had ever run before. Ovett had broken Coe's British record with 1 minute 44.1 seconds, the fastest he would ever run over the distance. And Coe, who would be almost universally criticised for his suicidal pace, had paid the penalty by finishing third in 1 minute 44.8 seconds, which was also a personal best for him. Nevertheless, the shock was Beyer.

The tall East German jogged to a halt, seemingly as surprised as everyone else. He turned, jogged back down the straight, and out of the tunnel, all inside a minute. He'd gone as quickly as he'd won, and, given the shock, there must have been those who thought it was all a mirage. The crowd looked to the Brits for their reaction. Coe was exhausted, and unable to register anything much, other than fatigue. As for Ovett, it is a measure of how some journalists never came to grips with him and his eccentricities that Coe's biographer David Miller wrote, 'he covered his face with his hands in dismay'. On the contrary, Ovett exhibited the panache which endeared him to so many people whose daily newspapers were trying to insist that he was the bad guy. He jogged to a halt, looked over at his parents in the crowd, grinned, maybe in embarrassment, and shrugged his shoulders. He says, 'I think a lot of people take their athletics far more seriously than I ever did. I have always enjoyed the sport, and I have never seen winning or losing as being a major concern. I mean, yes, it is lovely to win, but it is not life or death. You know, it is a sport at the end of the day.'

At the end of the Prague 800 metres, Ovett turned to find Coe, and they walked off together in commiseration towards the tunnel, with Ovett's arm draped over his younger colleague's shoulder. According to Coe, Ovett said, 'Who the hell was that?' Fast-forward a quarter of a century, to the Mommsen Stadium in a suburb of what was West Berlin, not far from the Wall which divided the city for three decades. The pate is starting to show through the sparse blond hair, but otherwise, Olaf Beyer is little changed physically from that day in 1978, when his tall, powerful figure, clad in the blue vest of East Germany, burst past first Coe then Ovett just before the line and strangled British celebrations in the throat.

No one, least of all the favourites, had given him a prayer. Even his colleagues were dumbfounded. Jürgen Straub – who would split Coe and Ovett in the Moscow Olympic 1500 metres two years later – says, 'We knew Olaf was capable of a great deal and was in good form, but we never expected him to beat both of them.' A race which had seemed destined to be won by one or the other of the British champions was stolen from under their noses. Inevitably, something smelled wrong.

Conventional wisdom has it that Beyer and his colleague Straub were products of the East German state-doping programme. Beyer's name (though not Straub's) *does* feature on a Stasi list of doped sportsmen and women which I have acquired from the acknowledged experts in the field, Brigitta Berendonk and her husband Dr Werner Franke. For the record, I asked both Beyer and Straub, whom I also met in Berlin, if they had ever taken performance-enhancing drugs, knowingly or otherwise. They both denied any involvement in doping. But, in the prevailing suspicion of the age, much was made of Beyer running off the track immediately after his victory in Prague, and submitting to his dope test in a record thirteen minutes, during which time his eyes were blank, and so on and so forth. This was standard Cold War fare, and about as reliable as tabloid astrology. The allegations are repeated in David Miller's first biography of Coe, and backed up in Ovett's autobiography.

But neither Beyer nor his coach Berndt Diessner were having any of it. Beyer said, 'I've read [Miller's] book, it came out in German. I don't know why it says there that I was wrapped in blankets; and as for the urine test, that's definitely not true, since I could never go to the toilet after a race! It took me hours to produce a sample; it's simply not true ... I'm the quiet type and, for me, the race is over when you cross the line. These days, people are allowed to celebrate, it's part of the show. I don't know if I could bring myself to do that. I always remember when John Akii-Bua, after his Olympic win, ran another lap over the hurdles. I couldn't understand why he did it. He'd done his race and it was over, why did he go on a lap of celebration with people applauding? Times change but, for me, I just wanted to get away. I never did a lap of honour because I was too much of a quiet type to do something like that.'

In a separate interview with Berlin journalist Jörg Wenig (who acted as my interpreter with Beyer and Straub), Beyer's coach Diessner backs up his charge's account, although he admits he was mystified by the runner's reaction. 'Right after the race, Olaf simply went out through the tunnel, which I didn't understand, but it was typical of him. Olaf is a very shy person and he would never have liked the idea of being celebrated. So he simply went through that tunnel and I later asked him, "Why did you do this, why didn't you run a lap of honour? You should have done so?" '

Beyer had been brought up in Tanzania, where his father was an engineer. It may well be that the youngster had drawn some then unrecognised advantage from living at altitude. By the time of Prague, however, he was back in East Germany, and had moved from the family home in Saxony to Potsdam, the training centre for the few top East German middle-distance runners, Straub included.

According to Beyer, 'Until 1976, I was coached by my father. Until I did *Abitur* [university entrance exams], I was training once a day. At times these were very tough sessions, which I couldn't often reproduce in later years. I ran 1 minute 46.8 seconds, just training once a day ... In 1976 I went to Potsdam and was able to do nothing but train for a whole year before I began studying in 1977. Training three times daily in camp had knocked me out, and in '77 I only improved by a few fractions of a second. I ran 1 minute 46.1 seconds against the best in the world in the World Cup in Düsseldorf, including Juantorena. I think the hard training only started to pay off a year later and the turning point was that from 1977 to '78 I could really train hard, injury-free. I was never able to repeat that.'

Diessner said, 'He was in absolutely superb form that year [1978]. He was a great talent. Before Prague we were training in high altitude in the Belmekken in Bulgaria. Ten days before Prague he clearly beat his personal best in the 1500 metres, running 3 minutes 36 seconds, then we had another test within a competition. He ran two 400 metres races, the first one in 47.3 seconds, the next one in 47.5 seconds, with a thirty-minute break. It was clear that Olaf could take on any pace in the final. I knew he could stand it. That was what I told him, and that was what he did . . . I knew if he ran tactically clever he would have a chance to win, and he would be OK. I expected that Coe and Ovett would kill each other off, so I told him to stay behind them. And Olaf was tactically a very clever runner. It all happened as expected. Maybe Coe was a bit too sure about himself. Running this speed for the first four hundred metres with a pacemaker would have been OK, but without a pacemaker? I think it was a bit too much, even for someone like Sebastian Coe.'

Beyer continues, 'I had already realised from their earlier results in the heats and semis that neither of them was going to be hanging about and would run from the front. That was obvious. My plan was to stay with them and do what I could. I had a strong kick, but so did they. I thought, You must stay with them, but at all costs not take the lead. Whenever I did that in my career, I lost. So I hung in and stayed with him. He [Coe] probably thought that if I was still with him, he had to run faster, and he did. I glanced at the clock and saw 49.5. I was feeling really good and thought, That must be a mistake, you've never run that fast in your life. Fifty-one seconds was very quick when I went on to run 1 minute 46 seconds, so I couldn't believe it. After five hundred metres he started to move aside, thinking Steve Ovett was behind him and wanted to let him pass. As he turned, he saw it was me and increased his pace again. I had no desire to go past. I didn't want to lose if they were coming from behind me. The tempo was relatively slow till six hundred metres, then Ovett went past me, I gathered myself again with two hundred metres left and I felt I still had a kick left. There was still a gap coming off the final bend and heading into the home straight, but somehow I managed it. A good day!'

That is something of an understatement. The fact is that neither Coe nor Ovett, nor anyone else for that matter, even his team colleagues, even the man himself, expected Beyer to do any better than third. He was truly a *deus ex machina*, in the same fashion as his colleague Straub would be in Moscow in 1980.

It is perhaps testimony to an unfulfilled career that Beyer is still competing today. After our interview in the Mommsen Stadium in May 2003, he competed in a veterans' (over-forty) relay, running 1000 metres in 2 minutes 48 seconds, a superlative time for a forty-eight-year-old. Beforehand, he had enthusiastically related how he had recently been training in Portugal for ten days, 'with a nineteen-year-old. We ran about a hundred and twenty kilometres in a week. If only I could do that every week!' Here was a man who clearly loved his sport.

Back in Prague, in 1978, there was some unfinished business: the 1500 metres. And Ovett was imperious. He recalls, 'I was pretty determined. It was the only chance of the UK winning a gold in those championships, so there was that pressure on me, and also pressure from myself to make sure I got a European gold medal, because I had two silvers, and that was enough. I made sure that I didn't do anything stupid, because I knew that I had one or two seconds to spare on the rest of them, so I made sure I wasn't in the position of being knocked over or bumped or whatever, and when I made the move, I was pretty straightforward, pretty cut-throat.'

The best judge of that was Eamonn Coghlan. Like many of his compatriots, going back to John Joe Barry in the late forties, and most famously to 1956 Olympic 1500 metres champion Ron Delany, Coghlan had won an athletics scholarship to a US college. He had liked New York so much he'd stayed on for years afterwards, living north of the city in the seaside community of Rye. In his house there, he had a collage of photographs on one of the walls. Pride of place was accorded to one of him in his Irish vest, arms aloft, crossing a finish line. If every picture tells a story, this is an ironic one. For Coghlan is finishing second. Out of shot, well ahead, is Ovett, who has slowed to a walk after winning in Prague. The picture is similar to those taken at the end of the Olympic 1500 metres in Moscow, when Jürgen Straub reaches for the sky, to celebrate beating Ovett. Except that Straub has finished second to Sebastian Coe. That's how it was for their opponents – finishing second to Ovett and Coe was a triumph in itself.

Coghlan is an extrovert character, and the New Yorkers, particularly and inevitably the 'Irish', loved him. He was the King of New York when either the Millrose Games or the Fifth Avenue Mile was on. At Millrose, in the carnival atmosphere of Madison Square Garden – where most of the staff are Irish–American – it was cut and dried. It was better than running in his home town of Dublin. Coghlan owned the Wanamaker Mile, the highlight of Millrose, winning it seven times in the late seventies and early eighties. That feat, since the track surface was then wood, earned him the sobriquet 'Chairman of the Boards'. Such was the affection in which he was held that, when he returned a decade later, to attempt the first sub-4-minute mile by a forty-year-old, the traditional US national anthem prior to the race was forgone in favour of 'A Soldier's Song'. He just failed to break the 4-minute barrier then, but did so a week later, in an even more Irish town – Boston.

There was an edge to Coghlan's self-publicising, however. Many even of his countrymen would have described him as a 'chancer'. There's nothing wrong with that, especially as a sportsman, even more so as a miler. One item in the chancer's repertoire is never to admit you're beaten. Ovett had a strong strain of that, too, as George Gandy, Coe's coach at Loughborough, once observed: 'You never beat Steve. Even when he lost.'

It always seemed to me that Coghlan would have loved to get Coe and Ovett onto the US indoor circuit, where he was practically unbeatable. How wrong can you be? A quarter of a century later, sitting just a few hundred metres from the Garden, scene of his greatest triumphs, when it might have been easy to equivocate, or drop in a throwaway justification, Coghlan was ruthlessly honest: 'No fucking way. I didn't want them on my patch. They were too good.'

They were certainly too good in their 1978 end-of-season encounters, in the Coke Meeting at Crystal Palace. But an opportunity for them to race against each other in front of an adoring British public was lost. According to Coe, 'I wanted to run in the two miles. Steve was running against Henry Rono, and I wanted to run, too. I don't think it was a decision by Steve, but I don't think Andy Norman was too keen to have me in there buggering up what was going to be a world-record attempt.'

What an intriguing possibility that might have been. Coe had begun his career at 3000 metres, the metric equivalent to two miles, but had percolated to 800s. This was the year that Rono had set world records for 3000 metres, the steeplechase, 5000 and 10,000 metres. Ovett had beaten the Kenyan in a 3000 metres at the end of the previous year. With Coe in there too, it would have been worth travelling across continents to see. But it was not to be, and after that, Coe never ran further than 2000 metres on the track outdoors.

At Crystal Palace he ran in the 800 metres instead, winning in 1 minute 44 seconds, breaking Ovett's week-old British record. In an exchange on the steps up to the press box, Peter Coe encountered Ovett's coach, Harry Wilson, and jibed him with, 'We told you it was only borrowed, Harry.' Wilson need not have been too bothered. In a year when Rono had carried all before him, Ovett blew away the Kenyan in the two miles, winning by eight metres in 8 minutes 13.51 seconds, clipping a fifth of a second off Brendan Foster's world record. Coe got caught up in the criticism of the 'Ovett wave', saying, 'I really cannot condone so much of Steve's behaviour on and off the track. He is without question a wonderful athlete, and my admiration of him as such is sincere and unbounded, but he does conduct himself in a way which regularly leaves so much to be desired. He should not belittle inferior opponents in lesser races the way he sometimes does. That is sheer bad manners.'

On the track, the couple's mastery of all but Beyer was complete when Coe emulated Ovett and ended his season with consecutive victories over Coghlan – in a 4-mile road race in Dublin's Phoenix Park – and Rono – in a slow mile at Gateshead. Ovett, meanwhile, ran what might be the fastest mile ever run at 4°C, in Oslo, winning in 3 minutes 52.8 seconds.

There was to be one more race for Ovett, which would be intriguing not simply for the result – another victory – but for the manner in which the event arose. It was something called the Dubai Golden Mile, but, in spite of the name, was held in Tokyo. Athletics was still amateur, in theory, but Ovett, and increasingly Coe, could command appearance fees of up to $3000. Neil Wilson had left journalism for a couple of years, and was working for one of the first sports management companies, West & Nally. 'It was fifty-one per cent owned by Horst Dassler and Adidas,' recalls Wilson. 'We were an Adidas front-company, and although Horst used federations for his own ends, he was very much pro the international federation. And he saw a threat to the IAAF from some rich people in Dubai, who suddenly had an idea that they were going to turn athletics professional, and run a circuit rather like the fledgling tennis circuit.

'But Horst manoeuvred them into using the same amount of money for one big spectacle, and it became the Golden Series. The first one was a mile in September '78. The whole idea started in early June, by mid-July it was all fixed, and to persuade the major stars of that year, who were Ovett and Henry Rono, to come along, they obviously had to dispense large sums of money. I was never a hundred per cent certain, but the word in West & Nally was that they were paying Ovett twenty-thousand, whether it was pounds or dollars, I'm not certain now. But it was the first time I ever heard of a race being that amount of money.'

Tokyo might have been the richest race at that point, but the most valuable lessons had been learned in Prague. Coe *père et fils* remained adamant that Prague was an experiment in front running. But, if anything, that experiment contributed to Coe's tactically impoverished run in the Moscow 800 metres two years later. Whereas Ovett maintains (and the Moscow 800 metres result backs him up) that he vowed never again to concentrate on just one man in a race.

The defeat by Beyer looked no more than a blip on the graph of the irresistible rise of Ovett. His all-round performance in Prague – silver in the 800 and gold in the 1500 metres – had earned him the Athlete of the Championships award, chosen by Czech all-time great Emil Zátopek. Back at home he won the BBC Sports Personality of the Year award. True to her lights, Gay refused to attend, but after a bit of soul-searching, given his media boycott, Ovett went along. Prior to that, he had to do another bit of searching – at the shops. Although he was now twenty-three, he'd never owned a suit.

One blemish was the British Athletics Writers' Association exacting some revenge on Ovett for his press boycott by voting Daley Thompson their Athlete of the Year. According to his pal Dave Cocksedge, this irked Ovett enormously, because Thompson was one contemporary that Ovett couldn't stand. In many respects they were similar characters: brash, opinionated, devil-may-care winners. Thompson was rarely gainsaid, but Ovett is responsible for one of the greatest put-downs in athletics history, when he described Thompson's event, the decathlon, as 'nine Mickey Mouse events and a slow 1500 metres'. Ovett denies it was intended as an insult to Thompson, but that was how everyone took it, and Cocksedge relates, 'I just thought he would laugh it off [the vote], but it obviously did affect him. He was quite stunned by that. And, to me, it was a vote of spite. Ironically, Thompson became more hated later by the press than Ovett. I think the press voted against Ovett rather than for Thompson. A few days after that, he said to me, "let's work out the average of Thompson's scores and see how that relates on the [event-comparison] scoring tables to 1500." It was 3 minutes 44 seconds. Steve said, "Christ, I could run three of those with a two-minute recovery." '

Despite his forthrightness, there was still a shy, private side to Ovett. Unlike Coe, who, according to close friend Steve Mitchell, had a succession of girlfriends at Loughborough, it seems that Ovett was never a ladies' man. But, four years after first noticing Rachel Waller training at Crystal Palace, Ovett finally plucked up the courage to ask her out.

14

Hare and Hounds

The worst thing that ever happened to British athletics was Roger Bannister breaking the 4-minute mile barrier. First of all, it fostered the impression that all was well with the sport in Britain when, just two years before, the team had won a meagre two bronze medals in the Helsinki Olympics, and would win just one gold in Melbourne 1956. But on a broader canvas it helped perpetuate the myth that Britain was still Great. Today, it's seen as one of the last gasps of Empire, along with the Festival of Britain, the coronation of a monarch who is still clinging on, and the ascent of Everest – by a New Zealander, led by a Nepalese.

But the worst aspect of the first sub-4 was the pacemaking. Because it wasn't just British athletics which suffered from the belief that this was the only way to do it, but the sport world-wide. And it persists to this day, to a degree that is ruining athletics. It didn't help that the sub-4 was accomplished by the sort of blokes portrayed by Nigel Havers in *Chariots of Fire* – fellows (in both senses of the word) who went out for a 'spin' rather than a run, and would celebrate the 3 minutes 59.4 seconds by going up to town and toasting it with champagne and cigars, and even, heaven forbid, some gels. Nothing wrong with a piss-up, of course, that's the bit of their Britishness that you can't fault. But their manner of securing the record, well, dammit, it just wasn't English!

Club athletics had begun a century beforehand, with the mob-run, where a guide would go out and lay a paper trail, and everyone else would follow. The practice – the origin of 'paper-chase' – gave rise to the first English running clubs, prominent among which, if only for its name, was Thames Hare and Hounds. So the practice has a long history of sorts, and Sydney Wooderson's mile world record in 1937 was set in a handicap race, itself a type of pace-making, since Wooderson was the scratch-man, or the back-marker, who would run the whole mile, while the lesser athletes would be off a variety of starts, a number of yards ahead of him, targets to draw him on. Reginald Thomas, ten yards ahead of Wooderson, acted as the main pacemaker.

There's nothing wrong with peers agreeing to pace one another, but that's on the understanding that they are taking a lap or a certain distance each in the lead, in an effort to improve their times. We frequently did it in inter-club races, two or three of us taking a lap each, but it was each man for himself on the last lap, with all of us out there to win, and that was the same philosophy espoused by the British Milers' Club when it was set up in the early 1960s with a view to raising the standards of national middle-distance running.

It's the paid pacemakers who are ruining athletics. Because they are effectively being paid to lose. How can this be ethical competition? Their forerunners were Chris Brasher and Chris Chataway, red-carpeting for Roger Bannister. They might not have been paid, but they provided the template. The rules of the international federation, laid down in part to prevent cheating in its many guises, used to be very clear on this one: everyone in the race/competition should be there to try to win – 'honest competition'. Self-evidently, pacemakers do not fulfil that criterion. There was also the understanding that everybody had to finish the race. That 'honest competition' rule has now been quietly dropped, and pacemakers drop out and are handsomely paid for their services. But the ethical question remains.

In 1953, the year before the first sub-4, Bannister had a rehearsal. Aussie international Don Macmillan paced for two and a half laps while Brasher trotted round a lap in arrears, waiting to pick up and pace Bannister over the fourth and final lap. Bannister recorded

4 minutes 2 seconds, but the AAA, to their credit, refused to recognise the time as valid for British record purposes, claiming 'manipulation'.

The trio finessed it a bit the following year in the context of the Oxford University AC versus AAA match at Iffley Road, and history was made, but at a price. By the same token, I was never partisan to the acclaim that Chris Chataway received for his world-record 5000 metres victory over Vladimir Kuts in London's White City Stadium in October 1954. Even as a kid, weaned on the those colonial moments – the Festival of Britain, the ascent of Everest, the coronation and the sub-4 – I could see that Kuts had led for 4,975 metres before Chataway drew level and edged ahead at the line.

Another Englishman, 'Galloping' Gordon Pirie, used similar tactics to beat Kuts, and break the 3000 metres world record the following year. But Kuts got his due in the torrid conditions at the 1956 Olympics in Melbourne. Pirie tracked Kuts in the Olympic 10,000 metres, and ran himself into a stupor following the Ukrainian, who at one stage veered off towards the outside lanes of the track, just to see if Pirie would follow. He did, Kuts turned to look him in the face, and they both knew then who would win. Kuts ran away, and Pirie disappeared back into the pack. In the 5000 metres later that week, Pirie let Kuts go, and ran for silver, which he duly won.

I occasionally run into Chris Chataway when we are trotting across Hampstead Heath doing what passes for training nowadays. Fifty years after his heyday, he is still an instantly recognisable figure, even from 400 metres away. The shock of hair is now grey, and he may have put on a pound or two, but he was always squarely built, and with those elbows round-housing for balance, he is unmistakable. About a decade ago, around the time of the fortieth-anniversary dinner for the sub-4, which he emceed very wittily – particularly with reference to Brasher, who responded the only way he knew, by chomping on his unlit pipe – Chataway said that there'd been no criticism immediately after that night of 6 May 1954 at Iffley Road, 'but a couple of months later, there started to be a bit of questioning of the tactics'.

It was the worst possible example of how to break a record. Unfortunately, it became an indispensable tool for Steve Ovett and Seb Coe, who, since they wouldn't, for whatever reason, race each other outside championships, made a virtue of pacemaking. In doing so, they must take considerable blame for the situation which prevails nowadays, where even they are forced to admit much of middle-distance racing is so predictable it's unwatchable. We have even had the spectacle of Hicham El Guerrouj, the leading middle-distance runner of his generation, agreeing to be paced in two World Championships, in 1999 and 2001, and in the 2000 Olympic Games.

It could be argued that countries 'new' to athletics – unsophisticated in the Corinthian nature of competition – are most likely to employ pacemaking in championships. The first example that I was aware of was Ben Jipcho of Kenya pacing compatriot Kipchoge Keino in the 1968 Olympic 1500 metres in Mexico City. Keino could have won it by himself, but he was afraid of world record-holder Jim Ryun of the USA. There is nothing wrong with being afraid of your opponent, but the crux of athletics competition is that the polarity of fight or flight becomes redundant – they blend into one. Keino had already run in the 10,000 metres, and finished second in the 5000 metres, and could argue that he was tired, and needed help to cope with Ryun, but it was already sufficiently established by then that Mexico City's altitude would militate in Keino's favour. He was born, nurtured and trained at an altitude even higher than that of Mexico City, close to 3000 metres up in Kenya's Western Highlands, whereas Ryun trained close to sea level, with its abundance of oxygen. Ryun would go into oxygen-debt when he tried to rival Keino, whose lungs were accustomed to the thin air of altitude. The Kenyan ran away to the biggest margin of victory in Olympic 1500 metres history. He and Jipcho doubtless argued that they were doing it for their country, newly a nation since gaining independence from Britain only six years earlier.

The Moroccans try to argue 'King and Country'. But Saïd Aouita, Morocco's first great athlete, does not agree. There's no love lost between the Aouita and El Guerrouj camps, but the former says, 'I think pacemaking is really good in the [independent] meetings: people come to watch the fast races. But in the World Championships and Olympic Games, I was always against. I don't like that. I don't like to name the people, [but] they are just not really champions. Show me that you are strong, show me that you are running faster. Show me that. If not, you are not a champion. I don't like to see some young athletes sacrifice their career for other people.'

Now, Hicham El Guerrouj is one of the nicest guys you could meet, personable, intelligent, accessible, yet there was widespread satisfaction when his paced tactics went awry in Sydney, where he folded in the final straight of the Olympic 1500 metres and conceded victory to Noah Ngeny of Kenya. I make no excuses for asking him, when he was in tears at the post-race press conference, why he thought it necessary to be paced in an Olympic final. He mumbled something about it being a decision of the Moroccan federation. That may be the case, but I doubt it. In any case, he was complicit to a tactic which demeans the Olympics, demeans athletic competition, demeans his competitors, and demeans the Moroccan youngster who was sacrificed like a lamb for a *meschoui*. But, most of all, it demeans Hicham El Guerrouj himself.

The worst thing in all of this is that El Guerrouj – an otherwise charming man – and his coach don't seem to think they're doing anything wrong. And why would they? Because the nation that gave the world the mile race, the nation that broke the 4-minute mile, the nation that produced Sebastian Coe and Steve Ovett, the men who changed the very nature of international athletics, well, if the Brits can do it, why can't everybody else? And that is the ultimate tragedy of Ovett and Coe's refusal to race each other outside championships.

The antidote, the cure for this malaise, should be apparent to anyone with even the most cursory knowledge of the sport's history. It should be as clear in the memory of those who witnessed it as the day it happened thirty years ago. The defining moment of twentieth-century middle-distance running didn't occur at Iffley Road, Oxford, on 6 May 1954, but at the Queen Elizabeth II

Stadium, Christchurch, New Zealand, on 2 February 1974. And the genius to whom we should all be paying homage is not Roger Bannister but Filbert Bayi of Tanzania.

When Bayi dared to run away from the field in the Commonwealth Games 1500 metres final in Christchurch, he created a template for Sebastian Coe, for Steve Ovett and for any middle-distance runner who wants to be proud of having stamped his or her personality and authority on the events which have done so much to define international athletics throughout the century and a half of organised competition. Bayi opened with a lap of 54.9 seconds and just kept going. John Walker, who had his breakthrough in that race, was catching Bayi throughout the last lap, and was barely a metre behind on the final bend. In those circumstances, 99 times out of 100, the pursuer bursts past to victory. With barely a backward glance at the big black-vested interloper, though, Bayi simply stretched away again, and won in 3 minutes 32.2 seconds, breaking Jim Ryun's world record by nine tenths of a second. Almost a second off the world record, and he had run every step of the way in front. What a man, what a hero! Bayi's performance is an indictment of every middle-distance man and woman who thinks that they have to be paced to turn in a decent time. The film of his Christchurch run should be compulsory viewing for every aspiring middle-distance runner.

It is the nature of athletics racing which causes the problem. Its essence, like that of any sport, is competition. Beating the other team, man or woman, and winning the contest is the end. But athletics has another yardstick of excellence – the world record. In running, that produces a parallel competition – runner against the clock. It has its place, but it should not take absolute precedence. The refusal of Ovett and Coe to race against each other, choosing instead to pursue paced world-record attempts, was the starting point for the barren situation we have today. Now, top middle-distance runners are led through a succession of paced races, with no effective opposition but the clock. Almost invariably, they get nowhere near the world record, and the result is dissatisfaction for all but the winner.

I was as frustrated as anyone by the refusal of Coe and Ovett to meet outside of championships, and criticised their solo world records as 'about as exciting as postal chess'. I admit to a measure of hyperbole because, since they were in the vanguard of reintroducing pacemaking as a means to an end, and they were succeeding so frequently, they built a high level of expectation, such that the excitement when they *did* meet in championships was as palpable to the public as their self-doubt was to themselves. Nevertheless, their example has led to a competitive wasteland much of the time in middle-distance running, and explains why athletics is going through a period of crisis which has nothing to do with drugs.

Steve Cram went some way to rectifying the situation, and two of his races, against Ovett in London in 1983 and against Coe in Oslo in 1985, are rightly remembered as great competitive victories. Both were as close as modern-day running gets to the nineteenth-century matches that Walter George and Willie Cummings enjoyed. Before Ovett and Coe, another great national rivalry – Gunder Hägg and Arne Andersson – provoked the Swedes into racing each other 23 times (compared to Ovett and Coe's 7), resulting in 20 world records. In Oslo in 1985, Cram justified the belief of Hägg and Andersson that more records would have inevitably ensued from more Coe–Ovett confrontations, because he passed the bell for the last lap thinking that a world record was out of the question. Hounded all the way to the line, he broke Coe's world mile record by over a second.

With impeccable continuity, I bumped into Chris Chataway on Hampstead Heath again recently, a few months before the fiftieth anniversary of the first sub-4. We trotted together for a while, and I mentioned this book. He stopped immediately, the better to impress on me, 'Of course, Roger's achievement was marvellous, but it wasn't in the same league. There's no doubt about it. Coe, Ovett and Cram were our three best middle-distance runners ever – by a mile!'

15

In the Zone

One of the reasons Ovett gives for he and Coe not racing each other more often is that their seasons were so different. Coe would invariably begin indoors, whereas Ovett would have a cross-country season, with heavy mileage, and would not be track-sharp until much later in the summer. 'Seb was obviously in better shape than I would have been to run against him earlier in the season at 800 and 1500. I'm still coming off a hundred miles-plus [per week]. He would have probably creamed me. Seb used to have a big Yorkshire Championships, running 1.44 or something like that, while I was still running 1.52 at the Sussex Championships.' For the rest of it, Ovett said, they'd be preparing for championships, and wouldn't want to get in each other's way. After the championships, they would have had enough of each other.

Notwithstanding the pained riposte of 'Yes, but seven races in seventeen years?', Coe's first 'big' year certainly began in the way that Ovett describes. Coe stepped up a distance and won the AAA Indoor title over 3000 metres at the end of January 1979. The first sight of Ovett was, as he remembers, on the cross-country circuit, finishing well up again in the National, sixth behind Olympic 10,000 metres silver medallist Mike McLeod. Ovett finished in a bunch of other great distance runners. It suited the pair somehow: the slight, fragile Coe running indoors, while the burly Ovett was braving the elements in nine miles of mud and ploughed fields.

Without a major championship that year, neither man was

looking to catch an early summer wave. Coe was preparing to take his final exams at Loughborough, and Ovett had announced that it was going to be 'a quiet year' in preparation for the Olympic Games in 1980. The athletics world was thus unaware that a tsunami was about to hit.

In his first outdoor race, Coe was reminded – if it were necessary – that he shouldn't run with a rough crowd. On the first lap of the 800 metres at the Northern Counties Centenary Championships in Stretford, he was bounced so far across the six-lane track that he was looking to the fence for support. He gathered himself, sped past the offending mob, and ran a championship best of 1 minute 46.3 seconds. He then negotiated the European Cup semi-finals in Malmö, Sweden, without any problems, another win, and prepared for his first trip to Oslo.

Ovett was making waves of a different sort. He ran in a British match in Bremen, Germany, on 23 June, winning the 1500 metres in 3 minutes 41.7 seconds, and headed off to race in Nijmegen in the Netherlands the next day. He won another 1500 in 3 minutes 37.7 seconds, the world's fastest of the year at that point. But an argument then ensued as to whether he'd had permission from the federation to go. There was a threat from new federation secretary, David Shaw, to suspend him. This was ultimately another dispute about amateurism, and who held the reins of power. Coincidentally, Coe would be involved in a similar dispute a week later, but little or nothing would be made of it. There seems little doubt that Ovett's stand-off with the majority of the media (he gave a big interview each year to *Athletics Weekly*, but that was it) fuelled the controversy, since no one knew he was going to run in Holland. Shaw admits that he wanted to suspend Ovett, but was overruled by his committee. In any case, as the federation's first professional secretary, Shaw had battles of his own to fight, against the 'amateur' clan. The result, however, was more bad press for Ovett.

Coe's late start in international athletics, compared to Ovett, meant that he had hardly travelled on the ad hoc European circuit. He had got into the Brussels meeting two years before only at the behest of Andy Norman, and had run there the following year. So Oslo was to be the start of his globetrotting, and it required Coe to show some of the bloody-mindedness that had not thus far been evident on the track. He mentioned to a team manager in Malmö that he was going on to Oslo, only to be told that he didn't have permission: 'I said, "I've got a passport, I've got a ticket, I'm going." In the end, they gave me permission.'

The team manager in question must still smile ruefully when he reflects on how he almost prevented the first chapter in Coe's rewriting of the record books. Compared to the 1500 metres and the mile, the 800 metres is a fairly simple race, in that it is an extended sprint. But maybe that's just how we've looked at it since 5 July 1979. Because Coe followed a pacemaker, Lennie Smith of Jamaica, through a first lap of 50.6 seconds – over a second slower than he'd run in Prague – with the pack twenty metres behind, before running the second lap alone, and steaming through the line – no winning tapes any more – in 1 minute 42.33 seconds.

When Alberto Juantorena had run his world record of 1 minute 43.5 seconds in winning Olympic gold in Montreal three years earlier, then reduced it by a tenth the following year, the consensus had been that the 800 metres was now in the 'Land of the Giants'. El Caballo stood 1.90 metres (6 foot 3) and weighed 84 kilos (185 pounds), and, in the estimation of those who had seen his temper, would have given his compatriot, Olympic triple-gold medallist Teofilio Stevenson, a few problems in the ring. The tale of the tape told another story. Sebastian Coe, standing 1.77 metres (5 foot 9), weighing in at 54 kilos (119 pounds), had taken over a second off the Cuban's record. Welcome to the real future of middle-distance running. John Walker was sitting in the stands: 'I remember putting the clock on him, and he went through at 1.42. I just didn't believe it, I didn't think anybody could run that fast.' In the seven decades of official IAAF records, only Sydney Wooderson, Rudolf Harbig and Peter Snell had taken more time off the world record, but the lower it falls, the more difficult it is to take off chunks. Coe had emulated those giants of the past, and taken his place in the pantheon of legends. But it was only the start.

Coe then had an impressive interlude, running his fastest 400 metres, 46.87 seconds – at last faster than Ovett! – to finish second in the AAA Championships. The better Coe ran, the worse, it seemed, Ovett behaved. The latter ran in the 1500 metres at the AAAs, did just enough to win, but incurred the displeasure of one of his admirers. The pathologically fair Mel Watman had conducted an interview with Ovett for *Athletics Weekly* during spring. Watman had urged readers to 'Forget the surly, vaguely hostile image fostered by certain sections of the press; don't be misled into dismissing Steve as cocky or arrogant because of all that waving to the crowd.' Three months later, Watman's exasperation showed through when he commented on Ovett's behaviour in the qualifying heats: 'Did he need to demean the efforts of those mere mortals scrapping for places in the final by running the last 30 metres across the track so that he finished, still comfortably ahead, out in the seventh or eighth lane?'

Unabashed, Ovett went on the offensive as Coe went back to Oslo twelve days later, to run in the Dubai Golden Mile. This was the big-money race that Ovett had won at the end of the previous year in Tokyo, but he was missing in Norway. He might not talk to the national press, but he had a way of making his feelings public, through the pages of *Athletics Weekly* and his pal Dave Cocksedge. The daily journos would transfer these thoughts directly to their back pages. Ovett would not run the Golden Mile, he said, because

> The race has got to be held here in Britain. We are supplying four of the field of 12 for the race, and if we have that many in it, we should hold it here in front of the British public and not have to trek over to Oslo for it. I've beaten the world's best in Düsseldorf and everyone who turned up in Tokyo, and now if the best milers in the world want to take me on, they must come here to do it. If they want to beat me, they must come here and race me – that's the right of the world champion, surely?

This was all great knockabout stuff, and, allied to the superlative results that Ovett and Coe were producing, was going to keep the back pages (and frequently the front pages) of Fleet Street in business for the best part of a decade. Neil Wilson's experience was common. He was back in journalism by this time, working for United Newspapers, which owned a series of provincial dailies. 'We didn't in those days send [a reporter] to athletics meetings; it was fairly rare. [But] I came home and suddenly found that Coe had broken the world [800 metres] record. He was from Sheffield, we had two papers there, so they said, "You'd better go anywhere this man goes in future." From then onwards, the press followed him everywhere. I mean literally *everywhere*.'

Surprisingly, given the way he had demolished the 800 metres record, no one among his rivals lent Coe much credence in the Golden Mile. One of the reasons was that he hadn't raced over a mile for two years, since beating Bayi in the Emsley Carr in an ordinary time of 3 minutes 57.7 seconds. Furthermore, in the two years prior to that, he had run in only a handful of 1500 or mile races. Walker was the world record-holder with 3 minutes 49.4 seconds, the only man under 3.50. He recalls, 'It was a funny night, because we didn't know who the pacemaker was going to be, and I thought Coe was an 800 metres runner, and wasn't going to run that fast, because his 1500 metres time wasn't that flash.'

Craig Masback, who was going to run the race of his life to finish third, had had an intriguing prelude to the race. Coe was thinking of doing a postgraduate course at Harvard. Since Masback was a Princeton graduate, Coe and his father sought him out for advice, and the trio had lunch together. 'Seb was viewed as a real curiosity. We obviously knew of his potential as an 800 metres runner, but frankly no one had thought of him as a 1500 metres runner. No one doubted that he deserved, from a promotional sense, from a potential sense, the right to be *in* the Golden Mile, [but] I don't think there was any particular expectation for him in that race, beyond the curiosity value. My recollection was that Eamonn Coghlan was the favourite in the race, given that Ovett wasn't present.'

It was the best mile field ever assembled, even without Ovett. The embryonic 'circuit' – and the money from the Dubai sponsors –

meant that it was possible to draw athletes from all over the world, instead of the occasional chance collision of top milers in one of the past Oxbridge–Ivy League matches, the two- or three-nation fixtures or even an Olympic 1500 metres final without a boycott or a banned 'star' – for there had already been plenty of those. Walker was Olympic champion and world mile record-holder and after a spate of injuries had come back to form with a world indoor 1500 metres record; Thomas Wessinghage was mile European record-holder with 3 minutes 52.5 seconds; Coghlan had recently set the world indoor mile record of 3 minutes 52.6 seconds; the slowest of the three Americans, Steve Scott, Steve Lacy and Craig Masback could still boast 3 minutes 54.7 seconds. Coe, by contrast, was the slowest of the four Brits. Commonwealth 1500 metres champion Dave Moorcroft and the Scots John Robson and Graham Williamson were ahead of him on paper, and made up the biggest national complement. Only the home entrant, Bjorge Ruud of Norway, and Takashi Ishii – in the field for Asian TV interest – were slower than the new 800 metres world record-holder.

Mindful perhaps of his slight frame and past misfortunes, Coe made a dash for the front. It was his best possible move as it strung out the field, and when Lacy took over after a hundred metres, the die was cast. None of the others seemed to know that Lacy was going to pace, but Scott, who always made sure he was near the front in any race, was in his lee, with Coe right behind. When Lacy dropped out at halfway at 1 minute 55 seconds – perfect pace for sub 3.50 – Scott readily took over. By now, the rest were ten or more metres behind.

Although Coe had run plenty of 1500s in the past, and had won his last mile, those races had not been at this pace, and he was now entering the unknown territory which had been a hazard for milers throughout the century of record chasing – the dreaded 'third lap'. 'Peter and I always knew the third lap would be critical for someone who was a jumped-up 800 metres runner and not, on experience, a true miler,' Coe told biographer David Miller. But Steve Scott was going to give him an unwitting lift.

'I took over the pace on that third lap,' explains the American, 'and, I mean, none of us thought that Coe was going to be a factor. He was a very good 800 metres runner but hadn't proved himself over a mile. It was like, OK, now you are running with the big boys and you've got to prove yourself. So when I took over the lead and felt someone on my shoulder, the last person I thought it was going to be was Coe. I don't remember exactly when he took over, but I know the one thing was we were all in kind of shock that not only would he kick all of our rear ends, but he also breaks the world record in his first mile attempt.'

Coe took over just before the bell for the final lap. He had six metres on Scott, and over twenty-five metres on the rest. The gap was still a dozen metres at the end, and Coe had shaved two fifths of a second from Walker's record. After almost a decade of planning and preparation, it had taken just thirteen days for him to annexe the middle-distance double that only Peter Snell and Sidney Wooderson had accomplished in the previous half-century. He was holder of the 800 metres and mile records at the same time.

Coe's most telling comment was: 'I was mentally prepared to be hurt on that [third] lap, and to go through a pain barrier, but it didn't happen. It was not all that hard.' Between them, Peter Coe and George Gandy had forged a stayer as strong as Sheffield steel. There was something more than simply the record: it was the manner of its acquisition that impressed his competitors. Eamonn Coghlan says, 'Seb Coe introduced something to me I'd never experienced before: running very fast from the start – he was gone.' Dave Moorcroft concurs: 'That's dead right. We'd kind of amble round the first lap. For example, I finished well down the field, and ran a personal best of 3.54. I never got on the pace, and it was the fastest first lap I'd ever run, must have been about 57 seconds. Years later, you'd occasionally go through in 55.'

Coe himself rightly points to Bayi as the precursor: 'I changed the face of 800 metres running. I don't think I changed the face of 1500 metres running. Bayi did that.' Nevertheless, Coe was the inheritor and the perfector. There have been few runners in history who would take this tactic to its limit, and Coe is the archetype. Another inveterate front-runner, the Ukrainian hard man Vladimir

Kuts had once said of the tactic, which early in his career had resulted in many defeats, 'I knew one day they would never come back.' In Kuts' case, the double gold at 5000/10,000 metres at the Melbourne Olympics would be his justification. The Golden Mile in Oslo in 1979 was only the second of many for Coe.

Craig Masback remembers the aftermath of the historic race: 'There was a dinner in a sort of dark room somewhere in central Oslo that only the milers were invited to. For some reason, three of us ended up being separated from the rest. I think it was because John Walker was getting a lot of phone calls, [wanting] his reaction from New Zealand and around the world. People wanted to know how he felt losing his record. Coe, I think, never had a chance to change [out of his kit].

'I'll never forget it, because John went in first and the entire room, which was primarily the people from the race and maybe a coach or two, stood up and applauded him. It was the first time to sort of recognise him for being the first sub 3.50 miler and for coming and racing in this great race where he knew he wasn't going to win and wasn't going to set a record but putting himself out there. Then Seb walked in and he got a standing ovation from the group, and it was the first time where I think it really sunk in for him what he had achieved. It was like he was almost in shock, to have his peers give him a standing ovation. That is what indicated to him that he had joined this incredibly small elite group of people who were world record-holders in the mile.'

Walker recalls, 'I was introduced as a world record-holder, as pride of the world. And five minutes later it was all over, and the whole focus of the thing shifted from me to him, in one night.' Well, not entirely to 'him', as there was, of course, a notable absentee.

Steve Scott believes Ovett played a tactical card. 'It was highly unusual that Ovett wasn't in that mile race, because Ovett had been the dominant force in the mile/1500 since '77, '78 and going into '79. He was undefeated. It was very suspicious. I mean, Oslo was always the big mile race of the year, and I think that was a pretty good indicator of Ovett's frailness in confidence that he wouldn't want to be there and show Coe a thing or two. I think that he purposely avoided racing him.'

This is a theme that Scott returned to a couple of times during our interview: that Ovett was not as confident as he seemed. And he was not alone in voicing that opinion. 'Steve was such a tremendous competitor and it showed by how he raced, but I don't know if he was putting on a façade or what, but when he was off the track it seemed to me that he was really not a very confident person in his ability. I don't know whether it was because we were his competitors and so he wanted to come across that way, or whether it truly is the case. But if you look at his career, he was always very dependent on [someone]. In the beginning his mum travelled with him wherever he went, to every race. Then it was Andy [Norman] and then it was his wife, so very rarely did you ever see him travel anywhere by himself.

'There always had to be someone there to keep building him up and keep stroking his confidence. And again, from my conversations with him, I don't think he was a real confident person. You certainly wouldn't see it when he stepped on the line – all of a sudden he became a lion – but in between times he wasn't that way. It was remarkable the things he would say. After a race, he would just be, like, "Gosh, I don't know where that came from, I just felt ghastly going into that." And I'm like, "Oh right!" So again, I don't know if he was just playing a game, but that was always my perception, that considering what he had accomplished he didn't really come across as someone that had a lot of confidence.'

I interviewed Scott quite early on in the research for this book, and at the time his comments came as quite a surprise. I'd always felt that Ovett was shy, something he readily admits, but this was something new. Yet others would back it up, prompted or otherwise. One of Ovett's later training partners, Bob Benn, put a different perspective on it: 'I think it was quite an astute observation from Steve Scott really, because you know he [Ovett] travelled a lot with Rachel and perhaps a lot of people would frown on that. You are going off to break a world record, you don't to the outside world turn it into a little "jolly", take your wife or the girlfriend along. But that was important to him, that human side to Steve, which a lot of people found difficult to understand – because of the way he was portrayed and conveyed to the public at large. They couldn't believe he had that side to him, but he certainly was a very sensitive person.'

In retrospect, I had had personal experience of Ovett's need for company, but I had not given it any credence at the time. Prior to the Olympics in Los Angeles in 1984, I had been the only British journalist at the Lausanne meeting. This was before the event became a Grand Prix and moved to the local football stadium. It was on a tiny municipal track down beside Lake Léman, and, similar to Koblenz on the Rhine, the floodlights would attract hordes of moths, lending the event an atmosphere of what Americans call a 'cow-pasture meet'. Right up Ovett's street, in fact. After the meeting, he asked if I wanted to accompany him on a training run the following morning. I gladly agreed, after being assured that it would be no more than a trot, to get the stiffness out of his legs. We ran down to the lakeside track, and when he said he wanted to do a few strides on the track, I turned to run back to the hotel. I was bemused when he insisted that I stay while he did his short session, but gave it no further thought until Scott and Benn started to discuss this side to his character.

If it was the case that Ovett harboured profound doubts about his ability, among the media adulation at Coe's mile record, there were a couple of writers who reminded Ovett what he'd missed. The *Guardian*'s John Rodda, who would be Ovett's biographer five years later, wrote, 'Last night's mile . . . was the greatest race of all time, with the tenth man to finish, Ken Hall of Australia, doing so in 3.55.3. Steve Ovett must really eat his words about the victory in the race he missed being hollow.' Frank McGhee in the *Daily Mirror* gloated: 'Sebastian Coe established himself as indisputably the world's greatest middle-distance runner. How does that feel, Steve Ovett?'

Provincial journalists – as Reg Hook, the Brighton *Argus* correspondent, pointed out – had a different agenda. Coe had brought the mile record back to Britain – its spiritual home. But residents of his adopted county would go a step further – he had brought it back to Yorkshire, since the previous British record-holder had been Derek Ibbotson, from Longwood Harriers, Huddersfield. And Granville Beckett, Ibbo's clubmate and *Yorkshire Post* athletics correspondent, could tell Scott, Walker, Coghlan and co., maybe even Coe, a thing or two, because after the 800 metres record two weeks earlier, Beckett had written, 'the next time Coe runs a mile, he'll break that world record as well'. The *Post* did a 'rag-out': they reprinted Beckett's forecast on the front page.

Ovett was canvassed for a response, which managed to be appreciative while carrying a sting in the tail. 'Congratulations to Seb, he is running brilliantly at the moment. To be honest, when you hear times like that they can be quite frightening, but for me it doesn't change anything. I don't get caught up in times. I never run against the clock. I run against men on the day.' This unequivocal philosophy would, however, be thrown out without a backward glance within the month.

Coe was in the zone, and underlined it with his most authoritative 800 metres victory, from a competitive point of view. Languishing near the back of the field on the opening lap of the European Cup final in Torino, he turned on the after-burners in the last 200 metres and flayed the opposition, which included Willi Wülbeck – who had elbowed him off the track in the same event two years before – and Olaf Beyer, who had outwitted him and Ovett in the European Championships the previous year. Coe then ran the last lap of the 4 x 400 metres relay in 45.5 seconds. This was off a rolling start, taking the baton on the run, but nevertheless put Ovett's time for the distance in the shade.

A middle-distance hat-trick beckoned, and Coe would respond with his third world record in forty-one days. He has always maintained that when an approach was made to include Ovett – whether Ovett knew about or not – in the field for Zurich on 15 August, he did not demur. 'What I did say in Zurich,' Coe recalls, 'was "I don't mind who runs, but you won't get a world record because there is no way I'm bloody going out there to do a pacemaking job for some guy who leeches off me and then comes by in the last thirty paces." I guess even then it was worth a hundred thousand dollars from [US network] NBC to get the record. So Brügger says, "No, I think I'll stick to the record rather than a head-to-head." And it suited me in a way, because I didn't particularly want that to occur before an Olympic championship.' Andreas Brügger was the patrician promoter of the Weltklasse in Zurich, and he would become a family friend of the Coes.

So Ovett was out, and the record attempt was on. Yet it almost went awry, and was a reminder of how inexperienced Coe was at this level. The pacemaker, Kip Koskei of Kenya, whisked through the first 400 metres in 54.25 seconds, with Coe right behind and the rest nowhere. This was the sort of pace that Coe was running on the first lap of an 800 metres just a couple of years earlier, and was almost suicidal in the longer race. Koskei throttled back, but the damage could have been done, had Coe not been in such superb form.

At 800 metres, he was still well ahead, both of the rest and of the world record. When Koskei dropped out, Coe had no option but to go for it alone. He managed it, but only just, taking one tenth of a second of Bayi's world record, with 3 minutes 32.1 seconds. Coe became the first man in history to hold the three classic middle-distance world records, although another all-time great, Jim Ryun, had once held the half-mile (negligible difference to 800 metres), 1500 metres and mile records. Being bracketed alongside Ryun was no shame. On the contrary, it was confirmation of Coe's elevation to the pantheon of middle-distance gods.

A decade and a half before the broadsheet newspaper sports supplement became commonplace, even the news-cluttered front page of the *Daily Telegraph* (*The Times* was on strike) found space for reports and photos of all of Coe's records. That had much to do with the enduring resonance of those 800 metres (or half-mile) and mile records. Former double world record-holder Sydney Wooderson was quoted: 'I could not keep up with the intense competition nowadays. It is incredible that Coe should break these records in such a short time.'

Ovett, in comparison, was looking increasingly mortal. And the bracketing of Coe with Ryun will have hit him especially hard, since Ryun had been Ovett's hero in his mid-teens, to the extent that, as will be recalled, Ovett tried to ape the American's training. But Ovett was about to pay Coe an even greater compliment, although it's doubtful he saw it that way. He was going to jettison his oft-stated philosophy of racing the man rather than the watch. Steve Ovett was going record chasing. It was apostasy! He shrugged it off, but even his pals were surprised, and maybe a little disappointed.

Coe recalls being taken aback, too. 'I was surprised that he went for it in such a big way, because he's a remarkably independent thinker, [but] it's human nature with competition. He suddenly looked at a guy who was beginning to trespass into his areas.' Dave Cocksedge, though, is still bemused by Ovett's decision: 'That was a strange thing, wasn't it? I couldn't really understand that. He may have been influenced by Andy [Norman] or someone [else] to start record chasing.'

Reg Hook, the Brighton club president, has a theory that Ovett's decision had something to do with the increasing problems at home over Rachel. 'It did surprise me that he was going for these world records with a pacemaker. If he was getting world records in a good race, that wouldn't have surprised me at all, because he had such talent. But I think he had this problem at home, so he wasn't getting any advice from home, and I think to a certain extent Andy Norman stepped in. He was going into these races where he had his pacemaker and that is not the type of event that he really enjoyed. It's nice to have a world record, but I'm certain he found competition much more attractive.'

Matt Paterson had been trying to get Ovett to go faster for years, and welcomed the move. 'Up to then, I don't think Steve was interested: he just wanted to win and win well. I would say to him, "Look, you can run faster than that, you are bloody just jogging. Why don't you start going for times?" If you are in a sport like athletics where it is very objective, you are measured according to how fast you run. I mean, you have to do it. But I think he got drawn into it because, as the sport became more professional, I think he had to start chasing times. I think Andy was behind a lot of that as well, you know. He wanted to see Steve going for records because Coe had started breaking the world records.'

Once he had decided, Ovett went at it full bore. And it says much for his talent and determination that he got so close to Coe's mile record at a venue not known for track world records – Crystal Palace. Paterson voices the view of the cognoscenti when he says, 'You know what Crystal Palace is like [in] September [in fact, 31 August] – usually windy, no one breaks world records there. And no one knew about it. I don't think even Harry Wilson [Ovett's coach] knew about it. Thomas Wessinghage was involved in the pace setting, I remember. I was sitting with all the other coaches, and I think they went through [the first two laps] in something like 54/55 seconds and 1.52/1.53 seconds. And they were all going, "What is going on here? This is world-record pace." And I said, "Oh yes, I think it is." And he ran 3.49 point something. It was a great race and I think he came away thinking to himself, God, I think I can go after some of these records. He got a big kick out of that, and it probably still is one of the fastest times ever run at Crystal Palace.'

Ovett ran 3 minutes 49.6 seconds. It was the fastest time ever recorded in Britain, but three fifths of a second slower than Coe's world record, and a fifth slower than John Walker's previous best. Ovett was the third fastest in history, and still had not lost a middle-distance race for over two years. Coe, nursing a minor injury that had ended his season, watched appreciatively from the stands. 'It was as perfect a race as I've ever seen, a real classy run,' he remembered.

When he had graduated from Loughborough earlier in the year, Coe had been planning a career in the City. He even had an interview lined up for the Foreign Desk at Barclays. The world records had changed all of that, and Coe was starting to get the spin-offs from his classy runs, one of which was a top-of-the-range Saab. His close friend and training partner at Loughborough Steve Mitchell recalls, 'He couldn't even drive at the time. I don't think those things changed him, he was very level-headed.' If Coe was ever embarrassed at the image he was projecting, one occasion was as a result of an impromptu remark following an interview with Frank Bough on BBC TV. Bough ended the exchange with Coe by saying, 'What an attractive young man.' As Coe told his biographer David Miller, 'I got the most impossible stick for months afterwards. I couldn't go anywhere without ribald remarks being made.'

Coe was also present at Ovett's next world-record attempt, at 1500 metres in Brussels. This had been Coe's first foreign independent meeting three years earlier, and he was fêted by the organisers – driven around the track to the strains of 'Land of Hope and Glory' and 'Rule Britannia'. Ovett took up the British baton, and ran with it. This time, he was just eight hundredths of a second from Coe's world record.

Coe had had an *annus mirabilis*, but Ovett had had a *finis proximus*. There was little doubt that, had they been on the track together in any of those races, the result could have gone either way. But the world records were all Coe's, and, for the first time, Ovett was in the lee. As he was in the final event of the year, the Coke Meeting at Crystal Palace, where he had another go in the mile. He clocked a 'disappointing' 3 minutes 55.3 seconds.

But the British public was justifiably agog, as was a reasonable part of the rest of the world. In the wake of Coe and Ovett (strictly in that order, for the first time), thirteen other Brits broke 4 minutes for a mile that year. It is a statistic which provokes awe and wonder at the start of the twenty-first century. The British hold on the golden distance – the mile (and its metric counterpart, the 1500 metres) – was total. In the wake of Ovett's win the previous year, Sir Roger Bannister presented Coe with the BBC Sports Personality of the Year award. All that remained for the pair at that point was to hold it all together for the Olympic Games.

16

Zen and the Art of Winning

Nothing becomes a champion more than a rival. A champion can exist in isolation, beating all-comers into submission and the rest of us into boredom. But, ultimately, it is rivalry which determines the champion, because the essence and *raison d'être* of sport is competition – between peers, with the result in doubt. It is a shame that so much credence has been given to that other arbiter of running excellence – the stopwatch. Both Coe and Ovett had proven they could run against the clock, but now they needed each other as foils to prove their greatness. And, finally, now they were both at their best, they were going to get the opportunity on the greatest stage – the Olympic Games.

By the time they reached the start line of the Olympic 800 metres final in Moscow on 26 July, the excitement was palpable, and a British TV audience of close to 20 million was testimony to that. The massive interest was partly because the build-up had begun the year before. Propagandists for heavyweight boxing bouts are probably the experts at 'selling' confrontation – often without the slightest notion of competitive excellence – but a couple of the most talented 'amateur' athletes in history managed to turn the game into an art-form in the months leading up to Moscow.

The bruiser Ovett must take a lot of the credit for that. Or maybe 'blame' is the appropriate word. He doesn't remember now, he says – and Coe has either forgotten or forgiven; and in the grand Olympic scheme of things maybe it doesn't matter so much – but in the early weeks of the 1980 summer season, Ovett tried to jump into a couple of Coe's domestic races, even going so far as to issue a challenge via the national press. It's difficult to see this as anything other than gamesmanship on Ovett's part, trying to unsettle his rival before Moscow. Ovett, who was due to run in the 800 metres at the Philips Night of Athletics at Crystal Palace on 21 May, switched to Coe's event, the Bannister Mile, a tribute race to Sir Roger. The upshot was that Coe moved to the 800 metres, which he won as comfortably as Ovett won the mile, neither man extending himself on the track.

Ovett did the same thing the following week at the Inter-Counties Championships, switching to the mile and again forcing Coe into the 800 metres. Ovett then compounded the insult by not turning up, and Coe turned to the media for revenge. 'Both the AAA and Ovett are well aware that any world-class athlete programmes his season to be at a racing peak at certain planned times,' he said. 'Steve Ovett has never in the past been prepared to run in a race which did not suit his purpose and has been known to manipulate the field for his races … It is wrong of him and the AAA, besides being unfair to the public, to contrive a race between us as short notice … I look forward to racing Ovett when I'm ready.'

Coe went back to what he did best, and completed a run of four 800 metres races in ten days, with the last two, 1 minute 45 seconds and 1 minute 44.7 seconds, the fastest in the world for the year. That was his two-lap preparation for Moscow. Ovett, meanwhile, dragged potential Moscow 1500 metres colleague Steve Cram to the fastest time for a teenager at Crystal Palace, 3 minutes 35.6 seconds, three tenths behind Ovett himself. Cram fuelled the hype by saying, 'I think someone will beat Steve this year. He doesn't seem to have that little bit of zap he has had in the past.'

With six weeks to go until Moscow, anticipation levels were hiked up to breaking point when the pair broke world records within an hour of each other in Oslo in late July. The Bislet Stadium was the venue for several of their records, and anyone who ever attended a meeting there on a calm, warm, sunny summer's night will testify to the magical quality of the place. Oslo is small and accessible for a capital city, and the Bislet Games and Oslo Games each summer became the focus for the knowledgeable citizens. The stadium is right in the middle of the town, across the road from a brewery, and flanked on either side by apartment blocks. The track had always been six lanes, which means that the spectators are much closer to the athletes than with the typical eight-lane track. It was common practice for the trackside spectators to lean over and bang on the metal advertising hoardings as the athletes passed, adding further noisy impetus to the races. Throughout this period, a 20,000 full house was guaranteed for the two big meetings each summer.

A year on from breaking the world records for 800 metres and the mile at Bislet, Coe set out to capture the rarely run 1000 metres record on the same track. The previous mark of 2 minutes 13.9 seconds had been set in Oslo six years before by the 1976 Olympic 800 metres bronze medallist, Rick Wolhuter of the USA. As with Coe's 1500 metres record at the end of the previous season, the pace seemed almost suicidal on the first lap. This was the start of a new pacing era, and there weren't sufficiently experienced athletes to undertake the job. Trinidad's Mike Solomon whisked through a lap of 50.1 seconds, which would have been fast for an 800 metres record attempt. But, again, Coe held on, although Willi Wülbeck pulled back thirty metres on the last lap. Coe crossed the line in 2 minutes 13.4 seconds, and was now, like Henry Rono the previous year, the holder of four world records concurrently. That status would last precisely one hour – until Ovett crossed the finish line in the mile.

That race had an extra significance for two of the younger Brits, Steve Cram and Graham Williamson, since they had been asked to treat it as a run-off for the remaining place in the 1500 metres team for Moscow. They were about to receive a master-class in miling, and a stunning riposte to Cram's contention that Ovett lacked 'zap'. The British 'third man' in the Moscow 800 metres, Dave Warren, supplied the early pace, and this time it was spot-on: 55.5 seconds and 1 minute 53.5 seconds. Ovett then took it on himself, ran the hard penultimate lap almost a second faster than Coe had done the previous year, before cruising the final lap to end with 3 minutes 48.8 seconds, taking a fifth of a second off Coe's record. Behind him, Cram finished second, getting the nod for Moscow over Williamson, who was third.

The shadow of Afghanistan lay over preparations for Moscow, but the *Daily Express* alluded to hardship at home with its front-page splash, adjacent to photos of Coe and Ovett. Under the headline 'Smashing For Britain', and the strapline, 'Gloom Beaters Coe and Ovett Stun Crowd', the intro ran, *'Super athletes Sebastian Coe and Steve Ovett put the life and fire back into gloomy Britain last night ... which can't be a bad tonic for a country suffering the economic blues.'*

One of the morale boosters' preparations for Moscow were truncated when Coe caught a bad cold and withdrew from a 1500 metres in Stockholm, but Ovett was still backing Britain abroad. Two weeks after his mile record, he returned to Oslo. Unlike the mile record race, there was a top-class international field this time for the 1500 metres, including many of the men who would be forced to miss Moscow because of their various governments' boycotts – John Walker of New Zealand, Thomas Wessinghage of West Germany, Steve Scott, Steve Lacy and Todd Harbour of the USA – as well as Graham Williamson, who was in the world's top ten, but 'only' British number four. These were also most of the men who had been destroyed by Coe in the Golden Mile the year before. Ovett was going to pay them the same compliment.

Chris Sly, another British sub-4 miler, was Ovett's pacemaker this time, but his opening lap of 57.8 seconds was a couple of seconds shy of the required first lap. Scott, always willing to take it on, rushed through the second lap in 55.8 seconds. They were back on schedule. Scott led with a lap to go and then folded. The others were powerless to respond when Ovett made his move with 200 metres to go. Once again, it was that unstoppable acceleration that killed off the pursuers.

Ovett gave the crowd a wave with fifty metres to go, which

doubtless cost him a tenth or two, and hit the line in 3 minutes 32.09 seconds. It was six hundredths slower than Coe had run in Zurich, but, under the prevailing rules, he had equalled Coe's world record of 3 minutes 32.1 seconds. More relevant was Wessinghage's evaluation: 'Never have I seen running like that, never! To run at that uneven pace, to fool around, to play to the crowd and to equal a world record . . . I cannot believe it. A year ago, I felt we were starting to run closer to Steve. I sensed he was human after all. Now I know I was wrong.'

Ovett was ready for Moscow, and there were ten days of wonder and speculation before the 800 metres heats. But there had been heat of a different nature. If the pressure to boycott Moscow was significant to either Ovett or Coe, it certainly didn't show in their races. They were both unbeaten for the year, with a world record or two to underline their superlative form. And, as far as the Thatcher government's call for them not to go was concerned, for once they were on the same track at the same time.

Most of the Moscow team members, but specially the prominent ones, were getting sackfuls of mail, either supportive or condemnatory, the latter often in the most vitriolic tones. Allan Wells, whose 100 metres victory in Moscow – on the same day as Daley Thompson's win in the decathlon – paved a golden path for the Ovett–Coe double, thought the pressure from Downing Street was a disgrace. In an interview with the *Daily Telegraph* in early 2004, Wells recalled, 'I must have received six letters from No. 10, the last of which included a picture of a young girl sprawled dead on the ground, with a doll lying six inches from the tips of her fingers. It made me so angry I became even more determined to compete as long as the British Olympic Association did not insist otherwise. It was a very distasteful and underhand tactic; if at any time I had thought that by boycotting the Olympics one child was not going to be killed, then I wouldn't have hesitated in staying behind, but in my heart I couldn't see how my presence in Moscow was going to cause more deaths.'

As a policeman, shot-putter Geoff Capes had a further burden, since civil servants were being put under extra pressure. Fortunately, each individual sports federation was given the choice, and the athletics federation overwhelmingly voted to go, so he was allowed to participate. Individually, Capes had an opportunity for the perfect response. When he retired a couple of years later, he voiced unequivocal criticism of commerce and industry being exempted from the boycott call – British companies supplied much of the field-event equipment to the Moscow organisers. For those who never saw Capes, either as a shot-putter, or as winner of the trash-TV show *World's Strongest Man*, picture, if you will, Bluto in the *Popeye* cartoon, because Capes could have been the model for the huge, burly, bearded character. 'There was a by-election the following year,' Capes related. 'And the Tory candidate came to my door. I pointed down the path and said, "There's the gate, son. Don't ever come through it again." '

Ovett was equally unsubtle, or rather, there were many who thought so. When he had broken the world mile record in Oslo, he had been wearing the Soviet vest that he had received in a swap following a European Cup match a couple of years earlier from Valery Abramov. He wore it frequently, he claimed, because it fitted perfectly, and there was no particular significance other than that. But, given the political furore over the Soviet invasion of Afghanistan, and how it was going to affect the Olympic Games, in tandem with Ovett's working-class-hero (and media hate-figure) status, this was seen as a left-wing statement. He recalls, 'I am not naïve enough [to think] that sport should be divorced from politics, but I can't see how politicians can argue the case for boycotts and whatever when they don't do the same. I mean, Thatcher getting on her high horse, saying we should boycott this regime and God knows what else, it's so naïve. I thought she was totally out of order. I'm glad that the Moscow Olympics didn't fold up under the pressure of politics, because I think the sport would have suffered. And I'm equally sad that in LA the Russians boycotted, because at the end of the day it's the athletes that suffer and no one else. There was no way I wasn't going to go to Moscow and I don't think there was any way Seb wasn't going to go to Moscow. And I think the Russians were more than happy that we went, because if we'd have chucked in the towel, I don't know what would have happened to the Olympics.'

The irony of Coe's opposition to the boycott was that he was a known Tory supporter, would end the decade as a candidate for the party, and ultimately be elected an MP in 1992. Now Lord Coe, he rubs shoulders occasionally with another Tory peer, Lord Hurd, later both home and foreign secretary but as Douglas Hurd a junior minister at the time of the Moscow Olympics. 'I think we were all really paranoid,' recalls Coe. 'I was paranoid because I had a rearguard action here [we were talking in the Houses of Parliament]. My dad was brought in by a young Douglas Hurd to say, "Look, call your son off." Dad always laughs about it, because when he was in the room, he could smell the perfume, and thought the PM [Thatcher] had been in. Four or five years ago, Douglas said, "I had a meeting with your father; he didn't half argue well." My dad said, "Look, he's twenty-two, he has a degree in economics and history. I coach him, I don't write the scripts. If you want to speak to him, I suggest you speak to him directly." '

The pressure was even worse in the USA, where at least President Jimmy Carter did try to suggest an alternative, even if it was risible. Kenny Moore, who had finished fourth in the Montreal Olympic marathon and was now athletics feature writer on *Sports Illustrated*, the world's biggest-selling weekly sport magazine, was summoned by Carter and promised 2 million dollars to organise an alternative Games. 'There was a lot of that going on,' says Coe. 'That was before we got there, but I was always aware, having made the point that I didn't then want to do anything that overstepped the mark, and have the accusations flying back, "Yeah, we told you, these guys only wanted to get you there for PR purposes." The joke of that is [Colin] Moynihan and I got portrayed as some sort of closest Commies. He ended up as Sports Minister and I ended up as Sports Council chairman, and members of the party, and still are. It was just grotesque.'

The political preliminaries over, the athletes could get down to business. And business as usual meant that while Coe held a press conference, to which a multitude of 600 turned up, Ovett avoided the media – apart from signing a contract for three 'exclusives' with the *Sunday People*. I put it to him that that was not just contradictory, but hypocritical. 'No, I don't think so,' he retorted. I genuinely thought that it was time to have my own say. I was getting an awful lot of rather malicious press, rather snidey press, at the time, and I thought, Well, I'm not like that, I am not what they are portraying, this sort of arrogant brat, bastard, would never speak to the press, waves at the crowd … And I wasn't like that and I thought, OK, I won't try and rectify this, but I can say what I feel, and the *People* came along and they offered me a reasonable amount of money for an exclusive and I said, "Why not?" '

The quotes were rehashed in ten thousand newspapers, magazines and television shows across the world. There might have been dozens of sports in the 1980 Olympic programme, with thousands of competitors, but, as Steve Scott said, and many other interviewees concurred, 'It wasn't the Moscow Olympics, it was the Coe–Ovett Olympics.' Dave Moorcroft says, 'It was an equal split: you were an Ovett person or a Coe person. It was brilliant. The world stopped at Moscow.' Even in the USA, which ultimately boycotted, of course, Craig Masback recalls, 'To the extent that the Moscow Games existed at all in the United States, the only significant stories related to Coe and Ovett and the 800 and 1500. My recollection was [that] those were the only races shown on television.'

Ovett and Coe and their rivalry were even going to alter perceptions in the USA, whose television had been – more than most national television – almost wholly dedicated to domestic issues and athletes. US citizen Michael Carlson – now a British television commentator on US sports – had just come to live in London, and was working at that time for a television news agency. 'One of the things we were interested in from the US point of view was the presence of American athletes in other guises, playing basketball for Spain, things like that. But, since athletics was still the focal point of the Games and since Coe and Ovett were as well known as anybody would have been in the States, there was a lot of interest. What it did do was give them the stage all to themselves, and create the impression for American TV that you didn't necessarily need the Americans in those events to be able to create a competition that the audience would be interested in. Then, after the Olympics, they went into that couple of years' span of breaking the records consecutively, and alternating, and although we did have American milers who would get in there – Steve Scott, Sydney Maree – it wasn't that important, because it was "Coe this, Ovett that".'

Carlson also crystallised a difference in attitude that many people saw in the pair. 'Coe was always a very reluctant interview once you were on camera. He'd be fine while you were talking, but when you turned the camera on, he'd be more guarded, as if there were secrets that were going to get out, that would do his opponents some good. You had the feeling he was looking at a larger agenda than at simply that interview at that moment, and was worried about the image he was projecting, or concerned, so wanted to keep control. With Ovett, you got the sense that he didn't really care, maybe because the British press, that he wasn't talking to, were going to say what they wanted anyway.'

Whatever the difference, they couldn't get away from each other. If Ovett had paid Coe the supreme compliment of changing his whole racing philosophy the previous year in order to chase records, then Coe and his father would return the compliment in kind in Moscow. In their discussions on tactics leading up to the Olympic races, the Coes decided that Seb should run them 'Ovett-style' – playing a waiting game before striking with 150–200 metres to go. It looked simple on paper, and so did the rest of the prognoses, because, on paper, Coe was fifteen metres faster than Ovett over 800 metres. But this was a race, not a time trial. There were no pacemakers here. What's more, it was the Olympic Games.

Athletes talk about a first Olympics being for 'experience', and that was certainly the case for Ovett. He had been out of his depth in Montreal. Yet, that begs a question about Ivo van Damme. He was a little older than Ovett, but had less experience. He had been in the European Junior 800 metres that Ovett had won in 1973, and the Belgian had failed to get a medal. He had not even reached the European Senior final the next year, when Ovett won silver. But in Montreal, van Damme had run out of his skin and it took two greats – Juantorena and Walker – to beat him. But van Damme had won two Olympic silver medals, at twenty-two! Did he 'know', somehow, that Montreal was going to be his only chance of Olympic glory? Did he have some sort of impetus, borne of pre-monition that he was going to die just three months later?

In a lower register, Coe was even less experienced than van Damme. His first international win had been indoors. In his first big Games, the European Championships two years earlier, he had got carried away, no matter what his father said in justification, and been relegated to a bronze medal. His mile world record had come in his first 'circuit' event outside a couple of hops over the Channel to Brussels – at the Memorial van Damme. But none of the pundits cared about the lack of experience; we were interested only in the stats, and the stats said Coe was in a different league to Ovett over 800 metres. The latter had run only three low-key 800s in 1980, the fastest in 1 minute 46.6 seconds, over four seconds (or thirty metres) adrift of Coe's world record. Similarly, Coe had run only one even lower-key 1500, a university match, in 3 minutes 45.1 seconds. It was plain: Coe would win the 800 metres and Ovett the 1500 metres.

That was most commentators' opinion. John Walker, the reigning 1500 metres champion, about to lose his crown no matter what, because of the boycott, was more ambivalent. Shortly after he had arrived in London that season, he had wandered from his nearby hotel down to the Crystal Palace Stadium, and clandestinely timed Ovett doing a session of interval training, also called 'repetitions', since the athlete repeats a number of fast runs over a determined distance – anything from 100 metres to a mile – with a brief period of jogging for recuperation between reps. The faster the rep and the shorter the recuperation, the fitter the athlete – in theory. 'He didn't know I was there,' recalls Walker. 'When I tried to repeat the session he did, I couldn't do it. The way he was running, he could have won anything. I mean, Ovett could have won the 800 and the 1500. But so could Coe.'

So there we were, no wiser. And the heats and semi-finals did nothing to disabuse anyone of their beliefs. Ovett won his in 1 minute 49.4 seconds, and 1 minute 46.6 seconds, equalling his year's fastest. Coe won his in 1 minute 48.5 seconds and 1 minute 46.7 seconds.

But even here Ovett was going to make, if not a song and dance of his victories, then certainly a mystery-trip. After his first-round win, he slowed to a walk, smiled and seemed a first to be waving. Even his close friend and training partner Matt Paterson, watching from the stands with Ovett's parents, remembers, 'I didn't know what was going on. I thought, Oh he's doing some sign language. I thought it was just Steve playing games, like he usually does.'

Few of us get to be actors even on a minor stage, let alone the biggest in the world – live at an Olympics when you are the focus of millions of people. If you get that chance, you can project whatever persona you like; you can be what you want to be. Ovett played a part, and the audience loved it. In the past it had been the wave – of fun, of joy, of victory and, to some, of arrogance. In Moscow, it became a personal message to his wife-to-be. When the audience, millions of times bigger than at Crystal Palace or any other athletics event, discovered what it was, they loved it even more. Ovett says, 'Women remember that more than the race.'

After his semi-final victory, Ovett repeated the gesture, and the television commentators were so intrigued that they asked viewers to call or write in with suggestions, since Ovett was keeping his counsel at that stage. David Coleman, the lead BBC commentator, reported dismissively that 'one lady' suggested that Ovett was tracing the letters 'ILY' in the sky. But even the object of the exercise was ignorant of its intent, as she watched back home in Maidstone. 'I didn't know what it was,' recalls the then Rachel Waller, but 'my brother turned to me and said, "That's for you. It's I Love You." I realised it then.'

That simple gesture was going to take on a life of its own. It started a process which would take a few days to come to fruition, but when it did, it was going to have a serious impact, not only on Steve Ovett's chances of an unforgettable Olympic double, but on his future relationship with his supportive and protective parents.

In the interim, just about the only people who thought Ovett was going to win the 800 metres were his family, his coach Harry Wilson and the ever-supportive Matt Paterson. 'When we got to the stadium, I said, "Steve, you'll win the 800," ' says Paterson. 'We knew he could win the 800 and even Steve knew he could win the 800. It was just like it was predetermined. He had never had any other thought about the races apart from winning the 800. We knew that Coe had never beaten Steve in any competitive 800 metres race. The last time was in Prague and Steve had beaten him. Steve was underestimated as an 800 metres runner, and he was in bloody good shape. He was full of confidence and he knew that he could handle the heats and the semis and the final, and everything else. Steve was that kind of person, he loved the competitive edge of these major championships and he looked forward to it. I remember walking to the stadium with his father and his mum, and Mick was saying, "What do you think?" and I said, "Well, who's going to beat him?" I was surprised that other people thought that he *wouldn't* win it.'

Coe himself had begun to have doubts. His father had realised there was something wrong, that his son was nervous, like he once had been as a schoolboy. But, for once, Peter went against his better judgement, and kept quiet. 'The day before the race, and particularly the day of it, I was saying to myself, "Do I give him a firm lecture about concentration, or do I compound it?" I think I should have said a lot more of the things that are natural to me.'

Brendan Foster was sharing a room in the Olympic village with Coe, and recalls, 'I remember seeing him going off to the track to run the 800 metres final and he looked really confused.' Coe admits that, for virtually the only time in his life, he had trouble sleeping: 'In the European Junior Championships, I nearly missed the race because I was asleep! I have never had a problem, but this was the first time I couldn't sleep. The following morning in the cafeteria, I dropped a jug of milk. I felt uncoordinated. By the time I got to the stadium, I remember thinking, Oh, let's just get through this. It wasn't: Let's go out there and kick some arse.'

To make matters worse, when Coe saw Ovett warming up with Dave Warren, he felt it was ominous, because, as neatly as there were Coe and Ovett camps, there are still those who believe that the short period that Warren spent at the front of the race was pre-arranged as pacing for Ovett. Warren, after all, had paced Ovett in several races prior to Moscow. Alan Pascoe, former European 400 metres hurdles champion, and long-time head of the company which markets British athletics, was just one of the people I interviewed who trotted this out as if it were scripture. Coe's biographer, David Miller, makes the same allegation in *Running Free*.

Ovett says he would never ask someone to do that in an Olympic final, and Warren continues to be exasperated by the suggestion: 'I'm disappointed, because when you get to the Olympic final, there is no one who could ask you, tell you. It wasn't even certain that I would get to the final, but once I did, it was never mentioned. And the way the race went was quite extraordinary. Everyone, myself included, thought Sebastian Coe would go off quickly, but he didn't.'

Until an hour before the race, Warren also thought that Coe was going to win: 'I did, until we were held in the warm-up room, in the bowels of the Moscow stadium. They got us into this room for a very long time, over forty-five minutes before the start of the race, in this airless, dim concrete room. And there were seven of us there, and no Ovett. It was last into the blocks, first one out, and I think he was applying this sort of psychology. He did trot in about ten minutes after the rest of us, and I have to say that Seb was very, very nervous. I mean, everyone was nervous, it would be unnatural if we weren't, but he was very nervous. I looked at him and I thought, My word, strange . . .'

Ovett admits that he got to the 'call-room' after the others, but all he was doing was utilising his experience: 'I didn't know I arrived late into the call-room. I always make sure that I don't spend any unnecessary time in there. I think a lot of athletes get panicky and they go in quickly. I remember saying to Harry, "I am not going to sit in there with that lot. That is the last thing I want to do." So we waited until the final "if you don't come now, you are disqualified" type of thing. I went into the call-up area, and they were sitting around and I thought, Well, I will shake everybody's hands now. I shook their hands, and Seb was looking terribly nervous, and I said, "Look, no matter what happens out there, the sun's gonna rise tomorrow." Nobody said anything at all. It was all hush, deathly quiet.'

Ovett says that this was ingenuous – 'that's the way I am' – which may be true. At the same time, it's the best bit of gamesmanship you could conceive: thanking your competitors for turning up, because you're not going to see them again. I suggested to Ovett that his were the actions of someone who was supremely confident. 'Not at all,' he claimed, 'probably quite the opposite. I was probably as nervous as any of them, you know. I generally felt empathy for all of us in there. I knew the sort of pressure I felt, and I knew what sort of pressure Seb felt inside, and Dave [Warren] was there as well. So I thought, Well, you know, shake their hands now, and if afterwards everybody is weeping and wailing, there might not be an opportunity to do the same thing.'

David Moorcroft, who could have run in the 1500 metres but had opted for the 5000, was an enthralled spectator, and an even more avid viewer afterwards. He has watched the race video dozens of times, as has Coe. Moorcroft recalls, 'As he walked out to the line, Steve Ovett was in control of that situation; he looked in control. Seb looked frightened, and as they were running round on that first lap, Seb lost control, and couldn't get in the right position and didn't know what to do and looked very tense. I just don't think he saw the escape route, and, the thing is, there is a dimension missing in TV, there's an extra dimension that TV doesn't show. Things are happening at speed, even at 54 seconds or whatever the pace was, things are happening quickly, and reaction time is much less than television gives the appearance, and Seb just didn't make the right choices at the right time.'

Dave Warren saw his opportunity, and took the lead. 'We ambled through the first lap, which raises all sorts of questions. I mean, when you're going through at that sort of pace ... I wasn't a fast finisher, so you decide what you're going to do. Everyone's watching Coe and Ovett, so you make the decision of trying to get ten metres, and if you get ten metres, who knows what's going to happen? You might get a bronze medal. And, in a way, today, I'm much happier at having had a go, rather than stay at the back, and end up eighth anyway, so no regrets there. But, to this day, I'm still surprised that Seb Coe didn't go out. Even more surprised he spent most of the first lap running in lane three. Very bizarre.'

Ovett admits, 'It was a scrappy race, a slow, scrappy race. And I think that was because everybody was assuming that both of us were going to go off like ten men. And I certainly wasn't going to do it, and Seb obviously decided that was going to be his tactic. Maybe that was Seb's mistake, because in a physical race, obviously, he is not very strong. He finds himself having to go wide, and not really wanting to make a physical challenge.'

The most extraordinary aspect of Coe's tactics in the race is related to that wide position he adopted. Because, out in lane three, he was well placed to see that Ovett was 'boxed', blocked by other competitors, in this case the two giant East Germans. It should have given him a crucial edge, and more than offset the fact that by running wide he was wasting precious energy. Coe can see it now: 'There's one point in the race where he's buried, absolutely buried. He is coming down the finishing straight for the first time, and there is a wall of East Germans, and they weren't small those guys. They were bigger than him.'

Well, in one sense they were. But, as Moorcroft says, 'Steve was patient, but there was a point down the back straight where there was an element of fortune. And [BBC TV's] David Coleman did it perfectly in the commentary. There was a head-on shot of Ovett, and he wasn't panicking, but he knew he had to do a bit of "physical", and Coleman said, "Ovett, those blue eyes, like chips of ice." It was spot-on, because you could see in his eyes absolute determination but no panic.'

If the East Germans reminded Ovett of anything, it would have been of Prague, where he had made the mistake of concentrating on one man – Coe. Ovett suggests now that, among everything that he had ever learned in training and racing, this was to be the lesson that would deliver him the Olympic gold medal: 'I didn't even think of Seb in that race. If you look at that race, I wasn't concentrating on Seb, I wasn't looking for him, I wasn't behind him waiting for him to move or whatever. I ran strictly on my own tempo, my own rhythm, I never watched anybody who was going to be a danger and I just went when I had to. And anybody that bumped off me, which a few of them did, then they just bumped off me.' That was putting it mildly. As everyone admits, Ovett included, his tactics would get him disqualified today. Because he ran through the tall figures in front of him, scattering them like cardboard cut-outs.

Call it Zen, call it the zone, call it total commitment, call it what you will, but Ovett had become the race. He was consumed by the race. There was nothing else in his world for those two minutes. He wasn't thinking of all the training he'd done over the years, all those Sunday mornings over the South Downs with Matt Paterson, all those dark, cold nights on Preston Park with his dad flashing the torch on and off to indicate another 400 metres of effort. He wasn't thinking of his failure in Montreal four years earlier, and how he had to rectify the fault. He wasn't thinking about all the times when he'd been in a similar situation, and had twitched into action, and left the opposition in the dust and rubber. He didn't need to think of any of those things; they were assimilated. Nor was he thinking about his mum, and her care and her chiding, and her righteous anger. He wasn't even thinking about Rachel, and her love for him and his love for her. He certainly wasn't thinking about Seb Coe. That was plain. He never gave him so much as a glance. The lesson of Prague had been assimilated. He didn't have to think about it. He didn't have to think about anything. He *was* the race.

Coe, on the other hand, was wandering in a dispirited world. Graham Williamson talked to me about sleepwalking through the 1982 Commonwealth Games 1500 metres final, not knowing where he was, not switched on. This is what Coe was doing in Moscow. I would venture that the sole reason was Steve Ovett. He had seen Ovett win too many times. He had seen Ovett beat him too many times: just twice, but that was two too many. Soon it was going to be three. When Coe lurched into action it was far too late, a lap too late, a lifetime too late. Those prior losses to Ovett had taken their toll. Ovett's whole demeanour, the bustle, the braggadocio, the hand-off, the panache, the wave, the handshake, even the 'ILY' – all staged as they may have been, on the testimony of many, who felt that this was not the 'real' Steve Ovett – conspired to convince Sebastian Coe that he could not beat Steve Ovett on that day and at that time.

Ovett cruised through the line, and into a twilight zone. The huge crowd was cheering and applauding, but it was muted. The great confrontation had not happened. It wasn't Ovett's fault: he had done everything necessary to win, frightened the life and speed out of his principal opponent, and all the others, and run the perfect race. He was entitled to grin, and raise a clenched fist, a gesture captured in a thousand photographs. He looked over to his parents and Matt Paterson and shared their joy. He wrote another love letter to Rachel, and then he looked up into the stands and became aware of what he'd done. 'I looked up at the press and the TV and the athletes and everybody there, and there was just indifference and shock and disbelief,' he recalls. 'And I thought, God, that is bloody amazing. In the Olympic stand with the press and the athletes, there were only two people standing there clapping: Geoff Capes and David Jenkins. It was very strange. You reached the pinnacle of your career, and I had won everything that I wanted to win up to the Olympics, and I wanted to win the Olympics, I won the Olympics, and I thought, There should be more than this. I am not saying it was something which I couldn't deal with, but I did feel that other people's reactions were strange.

'I went out to Moscow to win. I hadn't been beaten in any races. People forget that I beat Seb before at the 800, in Prague, and they said that he ran badly in the 800 metres in Moscow. I don't think they gave me credit for running the way that I ran. I ran to win. I had always dreamed of winning the Olympics, you know, and after the disappointment of Montreal, I said to my father, "Look, if I ever get to the Olympics again, I will not make any mistakes." So I was very determined that any chance of winning a medal was going to be given a hundred per cent. No matter who was in the race, no matter how their credentials stacked up.

'I think one of the headlines was "THE BAD GUY WINS"! And I thought, Where has this come from, where has this bad guy come from? Because I didn't ever think that I was a bad guy. I mean, OK, I was slightly unorthodox, but I thought I had won enough races to make people appreciate that I was talented enough to be accepted. In the village, there were a lot of people who didn't know what to say or do. That is probably one of the things that at the time was very hurtful to me.'

Ovett was equally disappointed by the reaction of the British media then, and later: 'Even Mary Peters. I recently heard her on the radio, saying that she was devastated, or something like that. She rushed off to see Seb at the Olympic village to sort of try and rally him, and I thought, What was the matter with me? Why didn't somebody say, "Well done, Steve?" It was like a vacuum, I ran into a vacuum. I ran the race, and no one seemed to be bothered, and it was a very strange thing. I remember walking back to the Olympic village and thinking, Is this all it is? Is this all you get for winning the Olympics? I thought, God, what have I done? It wasn't as if I had committed a heinous crime. I mean, OK, so I rubbed the press up the wrong way, but I still won for Britain. And yet I looked up, I literally crossed the line, looked up to the press box, and there were people sitting there with their arms folded. There weren't many people coming up to pat me on the back. They were generally shocked. I think there was a genuine feeling of shock throughout the team, and team management, and from the press.'

There is an intriguing, graphic footnote to the Moscow Olympics 800 metres, and Ovett's post-race clenched-fist salute. Prior to the Golden League meeting in Rome 2003, my good friend, former Italian international runner and now journalist Franco Fava, mentioned to another colleague, Augusto Frasca, that I was researching this book. Frasca turned up to the meeting in the Olympic Stadium carrying a large volume under his arm. It was a beautifully produced book – as only the Italians know how – reproductions of paintings by modern artist Angelo Titonel. Prominent on its pages are three dozen studies of Ovett's Moscow victory pose, entitled *Il Vincitore* (*The Winner*). Even better, one of the studies is on the front cover of the book. There is also a postcard of one of the images, with a very Italian interpretation of Ovett's gesture: the card has '*Ciao Mamma*' written across it. While we were leafing through the book, British photographer Mark Shearman came across to take a look. He immediately identified the painting as taken from one of his photos in Moscow. This could have raised copyright issues, but Titonel had foreseen the possibility: in place of the clenched fist, he has made Ovett's hand open, with fingers outstretched.

The last word on the Moscow 800 metres should go to Seb Coe. Over twenty years after the event, his summation is concise and damning, of himself: 'It was just a fuck-up from beginning to end. If you ever wanted to [show] somebody [how] to make every mistake in an 800 metres, just [tell them to] watch this! You won't need to watch another video of any race because every mistake you can make at 800, I made. I was too far off the back, too wide, too diffident, [there were] exit routes available which I didn't take, not covering the breaks, then coming too slow, too fast at the end. You know the whole thing was completely wrong, but actually we are talking logically and there was no logic that day.'

Coe admits that, had he lost the 1500 metres, too, he might have given up. That is not something to confess lightly. There were times during our interviews in 2003 that I felt he was glossing the past, which makes this admission – and the possibility – even more extraordinary. Having seen the way he ran in the Moscow 1500 metres, and in Los Angeles four years later, it's difficult to imagine that such resolution could have been short-circuited.

But Brendan Foster had little doubt that another defeat at Moscow would have finished Coe. 'That was the time when Seb literally could have given up his career, between that 800 metres final and the 1500. He was almost like, "This is not what I want to do any more," and I felt he was at breaking point then. If he hadn't won that 1500 in Moscow, he might never have run again.'

Peter Coe was going to leave no insult unsaid in his bid to ensure that 'his athlete' came good. It was not done privately, either. Even the media were shocked at the immediate, public dressing-down. 'When he came off the track after the 800,' Peter recalls, 'I said, "You ran like an idiot, I can't believe it." ' It only got worse. As Coe came into the press conference, Peter was already seated there, even more incensed, and told him bluntly, 'You ran like a cunt.' Coe told me it was mouthed, or whispered, but, to those present, it was as soft as a stage whisper at the Crucible Theatre in Sheffield. Alan Parry was BBC radio's athletics correspondent at the time, and was shocked to hear Peter's brusque assessment of his son. In a BBC radio programme in early 2003 – another example of the enduring interest in the pair – Parry recalled it as 'a very audible whisper. I thought it was a bit over the top to do that in front of all the press.'

Coe could not mask his disappointment on the victory rostrum, and Clive James, writing for the *Observer*, described his handshake with Ovett, 'as if he'd just been handed a turd'. Coe believes his attitude was misinterpreted: 'It's always taken out of context. I was grey and I was sullen, and it was nothing to do with Steve. I got the silver and I was disappointed. I knew how badly I'd run; nobody needed to tell me that.' Dave Moorcroft concurs: 'Seb was less good at hiding his frustration. Steve has always been better at treating success and failure with equanimity. But I've seen Steve in private moments, and he's not a great loser.'

But Ovett was not a loser, at least not this time. After all the years of effort, it was time for a little celebration, but first he went to find Harry Wilson, who had gone out to paint the town with fellow coach Ron Holman. Ovett scribbled a note to Wilson and left it on his pillow. It read, 'Tiger! I hope you're as proud of me as I am of you – Steve.' In his book *Running Dialogue*, Wilson describes finding the message: 'I couldn't speak, but really that little old bit of paper is probably the most important thing I've ever had out of athletics.'

While Coe went to face continuing recriminations with his father, Adrian Metcalfe, who would produce television documentaries with both men over the next two years, witnessed an unusual side to Ovett at his parents' hotel that evening. 'After the 800 metres, all the Ovett clan and Andy, of course, and lots of hangers-on, we all went back to the Ukrainia Hotel – dreadful thing, a skyscraper hotel, nasty, seedy sort of place. But we sort of took over the dining room and we ordered all the champagne that they had in the building. There was a little Irishman who suddenly appeared from nowhere, and he jumped up onto the table with all this cutlery and glasses, and food and champagne bottles and everything. And he starts dancing on the table and shouting, "Steve Ovett, you are bloody, fucking brilliant," and Steve started to laugh. It was like suddenly he let everything go and he was just weeping with laughter. He was laughing and laughing and laughing at this funny little leprechaun who was jumping up and down, and you could see finally he was beginning to understand what he'd done. That was two or three hours after the race.

'You are in a zone really once it's finished. The first thing you want to do is just go back to your bedroom and close the door. You don't go round saying, "I've won, I've won, great, let's celebrate." There is a huge tidal wave that comes after it, but it's almost plaintive, it's almost a kind of huge sadness that descends on you in a way because of the enormity of what you've gone through and the whole history behind you that has pushed you there, being on your back, this kind of liberation. It's like a man coming out of jail, just like Mandela coming out of Robben Island. Everybody wants him to cheer and in fact he's a stranger in this land, he's a different person now. Steve was a different person. And suddenly [there are] all these complicated things that you can't realise or analyse. Nevertheless, he burst into hysterical laughter at this leprechaun.'

Coe was having a rather more sober interlude with his father, which must have begun from the premise that he couldn't sink any lower. 'We had a long chat, but we didn't agonise. There was no long post-mortem, that wasn't the time. We had to get the wheels back on the bicycle as quickly as possible. The following morning, I went out for ten, twelve miles on the road. I didn't even notice all these photographers hanging out of a car, which is probably symptomatic of the way I was at the time. Of course, the Sunday papers came in a few days later. There was a photograph of me with the headline, "COE'S TRAIL OF SHAME".

'The following day I ran six-by-800 metres fast, and then I started to feel quite good about things. I was sleeping again, and feeling quite confident. Then I remember whacking somebody quite hard in the semi-final of the 1500. That is the only time he [Peter] bollocked me, and bollocked me big. It is the biggest bollocking I've ever had after a race. I ran a good race in the semi, and I just got caught on the bend and I got boxed. Now, two things came out of that. One was that I got the mother and father of all bollockings; I mean, I cannot begin to describe to you the language. It was the Somme without the mud. He just came at me big-time, and basically the general thrust of the argument was, "You do that tomorrow, and you're dead. Do that in the race with Ovett, and you are history." But the interesting thing was that I got into a tangle, and I came out of it, and I knew the speed was back. I had a great night's sleep, and I was genuinely looking forward to going out there and having a real punch-up.'

When the pendulum swings, it goes as far in one direction as the other. While Coe was crawling out of the pit, Ovett was sliding into it. The press back in England had finally tracked down Rachel Waller to her parents' home in Maidstone. Rachel had never understood the Ovett family's antagonism towards the media. As she argues, 'My parents are rather polite people, and if somebody knocks on the door and says, "May I take a picture of your daughter for the local paper?" they actually think that is rather nice. I was in this awful position where I knew that if I suddenly appeared on the front page, or whatever page, of the newspapers, it was all going to be very awkward. But then, Steve did actually put me in that position.'

Matt Paterson was at ground zero when the nuclear reaction was triggered. 'I think it was the semi-final of the 1500, and I was sitting having breakfast up in the lobby with Steve, and Mick was there and Nick [Ovett's younger brother]. And Gay came in with this bloody newspaper and slapped it down on the table and said, "What the fuck is all this about?" I didn't know what she was talking about. There was a picture of Rachel, and then all hell broke loose, screaming and shouting and everything else, and it must have affected Steve – big time. It was very, very humid in Moscow and I think Steve was suffering from the heat, and of course the pressure was on him to keep on winning all the 1500 metres races, because he was favourite. I was still certain that he was going to win the 1500. I thought he would win both gold medals, and even walking into the stadium on the day of the final I just could not see him getting beaten. I knew what shape he was in and everything else, but what I probably didn't know was the effect of his mother and the family upheaval on him as well.'

The people whom I was always going to be most interested in talking to for this history were Ovett and Coe's rivals. They were great athletes themselves, so would be better judges than any of us county-class runners and journalists. There was a hier-archy, even among the elite. Most of them – John Walker, Thomas Wessinghage, Eamonn Coghlan, Steve Scott, Ray Flynn, Craig Masback, and even Steve Cram, back then – knew that they could beat the British pair only by default. One of the leading questions about Moscow was: does winning one Olympic gold medal dimin-ish your desire to win another, especially if it is a few days later? Or do you receive extra impetus to do the double?

Ovett told me, 'Yes, definitely,' it *did* diminish his desire, and that he wasn't speaking here with hindsight. 'All I ever wanted to do was to become an Olympic champion. I have always said this: had the 1500 been first, and I'd won [it], I would have lost the 800. But that is not taking anything away from Seb or any other athlete. The pressure that was on us at the Olympics stopped for me after the 800. I had won it, but for Seb it was still there, if not more so.' Bob Benn, a training partner and sometime pacemaker, even went so far as to make the extraordinary suggestion that Ovett *let* Coe win the 1500.

Steve Cram has a different view: 'I think he was probably a little bit complacent and thought, I've beaten him on his territory. I don't think it was anything to do with Ovett not wanting to win it: he hadn't been beaten in goodness knows how long, [and] why on earth would you not want to be the double Olympic champion? It was his event. It's the blue ribbon; the 1500 is the big one. I just think that he probably went in a little bit under-prepared mentally than he might have been. He wasn't under-prepared because he was "Oh, I'm not that bothered." I think that's rubbish.'

Craig Masback says, 'You know, once he won the 800, it's a cliché of everyone who saw the race, I don't want to say he didn't care about the 1500, but it could not have been as important as it would have [been] if he had lost the 800 and didn't have the Olympic title.' Ray Flynn, though, feels that Ovett is being disingenuous: 'Of course he is, but that's typical Steve: he was always able to shrug off things that didn't go his way, but I didn't have any less admiration for him. That has always been Ovett's trait, he plays everything down: "I was just taking it easy," or, "I didn't train very hard," or whatever. He is one of those people who always played down what they achieved, and almost makes a joke of it. But I never really believed that.'

There's nothing like a parallel experience to effect a change of mind, as Coe admits: 'If you'd asked me that at the time, I'd have laughed. I would have said, "Well, he won the 800, he could have gone out there and historically put me in a box." But doing both is very difficult. I should have done it in '86 [European Championships] against Crammy in Stuttgart, and I didn't. I got caught up in traffic 600 metres from home, and he got five strides, and I closed it to two, and that wasn't enough. Having been there a couple of times myself, once you have won an Olympic title, it *is* very difficult.'

Information like this was difficult to come by in 1980. Accordingly, the British bookies had Ovett at 11–4 on to win the 1500 metres. As in the 800 preliminaries, both Ovett and Coe won their heats and semi-finals, although Coe's tactical problems in the semi had convinced many commentators – multi-world record-holder Ron Clarke and former Olympic champion and then *Observer* athletics correspondent Chris Brasher among them – that he had learned nothing from the 800, and that he was destined to lose the 1500 metres, too. Brasher and Clarke had written a letter to Coe prior to the heats, telling him he could win the 1500, but after the semi-final mess, Coe's biographer David Miller reported them saying, 'He's had it, he hasn't got a tactical brain.'

Ovett had other concerns. Following the 800 metres final, both he and Coe had been dope-tested. While Coe saw the short time – ten minutes – that it took him to provide a sample as more proof that he hadn't given his all in the race, Ovett found himself over-heating. He went red and became hotter and hotter, and had to lie down semi-conscious with wet towels over him for twenty minutes, with doctors feeding him cooling drinks before he recovered. A similar thing happened after his 1500 semi-final. 'On the bus going back to the village, I don't know if it was nervous tension or exhaustion. I superheated. I remember getting a towel out of my bag, and drenching it full of water and lying in this thinking, What is happening to me? I made another mistake of not going to the doctors back at the village and saying that is what happened, because when I got back to the village, it had gone. I should have perhaps taken some salt, or extra glucose or whatever to compensate for that, but . . .'

At the warm-up track prior to the final this time, it was Ovett who seemed unsure of himself. Steve Cram, who still saw the duo as untouchables, was shocked. Still only nineteen, Cram had done wonderfully well to edge into the final, another testament to Brit-ain's middle-distance domination. 'I saw Moscow at close quarters and I think that was where I realised that these guys aren't gods; they worry as much as I worry. Watching Ovett on the day of the 1500 final, travelling down to the stadium with him, and Seb for a little bit of the way, and then watching Steve's demeanour in and around the warm-up and then in the call-up room, I thought, Hang on, here's a guy who isn't exactly handling this, just breezing through it. He was as tense as anybody else and he was concerned about where Seb was – "Where's he warming up, what's he up to?" – which is just what we all do.

'Because once he won the 800, you thought, Well, he's just going to turn up and win the 1500. That's what we all thought. Bloody hell, Coe needn't bother turning up. I remember thinking, If I was in his position, I would just feel confident. And he was nervous and he was getting locked into "What's Seb doing?" In the call-up room, Seb was the one who was very, very focused. I've told this story quite a lot and I sometimes wonder whether in the telling I've made it more significant than it was at the time. But it must have made some impression on me, that in the call-up room Steve was trying to make conversation, which I think is the reaction of a nervous person who wants to have someone else sort of holding their hand. Whereas Seb [had a] frown on his brow . . . There were nine or ten of us in there and it was quite cramped, so it was better to sit down, [but] Seb was pacing up and down.'

If Coe was primed for action this time, so was Jürgen Straub. The East German had stretched Ovett in the heats, to a rapid 3 minutes 36.8 seconds. And he was going to stretch the final into a classic race. Straub had begun his career as a steeplechaser, but a hip problem, which would end his career altogether shortly after Moscow, caused him to switch to the 1500 metres flat. He had had some fine runs, notably beating Wessinghage earlier that year, but, because East Germany greatly restricted its athletes' freedom of movement, he rarely had an opportunity outside championships to prove himself. He was determined to do so in Moscow.

Sitting in the Mommsen Stadium in suburban Berlin a dozen years after the fall of the Wall, it seems ridiculous to think that these people were demonised, that this urbane, middle-aged man – whose daughter is coached by his former colleague Olaf Beyer – was the 'enemy'. I'd seen Coe a few days before going to Berlin, and asked if he had anything to say to Beyer and Straub. 'Yes,' he replied, 'ask Olaf what he was on, and tell Jürgen I owe my Olympic gold to him.' Well, as I said earlier, I did ask Beyer what he was on, and he said he wasn't on anything (as did Straub). But Straub agreed with Coe about the gold. Of the result in the 800 metres he had been 'Definitely surprised. Perhaps it would have been better for me if the results had been reversed. I considered Ovett the favourite [for the 1500], but I had to concentrate on my strengths; everything else was out of my hands. I knew that I was going well. I'd had a couple of problems which were later traced to my hip which affected me in the build-up and that gave me problems in trying to run the qualifying time. But otherwise I was in good shape and confident. I'd spent a long time working out the tactics. I ran the East German championships in similar fashion to Moscow. There I'd raised the tempo from 400 metres; it hadn't quite come off. So we decided in Moscow to wait till 800 metres before increasing the speed. I wanted a medal. I was annoyed in the build-up that Filbert Bayi had decided to run the steeplechase and not the 1500 metres. He would have gone out hard from the start. That would have been better for me. Everyone in the final had a good kick; they were all faster than me over the short sprint. So I had to work something out. My tactics grew out of that.'

Straub had studied his Olympic 1500 metres finals, and said he knew the first lap would be slow, but, because he wanted to be ready to go after 800, he found himself in the lead, with Coe right behind. The first 400 was run in 61.6 seconds. The second lap was even slower, 63.3 seconds. Coe was alongside Straub, with Ovett and Cram in tandem behind. Then, the torpor was suddenly shattered when Straub took off. And so, within a very short time, when he realised what was happening, did Peter Coe. 'I just whooped for joy,' he says. 'I thought no one could stand the extended pace like that, as Straub wound it up and wound it up. He was winding it up, and it was very good.'

Within fifty metres, the tight pack had sprung open like a ruptured concertina. From 2 minutes 5 seconds 800 metres pace, Straub had switched to 1 minute 46 seconds tempo. Only Coe and Ovett could respond. 'I concentrated completely on my race,' recalled Straub, 'you can't do anything else. From 800 to 1200 metres was a very fast split, just outside 54 seconds.'

If Ovett had been in the 'zone' in the 800 metres, Peter Coe had advised his son to do something similar in the 1500, but with a graphic difference. Seb recalls, 'He said, "I don't care if the guy goes off the track into the gents', I want you so close that you're in the gents' before you even realise you followed him there." ' The 'guy' to whom Peter Coe was referring, of course, was Ovett. But Ovett would not figure until it was too late. It was the 800 metres revisited, but with a different star sporting the same union flag.

Straub was still flying. With only 200 metres to run, he had four metres on Coe and half a dozen on Ovett. But, finally, here was to be justification for the adoption of that five-pace training that Peter Coe had borrowed from Frank Horwill and instilled into his son in session after painful session. Peter had seen it as the missing piece to the puzzle. And Seb was going to slot it into the final space. Coe raised the pace, and was level with Straub. Ovett remained two metres adrift. Coe raised the pace again, and was past Straub. Ovett was still two metres behind. And running out of track. Straub was in a zone of his own: 'I was thinking entirely about my running and I didn't even know who had gone past me, whether it was Ovett or Coe. I just ran.' George Gandy would say later that if anyone deserved a gold, it was Straub.

Dave Warren had had a go in the 800 metres final – all credit to him. It's the only way to approach any race, let alone an Olympic final. But Warren, as he knew himself, wasn't up to it. Straub was, and was giving his all. As he told me, 'There's no point saying afterwards, "If only this and that." What counts is the medal you've got and I was very happy with silver.' Because that final surge had taken Coe away to glory, and Ovett was not even going to make up the ground on Straub.

Ecstasy might seem a curious word to use in connection with sport. Its religious connotations and its modern sense of calm, quiet, even trance, run counter to the impulsive and explosive nature of physical, often violent movement. When we journalists talk of ecstatic reactions to success, it is usually trade hyperbole. But maybe this notion of ecstasy is an artistic one. In Death in the Afternoon, Hemingway writes about the ecstasy of the perfect 'faena', the use of muleta or cape in the prelude to the kill, when the bull has been subdued. Perhaps it is the trance of the bull that gives rise to the word, and many will argue that bull-fighting is not a sport anyway. But Hemingway is very convincing in his lengthy, pervasive argument that it is an art. The only other use of the term that I know relative to sport is in Werner Herzog's short film about ski-flying, The Great Ecstasy of Woodcarver Steiner. The use of slow-motion for the flying sequences, coupled with the quiet scenes of Walter Steiner sculpting wood, conjure calm and tranquillity. As do the slo-mo sequences of marathon man Abebe's impassive profile, emphasised by the pearls of sweat gathering on his brow, sliding slowly down the slope of his nose, and swinging into space in Kon Ichikawa's *Tokyo Olympiad*. Ichikawa heightens the effect with a monotone of shallow breathing counterpointing a sudden explosion of stadium noise. The artists saw a corollary in that quiet. But this is a relatively modern reading. For the ancient Greeks, ecstasy involved inhibition and the frantic movement of dance. It was part of the cult of Dionysus. Like the dance of dervishes, the object was an altered state.

Sebastian Coe's explosion of joy and relief is ecstasy of a yet another kind – one that relates to that other Sebastian, the saint martyred by arrows. It was the ecstasy of salvation. It may not look very pretty, and, over the years, Coe has spoken about his embarrassment at that crucifixion scene that he passionately played out when crossing the finishing line. Nevertheless, after he had thought that all was lost, perhaps irrevocably, he had won Olympic gold.

This time, the whole stadium was upstanding, arms outstretched, to join him in his ecstasy. They had witnessed a classic chase and race. And the better man, the *best* man, had won. But he had not only won the race; he had won back his life, vindicated his past and secured his future. Full house! 'It was complete relief,' he recalls. 'I don't think I ever thought that I had won until I crossed the line. It was the days before the diamond screen, so you didn't have the luxury of looking up and thinking, God, I'm clear here! I was just driving as hard as I could, thinking, At some stage . . . But it didn't happen!'

Straub had provided the springboard and Ovett had misjudged the result. Coe says, 'It was Christmas come early. We had two warm-up laps and an 800 metres. If anybody made any errors that day, anybody that allowed a race to develop like that with me in it, unless they really thought that I must have been so buried, so out of form after the 800 metres, that they risked it. We've only really touched upon the enormity of the occasion. Every morning, [the British] press conference was the first port of call for every international journalist. The French weren't going to their headquarters asking about Marajo, and the Italians weren't going to ask about Fontanella. It was "What did they have for breakfast? Were they sleeping? Are they both well." '

That was certainly true for Kenny Moore of *Sports Illustrated*. Although the USA had boycotted, there was a coterie of US press in Moscow. Coe's biographer David Miller bumped into an exasperated Moore in the stadium approaches on the day before the 1500 metres final. 'Every time I call my office and talk to them,' Moore told Miller, 'they say, "Fine, but you've only got half the story . . . It's *the* event of the whole Games back in the States." '

The disbelief at the result was equivalent to the aftermath of the 800 metres. One bemused competitor was Steve Cram. 'I got fairly detached once Straub started doing his stuff. I was fighting my own little personal battle not to come last. There were nine in the race and I was eighth. By the time we got to the bell we were pretty much strung out, so you were running and there was no big screen, we weren't watching anything. I came down the home straight having battled with the Yugoslavian guy [Zdravkovic]. I was determined not to be last across the line. And the scene I met as I crossed the line – and bearing in mind you were expecting Ovett to win – [was that] Ovett was nowhere to be seen, and Coe was prostrate on the ground. I did tap Seb on the back as if to say, "Tough luck, mate," and went to Steve as the winner, and I said, "Well done". It was only when I turned round and saw Seb getting up [that] I realised I had got it wrong.'

Almost everybody else had got it wrong, too. And anybody who said otherwise was either a blinkered fan of one of the pair or lying. They were good enough to win both, but too good to lose both. And there was plenty more to come; years of it. But, although Steve Ovett went on to break world records – the first just a month later, then in 1981 and 1983 – I would venture that his real career ended with the Moscow 800 metres, just as Coe's real career began with the Moscow 1500 metres.

Coe felt too drained even to celebrate what would be his greatest victory. 'I was absolutely exhausted by the whole thing,' he remembers. 'By about nine o'clock I'd had a couple of beers, and I thought, Sod this. It's a bit like graduating: you think you're going to go out and get blotto. But I just decided to turn in. But, about nine-thirty, the door burst open, and Daley [Thompson], Sharron Davies and, I think, Shirley Strong came in and pulled me out of bed, and threw flour and water over me, and told me I was coming out to party. I can't even remember what day I got back.'

Coe was just beginning, but Ovett had achieved everything he wanted to achieve. Yet, unlike a multitude of predecessors for whom international athletics was a rite of passage, even a passport to fame, running was his *métier*. He could earn a living at it, was already doing so. He hadn't been a good student, he hadn't gone to university. Unlike Coe, he didn't have political or pressing business ambitions, although he would invest (unwisely) in a couple of ventures. He had little option. He became a 'professional' runner. He still hated losing, but as many people acknowledged, winning was not the be-all and end-all for Ovett, and that became even more the case after the Moscow 800 metres.

Coe, in the meantime, had discovered what it was like to win a race, rather than a time trial. OK, in effect, the Olympic 1500 metres did end up having a pacemaker, Straub, but Coe wasn't to know that. He did what he had to do to win, just as Ovett had done in the 800 metres. What delicious irony. Each had won the other's event. It was unbelievable, but it had happened. the outcome was far better than if they had won the events they 'should' have won. But we – the public, the aficionados, even, heaven forbid, the media – were back where we began. When would they race each other again? Because, good as this was, it wasn't good enough. We wanted a result. We wanted a winner, and a loser.

Someone had the temerity to ask Coe the question at a post-race press conference at Crystal Palace the following week: 'When are you and Ovett going to race each other?' The 'new' Sebastian Coe nearly bit his head off. 'Where have you been the last couple of weeks,' the newly crowned, confident Olympic 1500 metres champion replied brusquely. Hang on, had we got the right one here? Yes, we had.

Coe had won a casual 800 metres that night, with Dave Warren second. Ovett was *too* casual in the 5000 metres, thinking that he had disposed of John Treacy at the bottom of the finishing straight. But Treacy, who had collapsed from dehydration in the Olympic 10,000 metres, and had shown his mettle by coming back and running better in the Olympic 5000, was not going to quit now. The Irishman came again, and ducked under Ovett's outstretched arms for a priceless photo-finish victory.

With the Olympic Games coming in mid-summer, there was still a good month to go before the end of the track season. Coe continued well enough, running within a tenth of his and Ovett's 1500 metres world record in Zurich, 3 minutes 32.2 seconds. But then he had another abrupt end to his campaign with a slipped disc, which came just before he *might* have run against Ovett in the third Golden Mile, at Crystal Palace. In any case, Ovett won that one, and several others, before he broke the 1500 metres world record that Coe had so narrowly missed.

Ovett was back in his traditional milieu – out in the sticks. If Coe loved the metropolitan glamour of Zurich, then Ovett favoured small-town venues, like Koblenz on the German Rhine. In mid-summer, the little town on the confluence of the Rhine and Moselle was enchanting. With its cobbled streets, its clock-tower with figurines waltzing out to celebrate the chiming of the hours, and its riverside restaurants, it was a place to relax after the frenzy of the big-city circuit, with its round of airports, hotels, stadia and feeding holes.

When the prior meeting was in Cologne on the Sunday, with Koblenz on Wednesday, there was an opportunity for everyone – athletes, coaches, managers, even journalists – to take a hydrofoil downriver to Mainz or, better still, to Rüdersheim on the Tuesday, have a stroll through the vineyards, take a funicular up to the Germania statue overlooking the Rhine, sample the *trochen*, and take a steamer back again, cruising past a selection of the baroque or plain barmy castles in the air, and still be in time for dinner in

Koblenz, and another relaxing day before the evening meeting. The weather in central Europe in mid-summer was invariably hot and humid, and the little wooden-benched stadium on the banks of the Rhine, packed with over 20,000 fans, was a wonderful venue for fast running. There was little or no wind, the moths kept out of the way, congregating around the floodlights, and it was still warm at ten o'clock at night; in short, perfect conditions.

Ovett made the most of them. While most of their colleagues had gone chasing the money in Dublin, Ovett and Wessinghage had hatched a plot to annexe the world record. Abetted by Gary Cook, yet another fine British middle-distance man – who would figure among the quartet who broke the world 4×800 metres record two years later – Wessinghage and Ovett were dragged through 800 metres in 1 minute 53 seconds, before the German forged ahead on the third lap.

Wessinghage was an interesting character. He managed to balance the impossible combination of qualifying as a medical doctor – with all the long hours that entailed – and being one of the world's leading middle-distance runners for half a dozen years. It was his misfortune that those years coincided with the era of Ovett and Coe, but he was not cowed. He would have his crowning glory in Athens in 1982, winning the European 5000 metres title. But Koblenz in 1980 was perhaps his second-finest race. He wasn't just in there to make up the numbers. He had agreed to pace Ovett on the third lap, but he failed by only a stride to beat him. He is now head of a hospital group on the Baltic coast of Germany, a post which he combines with managing a successful running consultancy with Markus Ryffel, the Swiss-German who won Olympic 5000 metres silver in 1984.

Wessinghage was paying his annual (competitive) visit to the London Marathon in 2003 when we met. As Craig Masback remarked of him, 'His facility with English was such that he was as much part of our group as anyone from an English-speaking country.' I have already quoted Wessinghage on Ovett, and he admitted as readily as any of that elite group that Coe was just as impossible to beat. But he was justly proud of his effort in Koblenz.

'That was quite a special situation. Koblenz is a stadium which holds about 22,000 to 24,000. I think they had 26,000 on that night. And the stands are very close to the track. So a perfect atmosphere on the Rhine, no wind, you couldn't imagine any better situation to run the world record in and it finally worked out. This time Steve didn't kick with a hundred to go; he kicked with fifty to go. But he won.'

Three men broke the world record that night. Ovett prevailed in 3 minutes 31.36 seconds, with Wessinghage on 3 minutes 31.58 seconds. Another German, the 'unknown' Harald Hudak, ran 3 minutes 31.96 seconds. The guys running in Dublin were distraught at the missed opportunity, as Masback recalls: 'We ran a sort of boring 3.56 mile at Santry and were back at the hotel. We turned on the news and Ovett had broken the world record. That was not remarkable. I mean, the Koblenz track was magic and I could go there today and run a fast time. But the report said Ovett dragged two others under . . .

'We were all kind of hanging our heads, because we had all gone to Dublin for the money instead of going to Koblenz, and everyone thought, Oh gee, maybe if I'd been in the race, maybe I would have been one of the ones to be dragged under the record. But none of us knew who it was. We figured Wessinghage for sure, and we thought it might be [Mike] Boit. We hoped it was Boit, because if it wasn't, we didn't know who it was. And some time later Ray Flynn, who was just slower showering or whatever, came down and said it was Hudak. Harald Hudak had gone from running 3.36 to running 3.31.9, a time which none of us ever ran. It reinforced that it could have been us.'

Ovett's uncle Dave recalls Mick displaying his son's Olympic medals at the front of the family stall on Brighton Market for a week, for all their customers to admire. But a show of the medals at another venue was going to mar a wonderful year for Ovett, and put the final dagger into his tumultuous relationship with his mother. The local Withdean Stadium, which had been closed throughout his Olympic preparation, so that an artificial track could be laid, was to be reopened by Ovett at the end of the season, with a mayoral reception to follow. Ovett was annoyed when he arrived at the opening ceremony to find his medals on display, without his consent. Then he became incensed when he learned that Rachel had been excluded from a seat at the top table. He saw the hand of Gay in the machinations. When he and Rachel returned to the family home after the celebration, a huge and terminal argument erupted, and Ovett stalked out, never to return.

Reg Hook, the Brighton & Hove club president, well remembers the build-up to the schism. He was presiding over the whole operation, the track opening and the banquet, and recalls, 'In his book [*Ovett*], he says he doesn't know how these medals got to this reception. Well, they got there because I had them, and I was given them by Gay. She said, "I can't give them, but they ought to see them," and I think she was right. But he never made a fuss about his medals or anything like that; he never made a fuss about records or winning things. I took them to the reception, and to the school afterwards, because he was quite happy with that. A lot of kids came to see these Olympic medals. But a couple of days later he came to my house and asked for them. He was perfectly all right, came in, had a chat, took the medals. There was no indication as far as I was concerned then that it had caused friction with his parents, nothing like that at all; he was perfectly affable. I'm certain if he wasn't having this problem at home because of Rachel, it wouldn't have been so important.'

It had been an abrupt and bitter end to a momentous year. But regret at the rupture with his parents was eased by the promise of a new life with Rachel. The pair quickly set up home in a nearby flat, and truly began their own adventure. Rachel recalls, 'It felt absolutely the right thing to do. There was a finality to the whole family relationship. It had reached an inevitable conclusion, sadly. Steve had probably stayed at home longer than most people. He was ready, absolutely ready, to move, and it was perfectly normal and natural that he should. It should have been perfectly normal and natural that Mum and Dad could have accepted that. Sadly, it wasn't. It all seemed so unnecessarily unaccepting. But it was great fun, lovely having our own place, and our own things. I think we coped remarkably well, considering everything. We just so wanted to be together and to do our own thing, and have our own space and time, like everybody else does, when they are embarking on their first relationship or future marriage.'

They were to be wed the following year. But that was to be just one of many momentous occasions in the lives of Steve Ovett and his great rival, Sebastian Coe, in 1981. Amateur athletics was unravelling, and Coe and Ovett were the principal architects of its demise. Their Olympic 'swap' had had the whole world riveted to their TV sets. The rivalry was even bigger now, and they were going to have the freedom to exploit it. A quarter of a century ago, there were not so many championships as there are nowadays, and 1981 was going to be a blank year. On the other hand, the embryonic circuit of Oslo, Zurich, Brussels, London and a host of other European and further-flung cities – not forgetting Ovett's preferred backwaters, like Koblenz and Rieti – provided a moving stage for their exploits. And there were plenty of promoters willing to pay ever-increasing sums of money for their appearances. Both would say later that 1981 was probably their best year. It was going to give even more impetus to the burgeoning legend that was Coe and Ovett.

17

Run – and Take the Money

From the moment they began running competitively, Steve Ovett and Sebastian Coe were governed by the rules of the Amateur Athletic Association. In the century since its foundation, the AAA had spawned myriad affiliate organisations and a panoply of regulations and restrictions. But one rule was paramount, and it was the very *raison d'être* for the AAA. It resides in a single word – amateur. Its root is the Latin *amare* – love. And that noble motivation – rather than money – was fostered by the AAA. Nowadays, 'amateur' is used pejoratively, but a hundred years ago, it was on the plus side of the philosophical divide.

There was no love lost between the amateurs and the professionals. The AAA was created in 1880 in an attempt to cleanse the professional swamp known as pedestrianism. The 'peds' were guilty of a multitude of sins, among them race fixing, deliberately losing, and competing in different parts of the country under assumed names. It was not unknown for rivals to be 'knobbled', that's to say poisoned. And there were early attempts by athletes to boost their own performances: strychnine was a popular tonic, in small doses. It was all designed to get a better starting mark in the handicap racing which was widespread at the time, and to get better prices with the bookmakers. For gambling was the ruling passion of the sport.

It was how the sport had come into being at least two centuries beforehand. The example of the Greeks and the ancient Olympics seemed to have been all but forgotten. (But the ancient Greeks were never amateur in the sense that was conceived by the English establishment, anyway. Victory at Olympia might only have realised a crown of olive twigs, but their home towns and cities rewarded winners royally. And those rewards didn't prevent them competing in the next Olympics, or the other Games – Nemean, Pythian, and so on – in the Hellenic world.) Pedestrianism grew out of the practice of noblemen betting on their servants racing against one another. Those early matches are probably also responsible for the predominance of the mile in English athletics, since many of the races would be held on highways and turnpikes, with the milestones marking the race distance. Despite the widespread cheating, by the middle of the nineteenth century there were legitimate great performances being recorded. But, since most of the races were 'matches' – one man (or very occasionally one woman) against another – if one of the competitors stopped before the end, as was also common, the match was deemed to be won, so the time was either not recorded or became incidental. In short, the time was unimportant. This is a practice which arguably could be reintroduced with much benefit to international athletics.

In the middle-distances, which have always been the touchstone of Anglo-Saxon – that is, British, Irish, American and Commonwealth (excuse the shorthand) – athletics meetings, times began to look impressive around 150 years ago. By today's standards, they would be good times for older schoolboys or good female club athletes. The latest edition of the *IAAF World Records* feels able, now the organisation has dropped 'Amateur' from its title, to record professional performances from as far back as the 1850s. (The IAAF, incidentally, was formed in 1914, two years after being mooted in Stockholm at the Olympic Games.)

On 25 April 1857, one J. Blackwood ran 2 minutes 5 seconds for 880 yards (the half-mile) at the College Sports, Addiscombe, which is not far from where the Crystal Palace had been transferred three years earlier. Two minutes was broken for the first time at the

Cambridge University track of Fenners by Arthur Pelham, who was clocked at 1 minute $59\frac{3}{4}$ seconds. There may have been pro times faster than these, because it sounds as if both Blackwood and Pelham were university runners, hence amateurs. But, although Lon Myers, the great US runner, might have been styled as an amateur, and doubtless did begin his career as one, he was competing in money matches by the mid-1880s.

In that decade match racing reached its peak, both in Britain and in the United States of America, notably on the East Coast – New York (where Myers ran) and Boston. Myers revised two-lap running in 1880, on the Manhattan AC track at 56th Street and Eighth Avenue. He ran 1 minute $56\frac{1}{8}$ seconds (an eighth of a second was the smallest fraction for stopwatches then). The IAAF book records that Myers was paced in the second half of the race, unusually on a 220-yard track. He went on to set four more half-mile records, eventually reaching 1 minute $55\frac{2}{5}$ seconds, again in New York. He was also a frequent visitor to England, since it was in the 1880s that matches between London and New York were instituted, effectively the first 'international' meetings. Myers would have some tight matches against the great Briton, Walter George.

It's another measure of the importance of the mile that 1500 metres times are considered incidental until close to the end of the nineteenth century, because they were so much inferior, compared to mile times. The 1500 metres (109 metres shorter than the mile) is a product of some of the original Continental tracks a century ago, many of which were 500 metres around, like a velodrome, since cycling was a much more popular sport across the Channel. The first world record in Oslo's Bislet Stadium, a location which features prominently in this history, was set at 500 metres by Adriaan Paulen of the Netherlands in 1924. He went on to become president of the IAAF and was quite a character. He distinguished himself under fire while helping the US military in Holland in the final days of the Second World War in Europe, and was awarded medals for bravery. He died following a fall on ice in the Alps in the mid-1980s, while stopping over on his way back home from a meeting in Monaco. He was eighty-three years old, and still driving a sports car.

More than a century prior to that, Charles Westhall probably ran the first sub-4-minute 30-second mile at Islington, north London, on 26 July 1852. I say 'probably', because the IAAF book records that initial reports claim 'four minutes and a half, and something under'. Westhall, a pro, was eventually accorded 4.28. The next seven records, over thirteen years, were all set in Manchester, one of the most important centres for professional running outside of London. It was there, at the Royal Oak running grounds, that the first sub-4.20 was recorded by William 'Crow-catcher' Lang *and* William Richards, who raced a dead-heat on the 651-yard cinder track on 19 August 1865. The pair ran in at 4 minutes 17$\frac{1}{4}$ seconds.

All the marks prior to this had been in matches, one-on-one, but this was the race for something called the Champion Cup, and eight men were competing. A Scot, McInstay, was given 4 minutes 18 seconds, estimated from the five-yard gap between himself and Lang and Richards. The 'winners' had a run-off a week later for the cup, which Lang lifted after running 4 minutes 22 seconds. But there was then a hiatus in record breaking for over fifteen years. That would prefigure events in Britain a century later, when out of the desert appeared two trailblazers.

Walter George and his Scottish rival Willie Cummings were pre-cursors of Steve Ovett and Sebastian Coe in several respects. At the very dawn of the sport, they were the first example of world-record rivals from the same country. They were the late nineteenth-century giants of the 'cinder path'. There would be a similar apotheosis during the Second World War, with Gunder Hägg and Arne Andersson in neutral Sweden. There have been many other minor national rivalries, but none so striking as these two pairs and the two subjects of this book, so it is worth comparing the earlier runners to our late twentieth-century heroes, to see how they measure up. At the press launch for their own proposed 'matches' in 1982, Ovett mentioned George and Cummings, and Hägg and Andersson, but, for a variety of reasons, principally injury and illness, the Ovett–Coe matches never happened, and the lessons of history remained unlearned.

There is a terrible symmetry in the stories of George and Cummings, who raced at the very inception of 'amateurism', of Hägg and Andersson, who succumbed to its strictures, and of Coe and Ovett, who hastened its demise. Much of what I know about George and Cummings I have cribbed from the work of Peter Lovesey, celebrated internationally as an award-winning crime writer, but whose writing career began as a member of that little-known specialist group NUTS, the National Union of Track Statisticians. Lovesey was never an athlete of any repute, as he freely admits, but he fell in love with the sport (and the stats) as a youngster, and is responsible for one of the few good, well-written books on athletics, *Kings of Distance*, published in 1968.

Athletics, incidentally, is not a sport that generally fosters good writing. The biggest problem for the journalist is trying to find a common theme in a meeting featuring such a disparate collection of disciplines, and then working against the tyranny of the deadline. The only way to write well is to concentrate on one event and put as much preparatory work into it as you can. But what if that event is a damp squib? Or what if there are three, four or five world-class performances in a single meeting? Aren't you letting down your readers if you don't mention them? But that would diminish the cohesiveness and impact of a piece. For example, trying to reconcile the sprint, pole vault and shot put – though all can be described as 'explosive' events, reliant on fast-twitch muscle fibres – in a comprehensive report isn't easy. Then again, it's the wrapping for tomorrow's fish and chips, as the critics of daily journalism would have it. As for books, in contrast to the lure of many other major sports, athletics has excited the interest of few talented writers. It is not for a shortage of 'characters'.

Walter Goodall George was a contemporary of another famous sporting 'W.G.' from the West Country – Dr Grace. They would have known each other, since the famous, fat cricketer was also a sprinter of some repute, despite that rapidly increasing girth. Born in 1858 in Wiltshire, George was the leading amateur of the day when athletics was riven by rivalry with pedestrianism. George was an intriguing character, and his domination of amateur middle- and long-distance running, and the fame which ensued from the extraordinary record he set in one of the final matches against Cummings, means that much was written about him.

He began his working life as a pharmacist, which involved long hours as an apprentice, and although he was attracted to sport in his youth, his job meant that he could barely train. Nevertheless, he brought a scientist's rigour to his sporting pursuit. Closeted most of the day amid the shelves of the pharmacy, the teenage George devised a system of exercises, later published, which he called 'The 100-Up'. They were a precursor of what became known as isometrics, using the body as its own resistance, in bounding, press-ups, sit-ups, and so on. George would practise these exercises at every free moment during the day, making up for the time he could not spend walking or running. There would be an echo of George's application and innovation almost a century later, when the neophyte coach Peter Coe would set out to educate himself well enough in athletics training and physiology to turn his son into a world beater and a worthy successor as world mile record-holder to Walter George.

Willie Jeffrey Cummings was born in Paisley, near Glasgow, in June 1858, two months before George. While his ultimate rival was cooped up in the pharmacy as an apprentice chemist, Cummings was learning and earning as a ped. Beginning in the handicaps at eighteen, he became one of the best runners in Scotland over the next two years. By 1879, his growing reputation earned him an invitation to race at Lillie Bridge Stadium in west London, which was equally famous for its promotions of both amateur and professional athletics, albeit not at the same time. Cummings won the English Champion's Belt, running the mile in 4 minutes 28 seconds.

In the ensuing years, despite the occasional setback, he extended his range to 10 miles, thus running the same events as George. The Scot set pro world records from the mile (4 minutes 16.2 seconds, exactly two seconds faster than George's amateur record) up to 10 miles (51 minutes 47.4 seconds). So good was he by this time, 1885, that the matches – wagers by and against rivals – had virtually dried up. He had to get the sort of job which was to become the staple of retiring professional footballers throughout much of the next century. Cummings opened a pub in Preston.

During the same period, on the same tracks, but assuredly not against Cummings – again a distant precursor of Coe and Ovett – George was dominating his amateur rivals. After an initial dalliance with cycling and track walking, he was invited to join Moseley Harriers in Birmingham. In the sort of coincidence that suggests predestination, George's first mile victory came, like Cummings', in a handicap, in 4 minutes 29 seconds, a similar time to that of the Scot, and in the same year, 1879. Over the next six years, George came to dominate the one version of the sport as comprehensively as Cummings did the other. If we were frustrated by the failure of Ovett and Coe to compete against each other more often, just imagine what it must have been like a century earlier. At least we got a match every couple of years, and two inside a week in 1980!

The feats of the nineteenth-century rivals were all the more extraordinary considering that the sort of training done by them would hardly stretch a twelve-year-old schoolgirl today. (Yet their training in preparation for their eventual match was considered excessive.) George jogged a couple of miles a day, interspersed with faster runs, from a quarter to three-quarters of a mile, and some sprints. Cummings did even less, his principal efforts being around ten miles of walking a day in four sessions, with a slow run over a mile, lots of rest in between, and a 'good spin on the track' when he felt like it.

Such a light training regimen led to frequent collapses during and after races, which would cause a national outcry today. For example, in the third of a series of races against Lon Myers in 1882, George fainted in the dressing room after his win at three-quarters of a mile, and remained 'insensible' for twenty minutes. But that was nothing compared with what Myers suffered. The American had collapsed in the final sprint – again a regular occurrence – and was out cold for two hours. Both were fine later, though, and

Myers, a noted drinker and poker player – his career positively yells out for a movie – was back in the gambling halls that night. He eventually died of consumption, a typical nineteenth-century demise.

Myers was, in short, the sort of man that Willie Cummings would have understood. Professional athletics survived the nineteenth-century rise of amateurism and its twentieth-century establishment around the world – in the USA, Canada, Australia, and Scotland, Cummings' birthplace. There was a brief heyday for pro marathon running in the two decades following the introduction of the race in the first modern Olympics, in Athens in 1896. And there were still six-day running events, similar to the cycling ones nowadays, which remain the legacy of the early days of both sports.

Indeed, when Peter Lovesey decided to become a crime writer, he used his researches into Victorian sport to write his first Sergeant Cribb book, *Wobble to Death*, a tale of 'murder most foul' committed during an indoor six-day walking race in gaslit London. 'Wobbling' was what the popular newspapers called walking. But the sprints were the best-known pro events, and exist to this day, the most famous being the Powderhall Sprints in Edinburgh and the Stawell Gift in Victoria, Australia. They have become somewhat incongruous in an era when the 'amateurs' can earn more than the pros, but they have the attraction of being handicaps, with the runner off scratch (at the back) often giving the others up to several metres start. They may be considered a curiosity nowadays, but it is only in the last thirty years or so that handicap racing has disappeared from mainstream athletics. Most of my summer track races when I began competing in the English Midlands in the early 1960s were at handicap events, often mixing cycling and running on grass tracks, organised as part of their annual sports day by local factories. Coe says he recalls the same thing in Yorkshire. The decline of industry, beginning in the late sixties, and the pit closures of the early eighties ultimately did for them.

George and Cummings were racing when the rivalry between amateur and professional athletics was at its most virulent. It was the 1870s in Victorian England, a period of efflorescence for many of the social movements which Western society now takes for granted – women's emancipation, universal education, organised labour, and the rise of the vocational clubs, whether in sports or the arts, a panoply of pastimes. The increasing leisure time of the working classes – fought for so valiantly by the labour movement against bitter opposition from the landed gentry and their factory-owning peers – meant that there was more time to spend on sport. But there were schisms in that area, across many disciplines.

The issue of 'broken-time' payments, time off from work for footballers, cricketers, rugby players, even runners, meant that professional sports were burgeoning. The split between the amateur fifteen-player Rugby Union and the professional thirteen-player Rugby League, the latter practised mostly in the factory towns of Yorkshire and Lancashire, dates from this period. The 'amateurs' – espousing the so-called Corinthian ethic of sport for its own sake, without the sullying influence of money, particularly through gambling, with its endemic hinterland of cheating and fixing – were very strong. They tended to be university men, better educated and connected, thus better able to maintain the status quo. But there were realists among them.

Clement Jackson, Montague Shearman and Bernard Wise, the Oxford graduates who created the Amateur Athletic Association in 1880, were not so hidebound that they did not recognise where the future lay. While many members wanted to exclude working men from joining the AAA, Jackson insisted that the proposed embargo on 'mechanic, artisan and labourer' be dropped before he would sign the articles of association.

It was against this background two years later that Walter George applied for an exemption to race against Cummings. George was so good that he had had to run the mile *alone* at the inaugural AAA Championships in 1880. No one dared risk the embarrassment of being beaten out of sight by him. At the championships of 1882, he won the half-mile, the mile, the 4 miles and the 10 miles. No one could touch him. At the same time, Willie Cummings was beating all-comers in the professional ranks, and setting times that were better than George's. The press was clamouring for a match between the two, but George didn't want to sacrifice his amateur status, and in his letter to the newly minted AAA suggested that he would race Cummings for nothing, and that he would donate his share of the gate-money to the charity of his choice, the Worcester Royal Infirmary.

The AAA had to refuse his offer because their credibility and whole *raison d'être* was at stake. Their definition of 'amateur' began, 'one who has never competed with or against a professional'. So the AAA committee unanimously turned down George's application for a dispensation, and he returned to record breaking, improving all the amateur world bests from 1 to 10 miles. However, he finally cracked three years later, having run up a debt of £1000, and turned professional in order to run against Cummings. They ran two series of three races in 1885 and 1886, one of which justified the later overworked sobriquet, 'Race of the Century'.

Thirty thousand paying customers – and many more having broken through the barriers or watching from adjacent buildings and rooftops – saw George win the first race, the mile, in London in 1885, in 4 minutes 20.2 seconds. But the time might have been much faster if Cummings had stayed the course. The Scot slowed halfway round the last lap, after they had passed the three-quarters in the extraordinary time of 3 minutes 7.5 seconds, only half a second down on the best time for that distance alone. When Cummings faltered, George relented, as was common practice in those days, even though a new record seemed inevitable.

The race was as much a collision of cultures as characters. As has been said, pedestrianism was rife with all sorts of cheating and sharp practice. With so many handicap events, it was relatively easy to look as if you were running hard, while deliberately failing to win. Thus your 'mark', or the number of extra yards' start you'd be given over the scratch man next time, would be increased. Similarly, with communications being far less sophisticated in the late nineteenth century, it was relatively common to run under assumed names in different parts of the country. Celebrity tended to militate against that practice, and the more famous athletes, like Cummings, had to essay other stunts, such as arranging results with rivals, either to influence future betting odds or simply to get a share of the prize money.

In the races themselves, it seemed to be accepted that baulking opponents was part of the game. In that first mile race at Lillie Bridge, Cummings ran close enough to George that he could employ a tried and tested pedestrian stunt, clipping the ex-amateur's heels as his feet kicked up, trying to break his stride and concentration. Obviously it made no difference to the result on that occasion.

Just to prove that good ideas are never outmoded, when the mass marathon-running boom began a century later, with big prizes for winners even in remote cities, there was an upsurge in blatant cheating and 'ringing'. One Rosie Ruiz feigned a fatal disease in order to gain an entry to the Boston Marathon in 1980. She ran the first couple of miles of the race, took a subway train to within reach of the finish, and ran in the 'winner'. Despite suspicions over her freshness and plumpness, particularly from the men's winner, Alberto Salazar, she was given the trophy. It was only because a sharp-eyed reader saw her picture in the next day's newspapers and reported having spotted her on the train during the race that her cover was blown. A disgruntled Jacqueline Gareau, who had questioned the result from the moment she crossed the line herself, saying she had never even seen Ruiz, was brought back from Canada the following week to receive the trophy from the mayor of Boston.

There are scores of such examples, one featuring twins, each of whom ran half the race, but the most ridiculous case was the coach who ran the second half of the race for his athlete after swapping vests and numbers in bushes mid-route. They were quickly busted, since the coach had a moustache, and the runner didn't.

There were strong suspicions that George 'threw' the next race in the first series, a 4 miles in Edinburgh, in order to keep the match alive. Cummings wasn't even required to race the whole distance, the race umpire telling him he had done enough with a quarter of a mile to go after George had dropped out.

There was more potential skulduggery in the final race, a 10 miles back in London, and maybe it was here that Lovesey got his inspiration for *Wobble to Death*. George's tactics were unusually reticent for a man known for his bold front running. He had collapsed several times during the day prior to the race, and later claimed that he had been poisoned, although there was no proof. After a slow start which confounded everyone, including the following Cummings, the Scot forged ahead and took George's world record in 51 minutes 6.6 seconds. On the brighter side, both had earned close to £1000, George had discharged his debts, and Cummings was able to invest in another pub.

Even over a century ago, there were the beginnings of a world circuit in pro and amateur sports. England and Australia had begun their home and away cricket 'test' matches, and boxers regularly criss-crossed the Atlantic. George ran in the USA and Australia, and a proposed match for Cummings in Russia was cancelled only at the last minute. It was just a decade before the inaugural modern Olympic Games were to be held in Athens, but it would be a long time, more than thirty years, before the Olympics would see the sorts of performances and times that George and Cummings produced in their next, final series. The highlight, appropriately for history and British tradition, was the mile, at Lillie Bridge Stadium in Fulham, south-west London, on the evening of Monday, 23 August 1886.

George was on the threshold of realising an ambition. Shortly after he had joined Moseley Harriers in 1878, he had announced to his astonished club-mates that he thought the mile could be run in 4 minutes 12 seconds. The amateur world record at the time was 4 minutes 24.5 seconds, although, as we know, Lang and Richards had run 4 minutes $17\frac{1}{4}$ seconds in Manchester in 1865. Even so! In training for the matches against Cummings, George reputedly returned times of 4.12 and even 4.10 (Cummings steered clear of time trials, preferring to husband his resources).

In the race, George led as usual, going through the first quarter in $58\frac{1}{4}$ seconds. A head taller than Cummings, the all-black-clad George slowed (again, as was the custom) to 2 minutes $1\frac{3}{4}$ seconds at half distance. Then, despite the frantic pace for these relatively poorly trained runners, as they approached the three-quarter-mile mark, Cummings did something which would ensure that this was to be the highlight race of the nineteenth century – he drew level. They passed the three-quarters together in 3 minutes $7\frac{3}{4}$ seconds. It was a fraction slower than in their mile of the previous year, but this time Cummings stayed in contention, and George could not ease down because Cummings then took the initiative. He sprinted ahead at the start of the final quarter, and had gained an eight-yard lead over George going into the back straight. But there was still a long way to go at such a pace, and George will have known that Cummings could not keep it up. Slowly, he began to catch the Scot, and the race became the model of how 800 metres races are won nowadays, as Coe has often characterised it: 'by the man who slows down the least'.

Unknown to George – the tumult drowning out any information – Cummings had collapsed just after being passed sixty yards from the line. So George drove on, and snapped the tape in 4 minutes $12\frac{3}{4}$ seconds. He had broken Cummings and shattered the Scot's mile record by over three seconds, or twenty metres. No amateur had come near it, and would not do so until well into the next century. George's time was beaten only in 1915, when Norm Taber of the USA ran 4 minutes 12.6 seconds in a handicap race in Harvard Stadium at Cambridge, Massachusetts. Just over a tenth of a second in twenty-nine years! That was just one measure of George's greatness. It took another all-time great, Paavo Nurmi, to reduce the time substantially, which the Finn did in 1923, recording 4 minutes 10.4 seconds in Stockholm's Olympic Stadium.

Sweden, fittingly, would be the backdrop for the next great national middle-distance rivalry in athletics history, that of Gunder Hägg and Arne Andersson during the Second World War. When the conflict broke out in 1939, the world mile record was once again held by an Englishman – the second of seven across the century. Sydney Wooderson, who had run 4 minutes 6.4 seconds in August 1937, was the least likely looking world record-holder in the history of athletics. After the well-built George, the sturdy Nurmi, the well-fed Americans Taber and Cunningham, and the lissom, elegant Lovelock, the spindly bank clerk with wispy hair and pebble glasses resembled an escapee from an internment camp. His reeds of arms and legs stuck out of the black bag of his Blackheath Harriers club kit, but Wooderson was one of the most successful runners in the considerable canon of English middle and long distance.

He broke world records for the 800 metres, the half-mile and the mile, and put off retirement a decade later in order to compete in the biggest and best cross-country race in the world, the English 9 Miles Championships, in 1947. He won that, too. Wooderson may have looked like a runt, but he was a giant. And his mile record was intriguing for other reasons. First, it came in a handicap race, where he was the scratch man. Second, he went through three-quarters of a mile in 3 minutes 7.2 seconds, that's to say less than half a second faster than George had some fifty years beforehand. The difference by this time, however, was that harder training sustained Wooderson over a last lap of 59.2 seconds. George, even though pushed by Cummings, had the strength to muster only a 65-second final quarter.

In 1942, Hägg and Andersson set about Wooderson's record with gusto. And tore it apart. Sweden remained neutral during the war, something which for years afterwards earned Swedes the contempt of many other Europeans, who suffered six years of death and destruction. There was inevitably some privation in the country, imports were scarce or non-existent, but in contrast to their Norwegian neighbours to the west, who fought the Nazis, or their Finnish neighbours to the north, who essayed a precarious balancing act between the Third Reich and the Soviet Union, life carried on much as normal. Including domestic sport.

Hägg and Andersson provided much distraction, and an even broader template than George and Cummings for the Coe–Ovett rivalry of forty years later. The Swedes raced each other twenty-three times, at distances ranging from three-quarters of a mile to 5000 metres. In all, they set twenty world records. They ultimately took five seconds off Wooderson's 4 minutes 6.4 seconds in six frantic steps, beginning and ending with Hägg, but with each setting three records en route. At distances from 1500 metres to 2 miles, they ran 38 of the world's top 50 times. As an encore, Hägg ran the first sub-14-minute 5000 metres, a record which lasted until another immortal, Emil Zátopek, got into his stride in 1954. While the rest of the athletics world was otherwise engaged, Hägg and Andersson rewrote the middle-distance record book.

As I write this book, they are still alive. No one, apart from other Swedes, had spoken to them in years. And they had become so much a part of the furniture that, aside from the well-worn anecdotes that were bandied around, they were simply lionised at occasional awards ceremonies but otherwise left alone. I had known about them for years, since I started running the half-mile and mile myself, in 1960. Forty-three years later, I went to visit them. On my way to the Bislet Games in Oslo, it was a relatively short detour, to Malmö, in south-western Sweden.

They are now both in their mid-eighties, and both have difficulty with mobility. Hägg is confined to a wheelchair in the second-floor apartment home he shares with Daisy, his wife of fifty years. The indisposition, he conceded, could have been a result of his training schedule. I was fortunate in having as a friend a former Swedish international, now an athletes' agent, Kenth Andersson. No relation to Arne, he was, however, a member of the same Malmö athletics club as Hägg, and had known the icon for years. We visited the Häggs' suburban apartment in June 2003 on a cool and overcast morning quite out of keeping with the torrid summer which Europe otherwise enjoyed that year. Hägg (shades of Ovett) has built a reputation for being dismissive about his career and his achievements. But he goes further than the English hero, saying he was never much interested in sport, and never watches it nowadays. That was reflected in our interview: he said he knew of Coe and Ovett, but hadn't seen any of their races, even on TV. However, another club colleague recalled visiting Hägg one morning in the early months of 2000 and finding him watching a football match on TV. The old man, when confronted about this apparent contradiction, said, 'The TV just happened to be on, and I couldn't be bothered changing the channels.' He was just as sharp with us, but grew more animated as the interview progressed.

He was the front-runner of the pair, but bore no ill-will towards Andersson, who would occasionally kick past him to victory, and a world record or two. 'We both had our own tactics, and that's the way it was,' he said, matter-of-factly, 'and Arne would lead occasionally. We had pacemakers in almost every race. It tended to be [Lennart] Strand in most races. First of all, he was a team-mate of mine, and also he had good pace judgement. We tended to dictate the races, since Arne didn't have a pacemaker of his own. In the beginning, Arne beat me many times at the finish, but I learned that if I went faster, it would draw out his final sprint. Speed kills!'

There is another similarity between Hägg and Andersson and Coe and Ovett, in that the 'third man' eventually succeeded them. Lennart Strand went on to become a world record-holder himself, at 1500 metres. Steve Cram never paced for Ovett and Coe, but he followed them into the record books, at the 1500 metres and the mile. There is another less welcome similarity between Strand and Cram: both failed to win Olympic titles for which they were earmarked as favourites, Strand in London in 1948 and Cram in Seoul in 1988.

By the time Hägg and Andersson were doing battle with each other, the elusive 4-minute mile was tantalisingly close. 'It was everyone's dream to break the four-minute mile,' says Hägg. 'That's why we ran it so often in Sweden at that time. We'd have done it too, if we'd run a little slower on the first two laps, say 1 minute 58 seconds. But it was the rivalry which determined the way we raced. We ran to win, not to break records. That was secondary.'

It must have been an extraordinary time for the pair of them. They were filling stadia around Sweden, albeit most of the races were either in the capital Stockholm, or in Gothenburg, where Hägg was based, and where his club, MAI, could ensure big crowds, and, perhaps, cover up the fact that both men were being paid. Hägg says that the most they got was 1000 kronor, but Kenth Andersson maintains that this has become part of the Hägg mantra, along with his 'disinterest'. A persistent rumour is that Hägg demanded a kronor per metre, which would have netted him 5000 kroners when he became the first man to break 14 minutes over 5000 metres, and those are the sorts of sums that Arne Andersson recalls. At that time, 5000 kronor would have been an average annual salary, quite in keeping with the $50,000 per race that Hicham El Guerrouj can command today.

Hägg travelled twice to the USA for a series of races during the war. According to Kenth Andersson, these races were the first sports events to be broadcast live transatlantic (during the night) on Swedish radio. Like the leading athletes in the Los Angeles Olympics of 1932, Hägg was invited to Hollywood, to meet the stars. His favourite moment, he says, was getting a cowboy outfit and six-shooters from William Holden. At which point, he entertained us with his imaginary pistols. True to form, he wasn't much interested in the athletics circuit in the USA. 'I enjoyed America enormously,' he says, 'but to get there, the boat had to zig-zag across the Atlantic, to avoid the U-boats and the mines. I didn't enjoy the races so much, because the track at Madison Square Garden was so small, and not in very good condition.' His autobiography, incidentally, was titled, *From Ålbaken* [his birthplace] *to Madison Square Garden*.

When Hägg returned from his second trip to the USA in 1945, there was just time for him to reclaim the mile world record from Andersson before the pair were banned for life, for receiving payments. This wasn't unusual. For the same reason, the French federation had banned a previous mile world record-holder, Jules Ladoumègue, in 1930; the great Paavo Nurmi was banned on the verge of the 1932 Olympics; and a decade after the Swedes, Wes Santee, the American challenger to beat Bannister to the first sub-4, was banned in 1955.

Andersson squeezed in a one mile race at peacetime London's White City before the ban. He beat Sydney Wooderson, who went on to win the European 5000 metres title in Oslo in 1946. Andersson tried to get reinstated, in order to run in the Olympic Games in London in 1948, but to no avail. He was mortified, but Hägg never even sought reinstatement. 'If you're a professional, you're a professional,' he says, phlegmatically. 'In any case, when I got the news, it was a sort of relief. I'd had enough, I didn't want to continue [only twenty-seven]. I never felt any bitterness about being banned; I was glad to get a bit of distance between myself and the sport.'

On that downbeat note, we left to drive north. Arne Andersson had eventually gone back to live in his home town of Vännersborg, in central Sweden, on the south-west side of Sweden's biggest lake, Vännern. The town is known as 'Little Paris', due principally to its theatrical tradition. There are half a dozen little theatres dotted around the town, with lots of old wooden houses rooted between the brick and concrete. The parks are pretty and filled with flowers, certainly so when we visited, and early afternoon sun brought temperatures into the high twenties. It was the sort of day I identified with strolling around the Scandinavian capitals – Oslo, Stockholm, Helsinki – waiting for an athletics meeting amid a knowledgeable, appreciative crowd.

Andersson's apartment was at the far end of the main street from the shops, a new, stylish block, with entry codes for each apartment at the front gate. The code for Andersson's apartment was 0007, and he could have passed for an ageing James Bond. Still a handsome man, he was easily recognisable as the tall, blond, wavy haired, lantern-jawed but intense competitor from the early forties. And, contrary to the historical accounts which painted him as a morose, monosyllabic character, he was chatty, courteous and very witty.

Andersson also had problems of mobility, with an arthritic left foot, but he could still get around, unlike his wheelchair-bound former rival. The pair still speak regularly, and, though they live about 400 kilometres apart, they manage to meet a couple of times each year, usually at the Sweden–Finland match, still the biggest fixture (for both countries) on the national athletics calendar. Andersson conceded that the press at the time had tried to depict him as the darker character, the dour, big-city slicker, in contrast to the fun-loving country boy Hägg. 'But it didn't really take off,' he said. Kenth Andersson interjected to say that Vännersborg was hardly a big city, but, sharp as a spoke, Arne shot backing admonishingly, 'Remember, I was living in Stockholm at the time.'

Hägg ultimately won 15 of their 23 encounters, but Andersson was quick to point out that he won 5 of their 6 races in 1944, implying that he was getting the upper hand towards the end of their rivalry. There is still a competitive edge to their relationship, albeit a joky one. Showing some photographs that morning, Hägg had mused, 'Arne looks very tired in this one.' Andersson had an unprompted riposte, referring to famous photos of Hägg training alongside a lake with the mountains in the background: 'Of course, Gunder would only run there when there was a photographer around.' He characterised Hägg's 'disinterest' as a form of naïveté: 'He certainly didn't know his winning times. It would always be approximate, so maybe he wasn't that interested,' he said, before adding with a grin, 'if you could believe what Gunder said.'

But he conceded that his rival, like Ovett prior to the 1980 Olympic 800 metres, 'was very relaxed. He would often fall asleep in the dressing room before races, whereas I would be pacing up and down.' Personally, I think sleep at such times reveals nerves just as much as pacing up and down: it's an attempted escape from confrontation, and certainly not a sign of relaxation. However . . .

Andersson admitted he'd been very angry after the ban, but he's long worked that out, and he's put a veneer of amusement onto the whole experience. 'We got tired of racing each other sometimes. We often went through 800 metres in 1 minute 57 seconds, when the rabbit dropped out. If I'd gone up to Gunder at that point, we probably could have run under four minutes [for the mile], but we were running to win, so we forgot about times and concentrated on each other.'

Hägg had earlier confirmed the story of how he began in athletics on the family farm, with his father timing him with an alarm clock: 'My father knew nothing about running; he was simply my timekeeper. I had a three- or four-kilometre circuit that I ran as fast as I could, to get an idea if I could be a world-class runner. What I didn't know was my father subtracted one minute from my real time, in order not to deter me.'

Andersson had a good tale of his own, from wartime, when he was conscripted into the Swedish Army. 'I was a bad soldier, the second lowest grade, a corporal. But when I got selected to represent the army in a cross-country match, I got a temporary promotion. It was a three-man team, and I told one of the officers not to go off too quickly, but he started to fall back, and I tied a rope around his waist, and was trying to pull him along. This incident became quite famous, because it got shown on the newsreels that preceded the movies in the cinemas. But when we'd got back from the race, I was demoted back to corporal.'

Both men would take three to four months off running at the end of the summer, which was necessary, as both admitted they trained intensively, although rarely, if ever, more than ten kilometres at a time. 'We had a saying in those days,' says Andersson, 'the further you ran, the more stupid you were. We were thinking particularly of marathon runners, so we were careful that we never ran too far.'

Unlike Hägg, Andersson has seen many of Ovett's and Coe's races. Like his rival, he feels that the Brits would have broken many more records if they had raced each other more often. 'I loved to watch Coe run,' he says. 'I got the impression that he and Ovett were real enemies, but I suppose that was the media.'

The circumstances of their ban were quite extraordinary. It does not appear that there was any outside pressure from the international federation for the move; it was simply a decision of the Swedish federation's president, Bo Ekelund. Andersson says, 'Everybody knew, including the federation. One of the officials actually said to me one time, "You guys are getting too much." What could I say? I could hardly deny it. It was bad book-keeping that did it for us. Someone was supposed to have offset the fees against other expenses, but it never got done. The public was very mad: I met people who told me they never went to an athletics meeting again after that. From one Friday – when we were banned – to the next, stadiums that would be completely full [i.e., have a crowd of twenty thousand] for our races had about four thousand people. Folks just stopped going.'

Andersson was very good company, and, like a good trouper, he saved the best till last. 'Do you know,' he began, 'I was contacted on my sixty-fifth birthday by Arne Lungqvist?' This is the Swedish official best known nowadays for being the hardline anti-drugs campaigner at the international federation. He was the Swedish federation's president at the time, 1983. 'Lungqvist announced to me that I had been reinstated as an amateur.' Andersson paused, to enjoy the anticipated reaction. 'I thought, That's some good to me now, at the age of sixty-five,' he said, feigning resentment, before continuing with a glint of satisfaction, 'But, after a while, I went to the fridge anyway, and cracked open a bottle of champagne. It was worth some sort of celebration.'

18

Milers

The mile! Four laps of the track. Like a four-act play. Prologue, Exposition, Action, Dénouement. All inside four minutes. Aristotle could not have conceived a better dramatic formula. It is the ultimate in audience involvement in track and field athletics – neither too short, nor too long. It is the fine balance between the blazing, witless energy of the sprint and the tactical ennui of the 10,000 metres. Such has been the history and impact of the mile on the sport, it is the only imperial distance which the authorities, the International Association of Athletics Federations (IAAF) retains on its world record lists. It is the Perfect Distance.

The mile has always had this special place in athletics folklore. Although it has never been run in the (wholly metric) Olympic Games, the mile is a seminal distance. The Olympic equivalent is the 1500 metres, three and three-quarter laps of the track, 109 metres shorter, sometimes known as the 'metric mile'. But its very awkwardness denies it the character of the mile.

When athletics became formalised in the mid-nineteenth century, the mile took pride of place. The early mile records were far superior to the times set at 1500 metres, the 'Continental' distance, probably a product of the 500-metre velodromes. In the 150-year history of the mile record, there has inevitably been a preponderance of Brits, mostly English. There was no one else running it for the first twenty years, and, despite regular trans-atlantic matches, it took the Americans another thirty years to make an impact. That was principally because Walter George had put the record 'out of sight'. His extraordinary time lasted until 1915, when Norman Taber finally ran a fifth of a second faster.

The late nineteenth-century London–New York matches, the subsequent Oxbridge–Ivy League matches, and the Commonwealth connection would ensure that Anglo-Saxons dominated thereafter. In the twentieth century, six Brits, three Americans, three New Zealanders, two Australians and an English-speaking Tanzanian, Filbert Bayi, held the mile world record. Nevertheless, a third of the record breakers have been non-Anglo-Saxons, drawn to the unfamiliar (for them) distance by the famed 4-minute barrier, a spurious blockage, as Dr Roger Bannister was first and loudest to acknowledge. Apart from being the first to run under 4 minutes, Bannister brought a scientist's rigour to his sport with his announcement immediately afterwards that 3 minutes 30 seconds would be breached one day.

The great Paavo Nurmi of Finland was the first non-English-speaker to hold the mile record, with his 4 minutes 10.4 seconds in 1923. Twenty years later, Gunder Hägg and Arne Andersson admitted that their obsession with the mile was due to a desire to break the 4-minute 'barrier'. The fact that they broke the record six times, bringing it down to just over a second shy of the target, is testament to that. But, for Bannister, as an Englishman, it was more than that. He had been brought up on the pre-war feats of Sydney Wooderson, the mile and half-mile world record-holder, and there was a whole historico-cultural framework into which Bannister's running of the first sub-4-minute mile would fit. Britain's role in the winning of the Second World War was still a fresh memory, despite continuing social and economic privation at home, Everest had just been conquered and a new monarch's reign had just begun.

Sir Roger Bannister still has his principal home in Oxford, about a mile from the Iffley Road track, where he became the first man to break 4 minutes on 6 May 1954. 'It did emerge as a consequence of the way in which we in Britain thought about running, thought about the mile as a particular British event and we were part of the

Wooderson tradition, with [Walter] George before him,' Bannister says. 'The mile was *the* race. It is the classic distance. In the 800, if you get a bad position at the start, the first bend, it's not easy to correct it, but with the mile it was a bit more so. The mile was more interesting. I wasn't aware at all that it would attract such attention, but it was not as easy to do as some people might have thought, because it depended on the weather. These are all parallels, if you like, with Everest: a gale blowing can add three or four seconds. So there was the weather and it depended on others: if the pacemaking is wrong then it can be virtually impossible. And it has this link that it was British. So I can understand why it caught the imagination.'

Thirty years later, John Walker of New Zealand became the first man under 3 minutes 50 seconds. Walker in full flow was a magnificent sight – big, broad-shouldered, long mane of blond hair streaming out behind, with a necklace of beads bouncing atop the stark black Kiwi vest as he pounded the track into submission. Walker was a force of nature, which must make his current predicament even harder to bear. When Walker retired, after clocking up over 100 sub-4-minute miles during fifteen years at the top, he contracted Parkinson's disease. Despite the aforementioned aberration behind Ovett in Düsseldorf, Walker was not a quitter on the track. Even Andy Norman was in awe of Walker's combativity: 'I'd always have Walker in a race,' he said in the mid-eighties. Walker is not a quitter off the track, either. He still works on the stud farm he runs with his wife near Auckland, New Zealand, and in the summer of 2003 he travelled to London for the fiftieth anniversary of the Emsley Carr Mile.

Walker does not harbour the slightest doubt about the pre-eminence of the mile. 'It was very special, the mile, and it still is today. It's quite amazing. I always regarded the world mile record as special. In fact, I'd put it higher than the Olympics, even though the Olympics is what you have to be judged by, your final career pinnacle. To be the world record-holder for the mile, and coming from an English-speaking country, was special. And to be a sub-3.50 miler was even more special. Everybody's gone crazy on it again. It's stood the test of time. To go through the fifties, sixties and seventies, then to die off through the eighties and nineties because of the 1500 metres, and now everybody is talking about the mile again. There have been many books written on the mile, and Bannister is still alive, and this anniversary is bringing it all back. It's gone full circle.' Walker was referring to the half-century of the first sub-4 in May 2004.

It's inevitable that the milers themselves should love the race. Ray Flynn called it the 'magical distance'; Steve Scott agreed that it was 'special'; Craig Masback virtually dictated a treatise on it. Because, apart from finishing third in the Golden Mile in 1979, Masback had another claim to fame: he was the second man to break 4 minutes on the Iffley Road track at Oxford, thirty-five years after Bannister had done it. Masback ran 3 minutes 59.6 seconds, a fifth of a second slower than Bannister. The first sub-4 man was present to congratulate him.

The second most famous doctor in mile running history, Thomas Wessinghage of Germany, was soon made aware of the significance of the distance in world athletics. 'When I, as a 1500 metres runner, entered the international scene, I found that there was something special about the mile. I recall a situation in New York: they wanted to make a mile within the Millrose Games in the Madison Square Garden. Before the race there were no stands for the athletes, so I walked through the arena and there was an empty seat and I asked if that space was free. The gentleman next to the space said, "Yeah, you may take it." So we talked and after two minutes he found out that I was running there. Then he asked what event and I said, "The mile." He stood up and said, "The mile? I am very pleased to meet you here." He shook my hand, he was really thrilled. So there is something special about the mile, always has been, and I was lucky to pick that distance.'

For Sebastian Coe, growing up in Yorkshire, there was no question: 'People at the club said, "You are going to be a miler," and my dad always referred to me as that. Trevor Wright [club colleague and international predecessor] said, "You're built like a miler. Don't waste your time, because you are going to be a miler." In

Yorkshire it was a huge thing. We'd had Derek Ibbotson, we'd had Alan Simpson, who finished fourth in the [1964] Olympics, and outside of international runners we still had runners like Ken Wood and Chris Mason who were all good local miling talent. Of all the counties, the mile in Yorkshire has always meant a lot.'

So it was on the South Coast, too. Despite all the other distances at which he excelled, Steve Ovett was a miler above all else. That three-year sequence of forty-five undefeated middle-distance races was eloquent testimony to that.

There were others who could never get a handle on it. Some middle-distance 'greats' set 1500 metres world records, or won the Olympic title, but never broke the mile record – Otto Pelzer of Germany, Luigi Beccali of Italy and Kipchoge Keino of Kenya. Saïd Aouita, who held five world records consecutively, but never the mile, used to refer to it as the 'English distance', and so it was. And when Coe and Ovett finished with it at the end of 1981, it was even more English than ever. For, despite their success at 800 metres, with Ovett as Olympic champion and Coe as world record-holder, their true *métier* was the mile. They were inheritors of the Great Tradition, and their individual talents would extend that tradition.

Ovett had been dragged from his record shyness by Coe's triple world-record feats in 1979. On either side of that little mid-season distraction in Moscow in 1980, he had broken the world records for the mile and the 1500 metres. Without a championship to beguile them in 1981, the two Brits set about their record-breaking chase again. The summer season can stretch to between four and five months, from May to September in the Northern Hemisphere, particularly Europe, which is where most top athletics is played out. But in the annals of the mile, nine days in 1981 stand out. In that brief period, Coe and Ovett swapped the world mile record three times.

But, inevitably, that wasn't all. They went wild, winning races across the globe. Coe went from backwaters such as RAF Cosford, in rural south-west Staffordshire, where an aircraft hangar housed Britain's only 200-metre indoor track, to the splendour of Rome's

Olympic Stadium, starting his competitive year in mid-February and ending it in early September. Ovett began in Antrim in Northern Ireland in mid-May and ended in a future Olympic venue, Sydney, Australia, in mid-October. Coe was unbeaten, including winning a Universities 400 metres title. Ovett lost narrowly twice, once by default, and once to Sydney Maree, who had his obligatory single great race of the season.

Both men agree that 1981 was their halcyon year. Everything went right. Coe was commuting between Loughborough, where he was doing postgraduate studies, and London, where he was living in Granny Coe's house in Fulham. Ovett and Rachel Waller were having a great time, scouring the antique shops and stalls in Brighton, setting up home prior to their marriage later that year. Both men had made their indelible marks on history. They were Olympic champions. They were famous throughout the world. There were no championships to distract them. They could go out and enjoy themselves.

Almost incidentally – 'I didn't think I was in that kind of shape' – Coe broke the world indoor 800 metres record at Cosford, with 1 minute 46 seconds on 11 February. In late May, Ovett flew into a beleaguered Belfast at the eleventh hour and rescued the recently minted UK National Championships (as opposed to the AAAs) by winning the 1500 metres at the Antrim Forum. 'I would not like to see the Championships disintegrate, especially as they are in Northern Ireland,' said Ovett.

In fact, both sides of the terrorist divide, Unionists and Nationalists, had made it clear that international sport was exempt from sectarian targeting. Nevertheless, persuading mainland Brits to go to the northern six counties, either to compete or to report, was not easy. As sports journalists, we went on several occasions during the eighties, and had the time of our lives. The pubs and clubs were livelier and friendlier than anything I ever experienced anywhere else in Britain or Ireland. It was as if the population had decided, after years of bombings and shootings, that they might as well enjoy themselves while they could.

The preliminaries over, the pair then got down to business. In a year of extraordinary performances, Coe's first international race was sublime. At the culmination of a particularly onerous Olympic decathlon, an Italian colleague once remarked to me, 'This medal should be heavy gold.' Coe's performance in Florence on 10 June deserved that sort of recognition. Any world record is out of the ordinary. That is its function. But to run 1 minute 41.73 seconds for 800 metres was something else again.

Billy Konchellah of Kenya, who would go on to win two world titles at 800 metres, served his apprenticeship at the feat (*sic*) of a master craftsman. Konchellah raced through the first lap in 49.7 seconds, with Coe right behind. When Coe had done that sort of time in Prague in 1978, it had seemed like a suicide mission, and he duly suffered the consequences. In athletics terminology, he 'died' in the straight. Three more years of conditioning and an Olympic title had honed his resistance. The world record would be the victim this time.

As soon as Konchellah began to flag, shortly into the second lap, Coe whisked past, and just kept sprinting, right to the line. His margin of victory over Dragan Zivotic of Yugoslavia, a world-class athlete, was five and a half seconds, or around forty metres. In a race of only 800 metres! It was the greatest margin of victory ever in a two-lap world-record run. And this was Coe's *fifth* world record, itself a record number for a British athlete.

There was only a minor gripe about the run, which came at the end of a night straight out of *commedia dell'arte*. Earlier in the evening, Carl Lewis had won the 100 metres in what was originally announced as a world record of 9.92 seconds. After Lewis had cavorted around the track a couple of times, and the applause had finally died down, it was discovered that the timing equipment was faulty, and it was switched off, with the American's mark being modified to a pedestrian 10.13 seconds. The photo-finish equipment also failed, and officials had to rely on something called Digicron photocells. These project laser beams across the track, which, when broken by the passage of an athlete, record times down to a thousandth of a second. Coe's times read 1 minute 41.724 seconds and 1 minute 41.727 seconds, while the mandatory three watches (manual timers) read 1 minute 41.6 seconds (twice) and 1 minute 41.7 seconds.

Dave Cocksedge, Ovett's pal in his teenage years, has been an enthusiastic guardian of the memory of that evening. As recently as December 1996, he wrote in *Athletics Weekly*, 'It's a great shame that Coe's run should be marred by confusion and official incompetence; and it's a mystery why the manual return of 1.41.6 was not forwarded for ratification. Photocell read-outs often placed by the finish line are provided as a guide for spectators. They are not official.' No one doubts that Coe shattered the world record, but the debate about the actual time became more heated when Joaquím Cruz of Brazil – who would beat Coe in the 1984 Olympic 800 metres final – ran 1 minute 41.77 seconds in a fully authenticated run in Cologne after the Los Angeles Games.

Ovett's next race was touched by even more farce, not something readily associated with the home of Henrik Ibsen and Edvard Munch. In the land of the midnight sun, someone drew the blinds on the man calling the 1500 metres lap times to Ovett and company in Oslo on 26 June. The athletes, particularly Ovett as the main man, should have realised something was wrong when Tom Byers of the USA – who had a reputation as a fast front-runner – was getting further and further ahead. What had happened was that the man on the watch was calling out Byers' splits instead of those of the chasing pack. By the time Ovett realised what was going on, with one lap to go, it was too late. But only just: Ovett ran a final lap of 52.3 seconds, which would not have disgraced an 800 metres race. He failed to catch Byers by a stride, and walked off the track laughing at his own stupidity.

Excellence is contagious. Five years after the disappointment of a single bronze medal for Britain at the Montreal Olympics, the national team won a semi-final of the European Cup for the first time. This was the heyday of Soviet and East German strength, yet Britain prevailed in Helsinki, with Coe winning the 800 and Ovett the 1500 metres easily. A week later, 11 July, they were back on world-record track in Oslo. It is difficult at this distance (in time) to appreciate that every time Coe and Ovett stepped onto a track, a world record was a distinct possibility. We were getting blasé, but we wanted more. And it did go on and on and on.

Coe ran 800 metres in 1 minute 44.6 seconds. Only he and Mike Boit (marginally) had beaten that time in 1979. But this was in a 1000 metres race, and Coe was en route to knocking a second off his world record of the previous year at the same venue. He recorded 2 minutes 12.18 seconds, a time comparable to his 800 metres record in Florence. And there was no question about timing equipment here. Later that evening, Ovett won what John Walker called 'the greatest mile race of all. I should know, I seem to have run in most of them.' It wasn't a record, but it was a closely competitive race, which Ovett won in 3 minutes 49.25 seconds. That was his third time under 3.50. Walker and Coe, and now José-Luis Gonzalez of Spain and Steve Scott of the USA, in the wake of Ovett, had done it once each. In all, eight men ran under 3 minutes 52.5 seconds that night. Hence the unqualified appraisal of Walker, who had recorded his second best time – 3 minutes 50.26 seconds.

Three days later in Lausanne, Ovett ran his fourth sub-3.50 mile. The bad news was that he announced that he was pulling out of the field for the fourth Golden Mile in Brussels the following month. Having won the first and third editions of the Golden Mile, with Coe winning the second, there seemed to be complicity and synchronicity. Coe was to have the fourth one to himself. If Ovett had known what was going to happen in Brussels, he might not have been so willing to step aside, but that was still over a month away. Coe rectified a curious omission, and won his first national outdoor title at 800 metres. Ovett went to Budapest for a crack at his 1500 metres world record.

When you're as good as Ovett and Coe were – and, of course, only they were as good as each other – maybe you can afford to be casual. Coe told me that on a couple of occasions he 'played' with a field that he knew he could beat, and he felt sure that Ovett had done the same. Bob Benn was doing a lot of pacing for Ovett by this time, and he saw another side to the coin in Budapest that night. 'I can remember warming up outside the stadium, and Steve was going to have another crack at the world record. There was a pretty good field there and I was kind of thinking about what I had to do and all the rest. And he just looked at me and said, "For goodness' sake, Bob, enjoy it!" It was incredible, I was more wound up than he was.' The Budapest meeting was not one of the usual televised events, but with one of our national treasures threatening to break a world record, BBC TV interrupted the *Nine O'clock News*. I watched in a pub in Kilburn High Road as Ovett ran the second-fastest 1500 metres in history, 3 minutes 31.57 seconds, just a fifth of a second shy of his own world record.

Ovett was building up a corpus of great times, but just failing to make the final breakthrough and add to his world-record tally. Coe would show him how it should be done. At the Letzigrund in Zurich on 19 August, he removed Ovett from the top of the mile list. He had made the mistake before the race of predicting a major reappraisal of the record, 'maybe 3.46, 3.47' (Ovett's record was 3 minutes 48.8 seconds). Coe had to make do with 3 minutes 48.53 seconds. If he wanted to send a message, other than breaking his record, to Ovett, he started off well, because Tom Byers was enlisted as the pacemaker. But the move almost backfired. Byers, suffering from a cold, wasn't up to it, and, after a decent first lap, he allowed the pace to drop. Coe had to take over himself and really work for it in the last 600 metres. Nevertheless, he prevailed and secured his sixth world record, with every other top miler (aside from Ovett) trailing home in his wake. So began a 'nine-day wonder'.

After the Oslo aberration against Byers, Ovett had suffered a leg injury, and watched, doubly impotent, as Coe broke his mile world record. There's nothing like a challenge to speed recuperation. One week after Zurich, Ovett was back in Koblenz, at the tiny Rhine-side stadium where he had broken the 1500 metres world record the previous year. He requested the 1500 metres be lengthened to a mile. Some of the others, already sick of being beaten week after week by the British pair, rebelled, and demanded the 1500 metres stay on the schedule. The promoters acquiesced and added the mile, rather than substituting it for the 1500. In the latter, Steve Scott broke the US record, with 3 minutes 31.96 seconds.

But Dave Moorcroft and Craig Masback went with Ovett to the mile. Maybe it was a diplomatic move, the sort of thinking which presaged their elevation to their current posts – as the heads respectively of the UK and US federations. Or maybe it was simply an awareness of the Great Tradition. Because they were involved in one of the mile's historic staging-posts. Bob Benn paced Ovett to the halfway, then US 800 metres runner James Robinson took over. He lasted until around fifty metres before the bell, when Ovett realised that he had to go it alone, something he was never too comfortable doing. But he hung on, and was rewarded with 3 minutes 48.4 seconds.

Moorcroft finished down the field, but he was to have his own *annus mirabilis* the next year, breaking the 5000 metres world record and winning another Commonwealth title, and beating Ovett en route. Moorcroft, from the wonderfully named Coventry Godiva club, recognised just how much he owed Coe and Ovett: '[They] took me to a new level, took me to under 3.50. For me, under 4 minutes was mind-boggling; under 3.55 was out of this world; to go under 3.50 was just beyond the pale. But, because Ovett and Coe did it, and I was racing them, I thought, If they can, I can. And then others came along and said, "So can I, so can I, so can I." And that was one of the great legacies of the Coe–Ovett generation, and Steve Cram. It lifted the likes of [Graham] Williamson, [John] Robson, [Steve] Crabb and [Peter] Elliott and others to think, We can do that as well.'

On the other hand, there was a potential downside. Ovett had retrieved the record, but in doing so he had contributed to a move that was as inevitable as it was unwelcome. The addition of Robinson to the mix meant that 'secondary' pacemakers were now being employed. But even they were nothing new. In perhaps the most seminal mile of them all, the first sub-4, Bannister had been paced by Brasher *and* Chataway. Not bad hares: one was a future Olympic champion and the other an imminent world record breaker. But resurrecting the ploy contributed to a fashion that has got completely out of control nowadays.

Coe was to have the final word in 1981. And it was at perhaps the most glamorous occasion of the season – the Golden Mile in Brussels. The mini-revolt in Koblenz had underlined their rivals' lack of belief that any of them could beat either Ovett or Coe. Eamonn Coghlan, who had recently broken the world indoor record with 3 minutes 50.6 seconds (itself an extraordinary time on an indoor track), puts it into perspective: 'My coach Gerry Farnham tried to instil in me that I was the only guy in the world who could beat Ovett, but I think he only managed to do it about ninety-nine per cent. One per cent, I have to admit in hindsight, was always there. Seb Coe, on the other hand, was a different kettle of fish. It was almost like, "Erm, you ain't gonna beat Coe." Because of that grace and elegance that he had, and the speed that he brought to it, it was just beyond my leg speed to handle him. I was now, at this stage, running more 5000 metres, and he was just blowing the world away every time he got on the track.'

Coe was going to do the same again that evening in Brussels. Thomas Wessinghage had a different, but equally bleak, perspective on his and his colleagues' prospects of threatening Coe. The German had finished eighth in the Golden Mile in 1979, and was to get another object lesson in Brussels. 'It was a surprise the way he did it [in 1979], the way his stamina was good enough to get him through four laps instead of two. From then on he dominated the scene by his personality for two or three years at least. He ran in a different way to the way we ran. He was not as [sociable] as the other runners were. He was a little special. But that meant he entered the race with a different attitude.

'In Brussels, he was set to break the world record and he did it. Ovett was not there and the rest of the field was competing for second place. First place was for Seb. Within our heads, we had kind of bowed to his superiority and he cultivated that situation. Maybe that was part of a few of the successes. I was in the car which Seb and Peter drove to the stadium. [Then] we were sitting on the grandstand and watching the track meet go on, wondering, as there was a delay of about twenty to twenty-five minutes, whether the mile would be on time. There was always the question of TV rights, and then there was the word that the mile would be delayed. So we went to the warm-up area about twenty-five minutes later than we originally had expected. When we had jogged over there, Seb was coming in the opposite direction on his way to the stadium, because *he* knew the mile would be on time. And that was the minute when he had won the race. That is what I felt. He was really outstanding in the way he approached the races and the way he cultivated his position as the best runner of his time.'

Brad Hunt, who later took over as Coe's agent at International Management Group, was immediately made aware of the depth of application that Wessinghage described. 'I had been working in athletics, managing some of the top American athletes, particularly middle-distance runners, for a couple of years. So when I arrived in the UK I had done a bit of background, a little bit of preparation, to sit with Sebastian Coe and talk about his upcoming schedule, and I had what I felt was a fairly comprehensive preliminary plan.

'I had spoken to several meet directors and taken their suggestions as to what it meant, what would be good for Seb that day, what the finances could potentially be for him to participate. I had what I thought was at least a working plan for Seb, and when I put it in front of him he studied it very carefully and then found a pen and crossed out at least half of the events that had been suggested. He said to me, and I remember it very clearly, "If I do my job well, we can make more money doing less events."

'And the light bulb went off. I mean, my background in college was economics, and he just summarised the most concrete theory of economics – reduce the supply to increase the demand. And as I got to know him, I realised that it wasn't about racing, it wasn't about competing; for Seb to get on the track, it was a command performance. It was everything prepared down to the finest detail, everything prepared in terms of race strategy to the hundredth of a second. It wasn't about the race [but] about a performance, and he maintained that for the years that I was involved with him. Every event had to be perfect.'

There were 50,000 people crammed into the Heysel Stadium, and Tom Byers was eager to make amends for his poor pacemaking in Zurich. At the end of a brisk first lap, only the veteran Mike Boit of Kenya was brave enough to go with Byers and Coe. Boit claimed to be thirty-two, but admitted that records were vague in rural Kenya in the late fifties. He might have been two years older. Whatever, he tracked Coe all the way, even when Byers finally gave up the ghost with 500 yards to go. Boit was on his way to joining that super-elite club of sub-3.50 milers. He ran an African record of 3 minutes 49.45 seconds. But he finished all of fifteen metres behind Coe, who had kept the cadence going, and crossed the line in 3 minutes 47.33 seconds. Ovett's world record had lasted for two days! And Coe had excised over a second from it. There was now no argument. Three world mile records in nine days, and Coe had come out the clear winner. Ovett would never get close to that time, and the record would last until after Coe had won his second successive Olympic title.

Both men were entitled to be exhausted, but the European Athletic Association came calling for their World Cup team. Coe duly won the 800 and Ovett the 1500 metres in front of capacity crowds in Rome's Olympic Stadium. Over the three days of competition, almost 200,000 people turned up, emphasising just how much of a draw international athletics, starring Seb Coe and Steve Ovett, had become.

At the end of the season, a tired Ovett succumbed to Sydney Maree in Rieti. The South African-born American won the mile in the fourth fastest time on record, 3 minutes 48.83 seconds, with Ovett ten metres back. Ovett then went on a short, successful trip to Australia, while Coe attended an International Olympic Committee convention in Baden-Baden, Germany. He was one of the founder members of the IOC Athletes' Commission, whose work would quickly develop into the acceptance of 'open' athletics.

The huge crowds in the Stadio Olimpico suggested professional athletics was going to happen sooner rather than later. That was in no small measure due to the influence of Coe and Ovett. It was clear that they had 'rescued' the Olympic Games the previous year. As many had admitted, it wasn't the Moscow Olympics but the Coe & Ovett Olympics. It was clear, too, that they weren't turning up in Oslo, Zurich, Brussels, Cologne, Rieti and Koblenz for nothing. They both recall getting low five-figure sums in dollars on the circuit at that point, with the Golden Mile and similar 'specials' occasioning more. As Coe recalls twenty-five years later, 'In 1979, when I went back to Oslo, after breaking the 800 record, and then when I went to Zurich for the third world record, I would say, from memory, that I was getting about eight to ten thousand pounds. The best advice I got was from Brendan Foster: "Get a good accountant. There's nothing the Board [British federation] or the IAAF can do any more. But there's a lot the Inland Revenue can do." '

Professionally, Coe would soon become the first track and field athlete to be represented by Mark McCormack's International Management Group. Personally, Coe would strike up a friendship with Swiss skier Irene Epple, whom he had met in Baden-Baden. This would blossom into a relationship which lasted through the next year or so. Ovett, meanwhile, would marry Rachel Waller. Andy Norman was his best man, and he persuaded Ovett's parents to turn up at the last minute. It seemed a reconciliation might be possible, but that never really happened. The honeymoon included a business trip ÷ three winning races in Australia – and the start of an appreciation of the country which would become their emigration destination twenty years later.

But what Ovett had called 'the best of years', 1981, was going to end on a sour note. Having had a couple of weeks' rest, he started back in training, and a run he had done dozens of times ended with a career-threatening injury. Like many accidents, it all began ordinarily and innocently enough. Matt Paterson felt that Ovett was going better than ever: 'Steve had just had his break. He used to have anything between four and six weeks [off] at the end of the track season. And I trained all the way through, because I was ready to take him to the cleaners when he came back into training! And he knew this. I would be ready for that first week when he came out with me and I'd be trying to run him into the ground. Then, I'd go home to my wife and say I screwed the bastard. He had only been training a couple of weeks, and, looking back on previous years, he was the fittest I've ever seen him. He was just absolutely champing at the bit. We had run a hard seven miles or something, and I really flogged him, and he was just absolutely relaxed and in really good shape.'

They had gone out with a group from Brighton & Hove AC, including Sam Lambourne, a long-distance specialist. Lambourne now owns a running shop in Brighton, but he was a handyman at the time, and doing some jobs for the newly-weds: 'I was painting his new house down in Adelaide Crescent, and Matt turned up and a couple of others, and we went for a run. As usual, Matt was sticking it and as usual it was fast. It always gnarls me a bit when people stick it in from the start; I always feel vengeful. Being more of a distance runner, I thought, If I can hang on to the pace, once I've settled in, I can then push it later. So it got to about five or six miles and I started to feel good and was pushing the pace. We were coming back and we had broken everyone, really. There was just Steve and I left. We were coming back in towards Hove from port side and I was running on the inside of the pavement and he was running on the outside. Then we turned right to cross the road at the zebra crossing. It's a sort of ninety-degree turn to cross, then another ninety-degree turn to go along the road. I took quite a tight little turn when we crossed the zebra crossing to go left on the other side of the road and he swung wide, and I was thinking, What is he doing? He wasn't looking where he was going. He was looking up at something and he just went straight into the railings, a really solid iron railing, and he just went straight into it with his knee. Oh, it was terrible, really awful. We had to carry him home.'

Ovett's first thought was that it was the end of his career: 'Without any question, yes. As I was lying on the road, and seeing what had happened to my leg, I thought it was the end of it. Because I was in great shape in '81, fabulous shape. I think '82 would have probably been my best year, without any question, if I was in that sort of form. I was at the peak of my career.'

Extraordinarily, Ovett did not call for a doctor immediately. Even Paterson, who had largely got used to his famous training partner's pathological bloody-mindedness and sense of personal well-being, could not believe it: 'He phoned me, and said, "I've had an accident." He came up that night to my house and showed me. It was like a balloon on his leg. I said, "For Christ's sake, get that fixed." So he phoned Andy Norman and got surgery on it straight away. Any time he had a cold, you'd say, "I think you should go to the doctor." "No, no, I'm all right," he'd say. He was his own person; you couldn't tell him what to do. That was his whole attitude about so many things.'

The Church Railings Incident, as it became known, happened on 7 December 1981. Ovett's recuperation was delayed, as his wife Rachel recalls: 'On the night, it all seemed quite drastic. He got this infection afterwards, and went off and had it lanced, which was probably the worst possible thing. Because it opened up the scar, and that elongated things.' Nevertheless, three months later, Steve Ovett appeared with Sebastian Coe at a press conference in central London to announce a series of three head-to-head races during the summer of 1982. The opening race, a 3000 metres, was scheduled for Crystal Palace on 17 July. It was to be their first encounter in Britain since the schoolboy cross-country in Hillingdon, west London, ten years earlier. At last!

19

Fools' Gold

I was working part-time at the London listings magazine *Time Out*, and a little subterfuge that I learned from a colleague there was to pay off handsomely, and effectively launch my career in national newspapers. I needed to make an impact outside of the cosy but penurious world of specialist magazines – whether *Athletics Weekly* or *Time Out* – so in early 1982 I called the sports editor of *The Times* and told him I had an interview one day the following week with the sports editor of the *Sunday Times*, which was housed in the adjacent building in London's Gray's Inn Road. Could I drop in and see him afterwards? He agreed to see me after my first interview. Except that I didn't have a first interview. Until I called the sports editor of the *Sunday Times*, and told him, truthfully this time, that I had a meeting next door.

I got a rapid result. Early one afternoon a month later, *The Times* asked if I could high-tail it to Loughborough to cover Coe's race for the Colleges in the annual match against the AAA. Driving up the M1, I got a blowout. On my first assignment! I arrived late and fairly flustered at the university track, only to discover that Coe had had to pull out, suffering from a fever. He was confined to the university sick bay, as I wrote, 'a mere hammer-throw away, but a hammer blow to the organisers'. When I went back to Loughborough twenty years later to interview long-time resident coach George Gandy for this book, he recounted to me that he'd had to take the sponsor's representative and the TV producer to Coe's bedside before they would believe that Gandy hadn't pulled a fast one on them. That incursion, in turn, annoyed Peter Coe, whose relationship with Gandy was strained at the best of times. By now, it had virtually broken down altogether.

Nevertheless, Coe or not, the event gave me my first piece in a national daily. It turned out that *The Times*' athletics man, Norman Fox, would be covering the World Cup football in Spain, and later that year was going to become sports editor. This was a try-out for me, as a prelude to being offered the job as the paper's athletics correspondent. I was on my way. And it wouldn't be long before I would encounter Ovett.

After a gentle reintroduction to track racing in mid-June, with a winning 1500 metres heat at the Southern Counties AAA (he withdrew from the final), Ovett had his first serious race in Oslo on 26 June, finishing second in a 3000 metres to Suleiman Nyambui, who was the only world-class Tanzanian, apart from the great Filbert Bayi.

I'd secured an interview with Ovett through Andy Norman. I later discovered that Norman was always trying to get Ovett back in touch with the media; for whatever reason, this time Ovett agreed. Norman got me to pick up Ovett and Rachel from Heathrow and ferry them to Gatwick, where they'd left their car when they had flown out to a race in Budapest. He had run in and won what was for him a rare outing over 2000 metres. Ovett was very laid-back and chatty, and everything went well, including him telling me he was going to run in Paris the following Friday, 9 July.

As a reward for my initial efforts, *The Times* sent me on my first international assignment to cover that race. The rest of the British athletics press corps had gone to Birmingham for the English Schools Championships, the annual meeting which regularly throws up prodigiously talented teenagers like Ovett, Coe, Cram *et al.* Indeed, the majority of British squads could point to their beginnings in schools athletics in those days, until the rot set in during the middle of the Thatcher administration, with the sale of school playing fields and pressure on the teachers' unions to 'modernise'. The result was that thousands of people who saw teaching as a vocation which benefited the whole populace started to see their work as a job, to be picked up and dropped as whim and bank balance determined. Fine athletes still emerge from the schools system, but nowhere near the numbers of two decades ago.

The Paris meeting that Ovett was to run in was held in the tiny Jean Bouin Stadium, tucked in the lee of the massive Parc des Princes, then the national rugby stadium, and subsequent home to Paris St Germain football team. Jean Bouin was a French Basque who won the silver medal in the 10,000 metres at the 1912 Olympic Games in Stockholm. He was killed in the First World War. It was an extremely humid evening, following a hot enervating day. As I strolled around the stadium, I found Ovett relaxing on the terraces with Rachel. This would be almost unthinkable nowadays – the stars mixing with the crowd pre-event – but it was a reflection both of Ovett's insouciance and the fact that there were only a couple of thousand spectators at that point. The atmosphere was very much that of a minor meeting. Ovett complained of the heat, maybe just for something to say, but I did notice that he was sweating profusely, and he hadn't even warmed up yet, something that seemed superfluous, given the conditions. A couple of laps of the field behind the stadium, and a few 'strides' (half-sprints) were probably all he was going to need before he went to the start.

There was plenty for the small crowd to cheer. Fernando Mamede of Portugal, a future world record-holder, ran a European best of 27 minutes 22.95 seconds for the 10,000 metres. The irrepressible American, Mary Decker, ran a women's world mile record. But I missed it, because I was a couple of kilometres away in the emergency ward of the Ambrose Paré Hospital. After looking distinctly uncomfortable through the first couple of minutes of the 1500 metres, Ovett had collapsed a lap from the end, and had been rushed there, with me alongside as his interpreter.

It had been clear that something was wrong with Ovett right from the gun. Even in a relatively low-key race such as this, he would not normally have lingered long near the back of the pack, especially with Mike Boit leading the charge. Boit may have been past his best, but he was still no slouch. Ovett certainly couldn't give the veteran Kenyan a thirty-metre lead with a lap to go and be sure of catching him. But that was the situation at the bell, and with everyone expecting a grandstand finish, Ovett just stopped and walked off the track. Then he stumbled to the middle of the infield and fell to his knees. He stayed on all fours for about ten minutes, while a collection of people – Andy Norman, assorted officials, Rachel and eventually myself, having come down from the press box – wondered what to do next. Ovett could barely talk, but readily acceded to an ambulance.

He was conscious, but contorted with stomach pains, and sweating even more profusely than he had been pre-race. Rachel held his hand and tried to comfort him, while he complained that he couldn't catch his breath. He was given a mild sedative and Rachel and I were asked to stay outside the emergency room while the doctor examined him. His condition didn't seem life threatening, so I was relaxed enough to smile wryly when the doctor asked if he was a tennis player. The Jean Bouin Stadium, and the hospital where we'd been taken, were adjacent to the Roland Garros tennis centre, venue for the French Open, which had been on the previous week. It was perhaps an inevitable mistake by a young intern who obviously wasn't into athletics, but I was thrown by her next question: 'Did he lose his race?' It was obvious that there was nothing radically wrong, and she was looking for psychological frailty rather than physical cause. In fact, Ovett was severely dehydrated as a result of the oppressive weather and had suffered stomach cramps. An hour on a saline drip did the trick.

I returned to the meeting, and by the time I called in at the hotel a couple of hours later, Ovett was tucking into a meal. He still didn't look 100 per cent, though, and admitted he'd been suffering stomach pains and wind all day: 'I could only take shallow breaths right from the start [of the race], there was no way I could go after Boit. I knew something was wrong, but I've never dropped out of a race before.' He and Rachel decided to put the incident as far behind them as quickly as possible. The organiser supplied a car, and they set off for the coast, to get the night boat from Dieppe.

They arrived in Newhaven, just along the coast from their home, at 6 a.m. on Saturday. With no public transport to Brighton available that early, and unable to raise a taxi, they hitch-hiked home. The driver who picked them up didn't recognise Ovett.

He suffered no further ill-effects from the incident, but it seems that many people in the sport – including the press contingent in Birmingham for the English Schools – were worried at the similarity of Ovett's collapse to the early stages of Lillian Board's problems. Board was the 'Golden Girl' of British athletics in the late sixties. She was young, extrovert, and widely loved for her determination on the track and her ebullience off it. She won Olympic silver in Mexico 1968 at 400 metres, and European gold the following year in the 800 metres. She was immediately dubbed favourite for the championship titles in the next three years: the 1970 Commonwealths in Edinburgh, the 1971 Europeans in Helsinki, and the 1972 Olympics in Munich.

She would end up in Munich far sooner than anyone expected, for at the beginning of 1970, she was diagnosed with Crohn's disease, a chronic disease of the intestines. Her rapid demise – including a series of operations, and a widely publicised attempted cure at the 'alternative' clinic of Josef Isserls in the Bavarian mountains – was reported in great tabloid detail. After yet another operation at Isserls' clinic, she was transferred to the Munich University Hospital just before Christmas 1970. She died on Boxing Day aged just twenty-two. A decade later, this startlingly sad sequence of events was still fresh in the memories of many in the sport. But, although Ovett would never really get back to his previous form during 1982, fears for his general health proved unfounded.

The proposed Coe–Ovett matches were foundering on the rocks of their indispositions. Because Coe had sustained a stress fracture of the shin, fine, hairline breaks caused by the continuous stress of pounding roads and track surfaces. The cracks knit quickly in fit athletes, but necessitate rest, so, after his usual introduction to outdoor track racing, a 1500 metres at the Yorkshire Championships and an unusual 2000 metres in Bordeaux – both wins –

Coe was forced to drop out of the Crystal Palace 3000 metres, and the subsequent 800 metres in Nice. Fortunately for British fans – and here was yet another example of the burgeoning talent in the middle-distances in Britain – there was a saviour at hand in the shape of Dave Moorcroft. Although he had disappointed with his first major race when he moved up to 5000 metres, at the Olympic Games in Moscow, Moorcroft had broken the world record, with 13 minutes 0.41 seconds in Oslo the month before.

There is no question that this was the greatest era in the history of British middle-distance running. The two biggest stars were indisposed, out of races for the rest of the season, and what happens? Two other guys lurking on the sidelines jump on to the track and beat all-comers. Steve Cram was to be one, winning European and Commonwealth titles, rehearsals for his even greater achievements. For Moorcroft, though, this was his year.

Moorcroft had decimated Henry Rono's long-standing world 5000 metres record in Oslo, and in doing so had had an experience that lesser mortals, even lesser athletes, barely recognise. That night changed his life. 'The first lap was quite slow, and I led from then on, and it felt so natural, just like one of those days when you're out for a run, and you just float, but you're normally running along Tipton High Street or something, and it just happened to be in Oslo. I can count on one hand the number of races I've run, literally four or five, when you just float. It didn't hurt, it just didn't hurt.

'It was only at the bell that I twigged I was going to break the world record. So the whole of the last lap I was aware of it, and that was bizarre. What frustrates me now is, could I have found something else, and got under 13 minutes? At the time I thought, Well, I'll do it next time. Someone once said to me, "Never be an 'if-only' person," and I'm a world record-holder, like Steve Ovett, Steve Cram, Seb Coe, but I'm not a multi-world record-holder. With that lot, they've got the frustration of not knowing which of their world records to pick. I've only got one and I'm dead lucky. I did race the 3000 at Crystal Palace ten days later, one of the races that was set up to be part of the Golden Challenge. Steve ran it, and wasn't at his best by any means; I think it was his last race of the season. Seb didn't run.

'I was part of a very special era. For that one period, I was a major player and experienced what it was like to be at the very highest level, which was great, it really is something special, it puts things into perspective. I'd have loved to have won an Olympic gold medal, and everything that goes with that, but I've absolutely no regrets about the breadth of experience, the ups and downs, it's a huge educational experience. There's a massive amount of cherished memories; the Coe–Ovett period and how Cram came into that, the laughs and the emotion that went with it were so special. It was particularly special because it was 1500 metres, the mile, the Bannister bit and everything else. It added an extra dimension.'

Moorcroft won the Golden Challenge 3000 metres at Crystal Palace, after a tight race with Sydney Maree, in 7 minutes 32.79 seconds, which was second only to Rono's world record of 7.32.1. Moorcroft also ran under 3 minutes 50 seconds for the mile that year, and improved all his personal bests from 800 metres upwards. But he ran too many races. By the time the European 5000 metres in Athens came around, he was exhausted, and Thomas Wessinghage, who admits he was forced up a distance by Coe and Ovett's excellence, won the race, with Moorcroft third. Moorcroft regrouped in time to win the Commonwealth title later that year in Brisbane.

When Coe returned to competition in the middle of Moorcroft's *annus mirabilis*, we were to see a side to him that no one had ever seen before. His stress fracture healed, he went on holiday with his parents and Irene Epple prior to racing in Zurich. Coe might have been a fighter on a track, but, with that slight frame, nobody ever expected to see him in a brawl. After all, he had the where-withal to escape confrontation if necessary. So it was something of a shock to get an agency report on 18 August, the day of the Zurich Weltklasse meeting, of Coe's involvement in a fracas at the Swiss resort of Interlaken.

An argument had started at the lakeside when a wind-surfing instructor, Peter Baumann, had accused Epple of leaving her equipment on his private beach. According to Andreas Brügger, the Weltklasse organiser, Baumann had tried to push Peter Coe into the lake, whereupon Seb had grabbed a lump of wood and clouted the instructor on the head. Both men suffered facial injuries, and were interviewed by a local judge a day later, but the matter was dropped. The most significant comment to come out of the affair was one of those throwaway lines which nonplusses you once you think about it. Baumann said, 'He hit me and ran off ... When I caught him ... '!

If Baumann was in the wrong sport, Coe certainly was not. Maybe the brawl had given him an edge in the crowd scenes which characterise 800 metres running, but after the injury setbacks and the lakeside incident, he was back on form in the Letzigrund that night. Following pacemaker Kip Koskei of Kenya through a first lap of 51.5 seconds, Coe was momentarily baulked before blazing away to win in 1 minute 44.48 seconds, just three hundredths outside Cram's best of the year thus far. Coe looked as if he could have run faster, but his satisfaction was short-lived. For, ominously, Cram's riposte a few minutes later was to dominate the 1500 metres. With the only absentee from the world's top ten being Dave Moorcroft, Cram ran 3 minutes 33.66 seconds. As he observed, 'That was as good as the world record, beating a field like that.'

Cram was, however, still the third string in the media's eyes. Two days later, I began my *Times* piece with, 'Whether in opposition or adversity, the names of Sebastian Coe and Steve Ovett seem destined to be linked.' The same evening that Coe was winning in the international spotlight in Zurich, Ovett was injuring himself in the relative calm of the Withdean Stadium, near his home in Hove. He had been running a time trial with his club-mates when he incurred the classic manifestation of the hamstring pull. 'I was halfway through the session when I suddenly shot up in the air,' he said.

There comes a stage in an injury-fraught season when efforts to return to premium form become counter-productive: the body gets pushed too hard, to make up for lost time, and it rebels and breaks down again. That, effectively, is what happened to Ovett. The collision with the church railing had caused him to lose four months' winter training, crucial to building up a solid endurance base from which to hone the speed for racing in the summer. This time the clock had beaten Ovett. Two weeks later, he withdrew from both the European and the Commonwealth championships.

Coe would go to the first of those, the Europeans, in Athens, but he would have another desolating 800 metres experience there, to add to those of Prague and Moscow. Everything seemed to be going well for him by then: he had been selected for the 800 and then added to the 1500 metres trio, after the withdrawal of Ovett, and finally here was an opportunity, without Ovett to confuse the issue, to win a 'double'. A prospective first 800 metres title for the man who held a superlative world record was made potentially easier by another withdrawal, that of Peter Elliott. The nineteen-year-old had been a revelation that season, as much for his work-rate as for his talent. I'd first seen him in the winter of 1980, when he'd won the National Youths Cross-Country at Leicester. In his all-black Rotherham Harriers outfit, he looked like a throwback to the days of Sydney Wooderson. But, whereas Wooderson was slight, the epitome of the cross-country runner (indeed, at the end of his miling career, he won the National Senior, over nine miles), Elliott was the most unlikely-looking cross-country runner I'd ever seen. He was built – in popular parlance – like a brick shithouse, and was correspondingly indefatigable. One year he ran thirty-eight races, all from the front. It was a tactic, if you could call it such, which endeared him to the whole world. Bravery or abandon is common currency, recognisable across the globe, and everyone loved Elliott. He had won the AAA title, thus earning selection for the Europeans, but a loss of form in the week leading up to Athens caused him to reconsider, and withdraw. Fit, he would have been Coe's major opponent. As it was, no one saw a threat.

An 'unknown' East German, Olaf Beyer, had done for both Ovett and Coe in Prague four years earlier. At least then the time had been world class. No one, least of all Coe, could explain the defeat in Athens by an 'unknown' *West* German, Hans-Peter Ferner, in a time of 1 minute 46.33 seconds. The potential gulf in class was illustrated on the electronic scoreboard: Coe's world record, at the top of the screen, was over four and half seconds faster; in terms of distance, around twenty-five metres. The gap in comprehension was bigger.

As Coe said after the race, he had done everything right: he had started briskly, to avoid getting boxed at the break from lanes, stayed in front through the bell, accelerated out of trouble in the back straight, 'then put daylight between myself and the others with ninety metres to go'. But that's where the trouble, or rather Ferner, began to come. Coe had easily outpaced him at the end of the first heat two days previously, and, although the West German had won the other semi-final the day before, his time was almost a second slower than Coe's semi victory. But when Ferner caught Coe with twenty metres to run, the world record-holder could not respond, and Ferner won by a couple of metres. Like Ovett, the lack of training had caught up with him. He had missed three and a half weeks in spring, then six weeks in mid-summer. If Ovett had broken down, Coe had ground to a halt. As he said, 'I've taken a lot out of a shallow well.'

The press, meanwhile, ensured that Ovett could not recover in peace. When he had dropped out of the Athens team, BBC TV had signed him up to do commentary. Having told the nation that there was no way Coe could lose, Ovett was caught on camera smiling embarrassedly at his gaffe after the race. At least one newspaper interpreted it as pleasure at Coe's demise. Ovett proved more accurate with his next comments: he asserted that something must be wrong with his rival. Coe withdrew from the 1500 metres a day later, and didn't go to the Commonwealth Games in Brisbane, either. Ferner, by the way, not only never won another major race; he hardly *competed* in another major race.

In the absence of both Ovett and Coe, Steve Cram seized the opportunity to begin his reign. His willingness to race all-comers, including Coe and Ovett themselves, was both a refreshing change and an indictment of their timorousness towards racing each other outside of championships.

21

The Third Man

Steve Cram never made a secret of the fact that he was an Ovett fan, citing a similar social background, with the traditional club experience of road and cross-country running as back-up. In any case, like most other people, he said he found Coe remote, and certainly couldn't get a handle on the father/coach situation. Cram himself can seem aloof, but it may simply be a manifestation of a seriousness of character. He certainly is not as immediately affable as Ovett was among his peers. But, like Ovett and Coe, he has also thought about his sport, and his position in it, and put that into a wider context than most. It took some time and several cancellations before we could fix up our interviews; his BBC commentary dates and commitments as chairman of the English Sports Institute must entail a lot of juggling. But we managed one session in Zurich, and a second at the World Championships in Paris in 2003. It says a lot about Cram that he broke off during one declamation to reflect, 'I've told this story so many times, I wonder if I've made it more important than it was?' That, of course, could serve as a critique of any recollection.

But Cram's thoughtfulness is representative of many middle- and long-distance runners. Maybe it has something to do with the long hours of training, for, even if you do much of it in company, there are inevitably many times when it is convenient only to be on your own. It's a great time for reflection, since for much of that time you're not extending yourself, not 'eyeballs-out', and the blood is thoroughly permeating the brain. In short, you're in prime thinking mode, to the extent sometimes that you're on cruise control physically. Occasionally at the end of a long run, I will reflect that to get from point A to point C, I must have gone through point B. But I cannot even 'see' point B in my mind, no matter how hard I try to summon it up. You're just somewhere else.

Cram was already established as a leading junior when the Ovett–Coe rivalry began in earnest in 1978. He was already physically different. None of the trio could remotely be described as well built, it was just that Ovett, with those beginnings of a barrel chest, seemed to be, in contrast to the light and elegant Coe. Cram was another contrast: lanky, with an aureole of blond curls which gave him a patrician look. Comparisons with a thoroughbred race-horse came easily, especially when you saw him high-stepping round a cross-country course, while those round him plodded, fought and dragged themselves through the mud. Like his elder peers, Cram had been an English Schools champion, but, while the young Geordie conceded that the pair had had an effect on his rise, there was someone much closer to home who would have a bigger influence initially. Even so far as to persuade Cram that his future lay in England rather than Germany.

Despite the family name, it was his mother not his father who was German. In early 1977, Cram had run a British record for a sixteen-year-old, of 3 minutes 47 seconds for 1500 metres. 'I remember going on holiday to Germany that summer, and there were real overtures, and talk about me running for Germany. But Brendan [Foster] was a big factor in me thinking, Hang on, you can be from the north-east of England, and get your chance. Brendan came from round the corner from where I lived. He had three or four fantastic years. He was the biggest athletics star in the country between, say, '73 and '77. When you turned your television set on, Crystal Palace on a Friday night, and then the European Cup, the European Championships as well, he won in Rome [1974], even the Olympics in Montreal, he was the only medal winner. [He was] a Geordie bloke who [didn't] seem any different to me, and I'd met him and talked to him. Then, suddenly,

I found that the 1500 was what I was doing best, and then these two guys came along and started setting the world alight.'

But Cram had a number of obstacles, or rather opponents, to overcome before he could even contemplate taking on those global fire-raisers. First of all, he had several national colleagues with better claims than his to being the 'third man' of British middle-distance running. That itself would be a major step. As Dave Moorcroft pointed out, 'You were the third-best miler in the world, but only the third best in Britain.' If Moorcroft was the most established of the 'rest', clipping at his heels were Frank Clement, John Robson and young Graham Williamson, as well as Cram. Peter Elliott, Jack Buckner, Tim Hutchings, John Gladwin and Steve Crabb would follow. And that was just at 1500 metres and the mile.

Moorcroft won the 1500 metres at the Commonwealth Games that Coe and Ovett chose to miss in 1978. Although that was Cram's first major Games for England, at the time he had yet to beat Graham Williamson, whose omission from the Edmonton team for Scotland – already represented by Robson and Clement – was disgracefully short-sighted by the Scottish selectors. The experience of a relatively laid-back championships like the Commonwealths would have been invaluable to Williamson. Ovett still claims that he might have done better in Montreal if he had gone to Christchurch in 1974, and Cram reckons that Edmonton contributed much to the realisation of his ambitions. 'There was a large group of new, very young eighteen- and nineteen-year-olds,' says Cram. 'I think you felt very much part of it, but a general buzz, rather than the Coe–Ovett thing.'

But Williamson remained a nemesis. With the Scot taking priority of selection for the European Junior Championship 1500 metres in 1979, which he duly won, Cram was selected to run in the 3000 metres in Bydgoscz, Poland. He won too. Williamson also took the Universiade (World Student Games) 1500 metres title in Mexico that year, with a neophyte Saïd Aouita finishing last in the final. But those promising results for the young British pair were obscured in the blitz of praise for Coe's three world records in forty-one days. The following year, competing on the fringes of celebrity, and with only weeks to go until the Olympic Games, Cram was still trying to figure out how to beat Williamson. And when Cram fell in the AAA Championships, the official selection race for Moscow, with Coe and Ovett already inked in for both 800 and 1500 metres, the Geordie thought his chance had gone for that year. But fate, or rather his mentor Brendan Foster, would lend a hand. Moorcroft had won the 1500 metres trial for Moscow, but opted for the 5000 metres at the Olympics, so the third 1500 place was still open. As has been mentioned the selectors ordered a run-off between Cram and Williamson, at the Bislet Games Mile in Oslo. Cram followed home the world record-breaking Ovett in 3 minutes 53.8 seconds, while Williamson, running with a bad cold and in borrowed kit, finished third two and a half seconds behind. Cram concedes he was fortunate even to be granted the run-off. 'I honestly thought my time had gone. I ran at a meeting for my club on the Monday [two days after his fall in the trial], and I ran seven races, I was that frustrated. I ran the two miles, the mile, the 800, the 400, the 4×100 and the 4×400 all in one night. Then I got home and there was a phone call, through Andy [Norman], asking if I can run in Bergen, I think on the Thursday. I ran a pretty decent time, and, from Bergen, they said, "OK, we'd better give Cram and Williamson a run-off."'

Williamson still believes he was shabbily treated. 'My old coach at the time said, "You lost your place because you were Scottish," and I said, "No, you're joking." But Brendan had got the ear of the selectors, and if I think now about it, you know there was no logical reason for the selectors to do what they did. They put me into an extra race, with Cram and myself. But the difference was that Cram had never beaten me. I had been in my bed the week before with a very, very heavy cold. So 3.56 straight out of your bed for a mile wasn't too bad, and two weeks later I ran 3.35 (for 1500 metres), so it was there, you know. But it wasn't there that night.'

And it wouldn't really be there for Williamson ever again. He was tripped in the 1982 European 1500 metres final – a stumble which gave Cram the impetus to take off and win. In the Commonwealth

Games later that year, Williamson admits he ran round in a daze, and finished fourth. The following year, he was among the first to witness the start of Aouita's rise to fame, comprehensively beaten by the Moroccan in an early season 1500 metres in Florence. He was in contention for the first World Championships in Helsinki, but injuries put paid to that and to the rest of his career.

Cram, in contrast, was only just beginning. 'Once [I'd] got the third spot and stopped looking behind, then [I could] start to focus on what's ahead. And it was those two. I didn't look any more at Graham Williamson, or anyone else. After that, it was much more "Right, how do I get up to their standard?" ' He would surprise himself in the run-up to Moscow, when, while not yet even selected for the Olympic Games, he ran Ovett so close in a 1500 metres at Crystal Palace that the Ovett wave broke on the reef of Cram's resistance. It says much for the unreliability of memory that, in recalling this in 2003, Cram thought the race had come in 1981, when it would have slotted better into the time-frame that he had in his mind charting his rise to prominence. In fact, it was in the Talbot Games, where Ovett was theoretically attempting to get close to Coe's world record of 3 minutes 32.1 seconds. A slow third lap ruined any chance of that, and Cram then caught back half a dozen metres on Ovett in the final lap. 'We'd already had three meetings at 1500 metres, and I was waiting for the Ovett "oomph". I came up on him on the last lap on the back straight, and I was with him going round the top bend. The first kick came, and I went with him. We got into the home straight and I was still on his shoulder. I remember thinking, There's something wrong here, you should be gone by now. And in that second, he was gone. He beat me by three tenths, which isn't a huge amount. I kind of walked off the track that night thinking, Right, I'm much closer now. That was the first time I really felt I had got closer to either of them.' His time, 3 minutes 35.6 seconds, made Cram the fastest teenager in history, yet, a month later, he was left so far behind in the Olympic final that he finished oblivious to who had won. While Coe was calming his hysteria, and kissing the tartan track of the Lenin Stadium (it's now the Luzhniki Stadium), having run the greatest race of his life, and Ovett was reflecting on his first defeat in forty-six mile and metric-mile races, Cram was so caught up in trying not to finish last, he crossed the line thinking Ovett has done the double.

Coe was going to give Cram another surprise in Moscow, with a bit of advice on how best to structure his future training. He told the younger man to forget going to Loughborough as the next step in his development. Cram had once been better known as an academic at school than as a runner, but then training and racing had become more important, and he'd had to do an extra year at school in order to pass his university entrance exams. His parents, inevitably, were 'really disappointed'. Like Ovett some years before, he had already visited Loughborough, with a view to going there. But, again like Ovett, he chose to stay at home. So we are left with a tantalising 'what-might-have-been' – the world's three top milers all living in a small town in the rural East Midlands of England, and competing for the same university team.

'It was the only real bit of advice that Seb gave me,' says Cram, 'but it was brilliant. He said, "Forget Loughborough, there's no magic wand, there's nothing there that you can't have at home." ' Accordingly, Cram chose a degree course in nearby Newcastle. He continued to train with his old club-mates and coach Jimmy Hedley. And remained near his folks and girlfriend Karen.

Coe may have had different reasons for wanting to get away from home himself, but as any serious athlete must recognise, the most important thing is a settled regime – the training, the meals, the social life, the racing – everything in its place, coupled with the recognition, the knowledge that this is what is going to work, this is what is going to produce results. Frank Duffy, the old Donegal coach to 800 metres Olympian Noel Carroll, once characterised the optimum day in the life of an athlete: 'Doing what or who you did the day before.' He was extolling the virtues of continuity.

Incongruously, given how his career would turn out, Cram still considered that he was going to end up as a 5000 metres runner. He said as much in the wake of the narrow defeat by Ovett in the Talbot Games. In Moscow, Ovett's coach Harry Wilson told him that by the time of the next Olympiad he would be running the longer distance. It was not necessarily the Coe–Ovett effect, driving others to different events, but rather a combination of his own background, in road and cross-country, and his win in the European Junior 3000 metres in 1979.

But in 1981, Cram suddenly found that his own improvement was bringing him closer to the untouchables at 'their' distances. First, he was called on to deputise for a briefly injured Ovett at the eleventh hour in the European Cup 1500 metres in Zagreb. Pitched into his biggest confrontation since the Moscow final, he ran ably enough and finished third, to Olaf Beyer, who was having his best race since Prague. It is a Beyer victory that is conveniently forgotten by those who want to dismiss the East German's earlier run as an aberration. But Beyer had had an ankle operation in late 1978, after his shock defeat of Ovett and Coe in the European Championships, and, although he had competed without distinction in Moscow, that was following another injury. By mid-1981, he was back in form. He finished a very close third to Coe in the 800 metres on the first of the two-day competition in Zagreb, then put his exhilarating finishing speed to good use with a 50-second last lap in the 1500 metres the next day.

'With the benefit of hindsight, I could say I might have beaten anyone in the world that day,' Beyer recalls. 'I wanted to race against Steve Ovett and beat him, but Steve Cram ran instead. The time wasn't anything special, but I knew that I could do anything that day, I was in really good form. That was only the second time that I felt that good. In 1981 there were no European Championships, no Olympics, but that was my bad luck, that's sport, I don't regret it. Ovett wasn't there, and no one knew Steve Cram at the time.'

The last remark is an interesting reflection on just how much the famous pair obscured everyone else, particularly their young pretenders in Britain. Cram, after all, had been an Olympic finalist. Yet he still saw himself as a tyro, despite his mentor Brendan Foster doing his best to make the youngster consider himself otherwise. Like Peter Coe, Foster knew how and when to put in the verbal boot. 'I was sitting in his office in May 1982,' recalls Cram, 'and I remember Brendan saying to me, "When are you going to stop being a promising youngster, and when are you going to win something?" I walked out thinking, Shit!'

Race of the Century

Coe's first act immediately after the disappointment of the Athens 800 metres was a generous one. He went straight to Cram and told the youngster, still only twenty-one, that he (Coe) would not be contesting the 1500 metres in the European Championships. Cram was primed for his first major success as a senior. His resounding victory over a world-class field at the Zurich Weltklasse a month earlier had made him a clear favourite, now that Coe was out, but it remained to be seen what he could do in a senior championship. He had won the European Junior title, of course, but this was a different league. Was he going to be an Ovett, that's to say a winner in the rough and tumble of a championship? Or was he going to do a Coe, and fall at one of his first competitive hurdles? In fact, he was going to be his own man, and win in his own way.

Circumstances were going to provide him with the opportunity to underline his success with a cavalier touch. Given the cool and rainy conditions, unusual for Athens, even in mid-September, the two Brits, Cram and his former nemesis Graham Williamson, had good reason to feel at home. But, after a couple of steady laps up-front for Irishman Ray Flynn, misfortune blighted Williamson's chances again. He was moving up towards Cram and Flynn when he clashed with José-Manuel Abascal. The Spaniard was sent reeling, but Williamson went down. There was mayhem in the middle of the pack.

Cram quickly sized up the situation. 'If nobody had moved by then, I was going to wind it up from maybe 500 metres out. This was just after 600 metres, when Graham goes down, and someone clips my heels. You react quickly, and move forward a bit, but there was a big screen, and I could see something had happened behind me. I thought, Right, I'm off, but by the time I got to two hundred or a hundred and fifty to go, I'm thinking, Oh, you daft bugger.'

Cram had nothing to worry about. He had seized the moment. His decisiveness had made the difference. He had displayed the courage that separates the champion from the support act, the also-ran. He was running the last 800 metres in 1 minute 52.5 seconds, that's to say as fast as Gunder Hägg ever ran for a solo two-lapper, and he was away to his first senior international championship title. It was due reward for his audacity, and the rest of Europe's middle-distance men were left struggling in his wake. Their frustration would have been compounded by Nikolai Kirov finishing second. The Russian had finished third behind Ovett and Coe in the Olympic 800 metres two years earlier. The lesson was as clear as those signs at railway road crossings in France: 'Be careful, one passing train can obscure another.' This was worse. Even with Coe and Ovett indisposed, the Brits had found someone else to take on and beat the rest of the world. And so it was to prove over the next twelve months.

A month later, Cram went on to win the Commonwealth 1500 metres in Brisbane, more or less as he pleased. He now had two major titles, as well as the win in Zurich over the best of the rest, including the leading Americans Steve Scott and Todd Harbour. He had beaten everybody whom Ovett and Coe would expect to beat, and no matter what the media might say – and I was one of them – about his times being slower than theirs, at a rate of progress like his, the good times and records were going to come. More importantly, in that extraordinary context that Dave Moorcroft had mentioned – 'You were number three in the world, but only number three in Britain' – Cram's attitude now was 'I banished all thoughts of I can't beat 'em.'

Nevertheless, he began 1983 with injury problems of his own, first a groin strain then an unlikely incident while training which resulted in a turned ankle – stepping on a soft-drink can! Meanwhile, the Old Firm were making their tentative comebacks. Coe, gloriously, set a couple of indoor world records – 800 metres in 1 minute 44.91 seconds and 1000 metres in 2.18.58 (three and six seconds respectively slower than his outdoor records over the same distances, incidentally). He followed those with an early summer win in the Emsley Carr Mile, which, despite a slow time, was a further reminder to their rivals that no matter the indisposition, they were still the men to beat, because second yet again was Soviet fall-guy Nikolai Kirov. The Russian edged on to Coe's shoulder on the final bend, but the Brit refused to let him pass and won easily in the end.

A track race would have been too easy for Ovett. True to type, he chose to demonstrate that the breadth of his range and talent was undiminished by competing in a 10-kilometre road race in one of his old stamping grounds, Oslo. He didn't win, but finishing second behind specialist colleague Eamonn Martin was no disgrace.

By the middle of June, Seb 'n' Steve were back in the roles they had long created for themselves: both running an 800 metres race, but 1000 miles apart. Coe won in 1 minute 45 seconds in his backyard in Loughborough, with Graham Williamson, still attempting to challenge for a place on the rostrum, setting a Scottish record six tenths behind in second place. Ovett, in the meantime, was struggling against a mediocre field in Udine, Italy. But, tellingly, he still won, 1 minute 47.64 seconds.

Despite these victories, the pair were far from their previous dominating form, and there were doubts that they were going to regain sufficient ground in time to stage duels of Moscow intensity at the inaugural Athletics World Championships in Helsinki in mid-August. Against a background of controversy over whether Coe was being paid in the first European meeting under the new trust fund system (his agents IMG were upsetting promoters with their inflated demands), he was defeated in a 1500 metres in the same Jean Bouin Stadium in Paris where Ovett had dropped out the previous year. That was one unwelcome coincidence, but another was worse for Coe. His defeat by the Spaniard José-Luis Gonzalez had uncomfortable echoes of his loss in the European Championships in Athens.

The meeting was a novelty for reasons other than the payment debate and a rare win for Gonzalez (which he would repeat against Cram, with similar repercussions for the Briton, in the European Cup in Prague in 1987). It was the first time I'd heard music used as a background to a race. The organisers chose a disco version of 'Ride of the Valkyries' – this was the country which gave us Johnny Halliday, remember. Speaking immediately after his defeat, Coe, to his credit, said it should have been the 'Death March'. For he folded in the finishing straight, exactly as he had done against Ferner in Athens. Similarly, Coe was again at a loss to explain his loss of power in the final metres.

Intriguingly, this should have been Saïd Aouita's first big race after his early season crushing of Graham Williamson in Florence, where the Moroccan had posted the fastest 1500 metres time of the year, 3 minutes 32.54 seconds. But another argument over appearance money had resulted in his withdrawal. Which was a great shame, because Coe and Aouita never got to race each other. What a match that would have been! I suspect that Aouita was content not to show anything more pre-Helsinki than he had already demonstrated against Williamson. Despite his defeat in the 1500 metres, Coe had run 3 minutes 35.17 seconds, a qualifying time for the World Championships, for which he'd already been selected at 800.

Ovett was having problems of a different order. The previous weekend, he had been knocked off the track in the Southern Counties 800 metres at Barnet, north London, by his old pal Bob Benn. Ovett had dropped out, and characteristically couldn't remember this incident, blaming it on cramp. Nor could he recall the reason for the fall-out with Benn. And Benn had been reluctant to tell me. In fact, it was one of those fortuitous questions that an interviewer throws out in passing, or, in this case, in leaving. I'd concluded my interview with Benn, at the offices of his architectural consultancy in Portsmouth, and casually said, 'I suppose you know Steve lives in Australia nowadays.' 'No, I didn't,' he replied 'we haven't spoken in twenty years.' I virtually had to force it out of him, switching my recorder back on and badgering him. I took it for a sort of fidelity to the memory of their times together, and he'd certainly given me no indication during the hour we'd been talking that there had ever been bad blood between them. On the contrary, he'd been as complimentary towards Ovett as Matt Paterson was. (Then again, Paterson and Ovett had had their fallings out.) But I'd even asked Benn about Ovett's disputes with various people, and Benn had come up with a 'black-and-white' characterisation, without so much as an indication that he'd been excommunicated too.

The spat went back to a bout of glandular fever Benn had had before Ovett's accident with the church railings. 'I became quite ill at one point,' he recalled, 'and Rachel, who I'd been speaking to on the phone, said, "Come over to Brighton and spend the weekend with us. Steve is racing round Preston Park." I said, "Well, I'm not sure I'm up to it." I was pretty groggy at the time. But I eventually decided to jump in the car and go over there, and what became patently apparent in the meantime was that she had mentioned to Steve that that was the case. And she shouldn't have done that, she shouldn't have invited me, because he was worried about picking something up, even though he'd already had glandular fever. No one rang me to say don't come over, so I drove all the way to Brighton and got out of the car ... Gradually [I] realised I was being blanked and came away from that feeling very upset about it and drove all the way back to Portsmouth. I dropped him a line and said I was upset about that, but I had checked with the doctor and once you've had glandular fever, you can't get it again.'

I put this to Ovett, who maintained that you *could* contract glandular fever again, and had said as much to Benn at a Sportswriters' Dinner later that year. In fact, Benn is right, but that's not really the issue: it was the lack of contact that had upset Benn. He never received a reply to the letter he sent to Ovett. The next time they met was on the track at Barnet.

Benn recalls, 'He was boxed actually, on the inside, and he got in the straight and started pushing his way round. I wasn't going to be pushed out of the way by him, given the slight bad taste in the mouth that I had. I gave him a good old shove and then he pulled up with his hamstring. I don't know if it was for real or not, but Andy Norman came up to me and said ... fight outside, you know. So that was that. That was the last time I saw him.'

It *was* only cramp, as Ovett recalls, and after a massage he ran and won the 1500 metres at the same meeting. A week later, and two days after Coe's disappointment in Paris, Ovett ran at a meeting in Edinburgh. With everyone eager to see whether he could still cut it at international level, he kept us all guessing with typical Ovett serendipity. In a 1000 metres race, he tripped over local international Geoff Turnbull, got spiked in the process, then waited to see that Turnbull was OK before giving chase to the leaders. Despite a last 400 metres in 53.6 seconds, he could make no impact, and trailed in well behind Peter Elliott, who won in 2 minutes 21.92 seconds.

But at the Bislet Games in Oslo a week later, Ovett and Coe were back to their copy-book best. Which is to say that Coe won the 800 metres in a rapid 1 minute 43.8 seconds, after being paced away from his pursuers. And Ovett outstripped Coe's Paris vanquisher Gonzalez to win the 1500 metres, but only after barging his way out of a box behind Ray Flynn, knocking the Irishman into the other leading Spaniard, José-Manuel Abascal, who went sprawling to the track. Abascal was furious, as was Flynn. But that was then. True to his good nature, Flynn cannot help laughing at the memory now. After all, he had once conceded, 'If Ovett ran a mile in 4.16, I'd run 4.16.1.'

Of Bislet, Flynn says, 'It was typical Ovett. He always waited very late in races, and liked to find himself involved in situations. He probably could have found a way around a lot earlier, but Ovett was dramatic, if anything, and maybe he was always going to win the race anyway. I mean, anybody else probably would have been disqualified, but Steve Ovett, with Andy Norman, in Oslo, was not ever going to be disqualified, despite any kinds of criticism from athletes or officials.'

Ovett admitted that his aggressive tactics, worse even than those he'd employed in Moscow, would deserve disqualification in a championship, but he was well pleased with his time of 3 minutes 33.81 seconds, his fastest since the halcyon days of 1981. He followed Bislet with another 1500 metres win in Birmingham, and, although it was much slower, the fact that he'd come through three races in six days was enough to convince him that he should attempt the double in Helsinki. It was not going to be so easy convincing the selectors and public this time, however. But Ovett was back on a roll, and at his anarchic best.

Cram had a low-key reintroduction to competition, running 3 minutes 37.53 seconds on his home track at Gateshead, fast enough to qualify for Helsinki, and sketching out a makeshift programme, which he hoped would deliver him to the World Championships with at least a chance of adding to his titles of the previous year. After his injuries, the biography he was shooting with Tyne-Tees TV had all the makings of a disaster movie, but he was doing his best to salvage it. Ovett, meanwhile, seemed to be doing his best to sabotage it.

With only six weeks to go to the World Championships, Cram wanted to run an international 1500 metres in Enschede in the Netherlands, but Ovett entered the race at the eleventh hour. Ovett says that he can't recall doing this deliberately, but Cram has no doubts about his elder rival's intentions. In retrospect, the Ovett plan backfired, because Cram switched to the 800 metres and won in a qualifying time for the distance. Ovett still had not run one at that stage. He won a slow 1500 metres.

Cram's take on such tactics is illuminating. 'I was doing a documentary at the time, and did a walking piece with the camera. I can't believe I did this on the day of the meet, [but I said], "Ovett has come here, I'm sure it's part of a plan to mess up my preparations. I'm not ready to run against him yet." This gives you an insight into my mindset then, because, had I still been thinking he was better than me, I wouldn't have minded getting beaten by him.'

This begged the question, did Cram ever indulge in such tactics himself? When I interviewed him at length in 1986, after the Commonwealth Games in Edinburgh (where he had won the middle-distance double after Coe had dropped out of the 800 metres with another illness, and Ovett had won the 5000 metres), Cram had admitted using the media to 'get at' his rivals. The piece ran over three days in *The Times*. Kim McDonald, by then the world's leading athletes' agent, told me later that he was astonished by this admission, believing Cram was too honest for his own good. Maybe that said more about McDonald, a notoriously hermetic man, than it said about Cram, and Cram remains forthright. 'I think we all played these games occasionally. I was getting to know the meet promoters quite well, and, yeah, there was a little bit of chess about where you ran, and obviously we didn't want to run against each other. But I realised then [that] I didn't mind running against them. But you've got to run against people when you're ready to run against them.' In living up to this testament at the end of that 1983 season, Cram (and Ovett) would provide us with one of the twentieth century's indelible athletics memories.

The prelude was equally unforgettable, since it produced a media frenzy, which almost equalled the pre-Moscow rigmarole. But this time there was a significant difference, since there was something other than 'who will win what?' to debate. Cram's return to form meant that we still didn't even know who would line up at the start. The International Amateur Athletics Federation, which was organising its World Championships for the first time, had chosen to follow the example of the Olympic Games, where a maximum of three competitors per event per country was allowed. There had been much debate on the subject. Many commentators and coaches pointed out that if six of the top ten sprinters in the world were from the USA, as was regularly the case, then why shouldn't they all be given the opportunity to compete in a world championships? (Incidentally, the Olympics had started way back in 1896 as an open house. Three per event was introduced as late as 1928.) The argument was the same for Soviet hammer throwers, who dominated the event world-wide. Ditto the British middle-distance runners. But, mindful of Olympic boycotts, the IAAF wanted as large a representation of countries as possible, even if some sent just one athlete, and it was a case of keeping the numbers of entrants manageable, as well as ensuring that a handful of countries would not overwhelm the rest.

Ovett and Coe, the Olympic middle-distance champions, wanted to double up again, to run both the 800 and 1500 metres, in Helsinki. But neither was running well at his title event. Ovett had barely raced at 800 metres since Moscow, and Coe was looking vulnerable at 1500, something that was underlined when he lost again, at Crystal Palace this time, to Dragan Zdravkovic, the Yugoslav whom Cram had battled with to avoid the final place in the Moscow 1500 metres. Coe conceded that he was 'mentally shattered' by the defeat. Cram, on the other hand, having been told after winning two titles the previous year that he only had to prove his fitness to gain selection, was clearly on the way back. After Enschede, he won a fast 1500 metres in Nice. And the ill-fated Graham Williamson, in the best form of his life, had run the fourth fastest time in the world for 1500 metres. He'd backed that up with a silver medal over 800 metres in the Universiade, a major championship that has never been accorded the significance it deserves in the UK. But, as far as Coe and Ovett were concerned, neither had been so vulnerable since Olaf Beyer had eased past them five years earlier in Prague. Yet, extraordinarily, this was still a domestic argument. Whoever was selected would immediately be installed as a favourite to reach the podium, if not to win.

This time round, Andy Norman, made it public that, in view of these uncharacteristic weaknesses for Coe and Ovett, there should be no doubling up this time. When the selectors took him at his word, and pencilled in Coe for just the 800 and Ovett for the 1500 metres, Norman spent the weekend on the phone trying to convince them otherwise. There was a furore, because a list of selectees was issued which included Ovett, Cram and Williamson in the 1500. It was given to the press agencies, but then changed late on Sunday evening, and published on Monday morning without the two youngsters, and with just Coe at 800 and Ovett at 1500 metres. The implication was that Cram and Williamson, who would be welcomed into any other national team with open cheque-books, would have to race-off *again*.

'Joke', 'farce', 'farrago', 'fiasco', we wrote, and the sub-editors splashed our words in headlines. The audio-visual media followed suit, as is their wont. It was all wheeling up into the national talking point that it had been before Moscow. Cram stayed cool (he could afford to), saying he never expected to be selected straight away. Williamson tried to avoid the press, but I had a phone number for him, and, after a few fruitless attempts, essayed the time-honoured trick of letting the phone ring once, ringing off and calling back immediately. Williamson is such a sweet guy, he didn't put the phone back down when he realised it was me. 'This is getting beyond a joke,' he said. 'The selectors should get off the fence and pick the team properly. What they're effectively doing is giving Coe another chance, when I've done three times faster than him.'

With respect to Williamson, most of us were getting carried away, being burned and blinded with the heat and light generated by this debate. Coe, after all, or rather before all, was the Olympic 1500 metres champion, and the sort of character who would not go to Helsinki if he thought he couldn't do himself justice. As I recall, the only member of the media championing this eminently sensible point of view was John Rodda of the *Guardian*.

Then something happened that no one was expecting. Williamson and Cram did not initially even believe it. Coe opted out of the 1500 metres. In a statement prepared for him by his biographer, David Miller, Coe attacked the selectors, saying they had made his position untenable. In 2003, Cram recalled, 'I was, like, what is he on about? "Untenable?" I had to go and look it up in the dictionary. I didn't know what it meant.' What it meant was that Cram and Williamson were selected for the 1500 metres in Helsinki.

But Ovett kept the media pot boiling when he suffered a surprising setback. Poised at Peter Elliott's shoulder on the final bend of the AAA Championships 800 metres, Ovett clutched at his thigh and dropped out. He had been spiked on the first lap, and had a three-inch gash on his right foot. He then suffered an attack of cramp. With a quote that should be put up in lights at the Olympic Academy in Lausanne, Ovett complained, 'It seems that the 800 metres is getting more and more physical, and I seem to be on the receiving end.' The selectors remained oblivious to Ovett's thus far undiscovered talent for irony, but they finally decided that he would not compete in the 800 metres in Helsinki.

More astonishingly, neither would Coe. After another defeat, by an in-form Steve Scott in the mile at the AAA Championships, Coe chose to run in an 800 metres in Gateshead, Cram's stamping ground. Horror at Coe's ultimate demise that season was equalled only by the elation and amazement of Cram and his home crowd, when the local man surged past the leading group, including Coe, in the home straight to win. Coe could finish only a dejected fourth. The packed stadium erupted. Cram recalls, 'A lot of people remember that as one of the great races at Gateshead.' At this juncture, remember, Cram still thought that he was on his way to eventually becoming a 5000 metres runner. 'I didn't consider myself an 800 metres runner. I didn't win 800s, I just didn't win. But in those days, you always thought that championship races were slow, tactical affairs, so speed was the thing you wanted to work on.'

Ovett won the 1000 metres at Gateshead, holding off a fast-finishing Don Paige, who Steve Scott felt would have challenged for Olympic 800 metres gold had the USA gone to Moscow. Paige had once beaten Coe over two laps, but most people ridicule Scott's assessment, pointing out Paige was a good man for a one-off race, but would have toiled with heats and finals.

Unusually, Coe fled Gateshead without talking to the media. His despair on the track post-race when he shook Cram's hand was tangible. The following day, Coe withdrew from Helsinki completely. When he got home to Sheffield, a fortuitous first visitor was a family friend, Dr Bob Hague, who took a look at him, and quickly counselled a visit to the specialist who had treated him for a lymph-gland infection after Athens.

One man's disaster could prove another's opportunity, but an application from Ovett to replace Coe in the 800 metres in Helsinki was turned down by the organising committee because it had arrived four days late. Who knows, four races at 800 metres might have tuned him up to win the 1500m title rather than breaking the world record later in the season? But Ovett was going into Helsinki lacking the sort of spark he had shown for the six previous summers, and it was the Third Man who was coming into world title-winning form.

Helsinki is one of the world's greatest venues to watch athletics. IAAF boss Primo Nebiolo found no dissenters when he referred to the 1952 Olympic Stadium as the Temple of Athletics. The broad, clean curves of the stands afford integral sight-lines, and the giant pines lofting against a Klein-blue sky offer a perfect backdrop. Of course, you got wet when it rained, but that only happened once, as far as I recall. And, thanks to Paavo Nurmi, whose statue stands on the stadium forecourt; thanks to Matti Järvinen, whose 1933 world record (one of eleven) in the javelin determined the 76.10-metre height of the stadium tower; thanks to those legions of distance runners, pre- and post-Nurmi, and those battalions of javelin throwers, men and women, a Helsinki athletics crowd is the most knowledgeable on the planet. It was the ideal place for the inaugural championships. And we got some great competition.

Denied an outing in Moscow at the 1980 Olympics, when he might in any case have been a little too young, Carl Lewis set out on a major championships career which would end with him emulating the great Nurmi, with nine Olympic golds. Jarmila Kratochvilova confounded commentators and opponents alike, winning the 400/800 metres double. Alberto 'Caballo' Juantorena looked to have ended his career when he stepped on a kerb and broke an ankle. Willi Wülbeck gave West Germany its second major 800 metres title in successive years. After finishing fourth, which he aptly characterised as 'the loneliest place in the athletics', in two Olympic Games, Eamonn Coghlan finally won gold, in the 5000 metres. In winning the javelin with her final throw, Tiina Lillak raised the national sperm count (well, at least in the case of *Sports Illustrated*'s Kenny Moore, who wrote what many people joked was a soft-porn piece on her). And Steve Cram won the blue riband, the 1500 metres. In doing so, he relegated Ovett to fourth, and set up a show-stopping season's finale at Crystal Palace.

The pair had met in a semi-final in Helsinki whose line-up was announced only at close to midnight the day before. Only a year in the job at that point, I raced to a phone, got on to 'copy', and surprised myself by ad-libbing 400 words which were eminently readable the following day. I rank this as second only to having my expenses queried as one of the staging-posts in becoming a fully paid-up journalist.

In the semi-final, it was telling that Ovett did not challenge Cram's intent to cross the line first. And in the final, Cram gave a master-class of how to plan your way to victory, again with a bit of help from Brendan Foster, his friend and mentor. Cram still believed that Ovett would be the major threat, along with Steve Scott. For the first time in ages, neither Ovett nor Coe, nor Cram, had run in the second Oslo meeting of that season (there would be a third Oslo meeting after Helsinki, an indication of the drawing power of athletics at that time). But Scott, who had finished close to Coe in two world-record races, had finally won the Oslo mile in 3 minutes 49.49 seconds, close to the world record. He had also beaten Coe at the AAA Championships, of course. It was to be his best season.

Few would argue with Cram's assessment: 'Although we'd never seen Scotty as a winner, he was in the best form of his life. I was more worried about Scotty than Aouita, but my tactic was to make a long run for home, and I heard that Aouita was thinking of the same. I thought, Great, but you take those things with a pinch of salt.' Foster had identified that Aouita had struck for home with 500 metres to run in both his heat and semi-final, and Aouita did go at 500, but Cram was right there, waiting. Not for long, though. He used the Moroccan as a springboard, and was away to victory before Ovett could respond. Scott claimed silver and Aouita bronze. It had been a perfect summation by Cram and Foster, a disaster for fourth-placed Ovett.

Despite the weeks out injured, Cram was still in his prime, when self-belief can make up for a lot that is lacking. It may seem contradictory, when I have emphasised so much how anything other than optimum fitness is a recipe for disaster in a runner, but there is also a phenomenon which we club runners used to call 'fresh-fitness'. That is when you are back from a lengthy illness or injury when you are young, and you are so in thrall to your sport, so overjoyed to get back into competition, that you can outdo yourself. Or you could just say that Cram was 'in the zone'. He did not even contemplate defeat, and there is a lot in that.

As for Ovett, he was barely recognisable. This was not the Ovett of old. He had not responded when Cram had taken off; he looked jaded and lacklustre. Back at home a week later, Matt Paterson would give his appraisal in typically forthright style. Ovett was surprised by the reaction of the folks in Brighton, and particularly his club-mates. They didn't speak, went out of their way to avoid him. It was embarrassment more than anything. They didn't know what to say. Where once they'd avoided him, thinking he was a young god, now it was because they saw him as a lost soul. This was the first time they'd seen him truly beaten. Yes, he'd lost before, most obviously to Coe in Moscow, but he'd lost with honour, with a gold medal already in his pocket, and his dignity intact. Here, it seemed that he hadn't even tried. Or, as Paterson put it to him, with candour as sharp as a Gorbals smile, 'Boy! You ran like a cunt.' 'He laughed,' recalls Paterson: ' "Thank God somebody can tell me the truth," he said.'

Ovett takes up the tale: 'I think people don't understand failure, and not just in sport. It's naïve, because they think winning will go on. I don't think there is failure as long as you try your best. True failure is not even bothering to try. I mean, I wasn't in great shape [in Helsinki], and tactically I was all over the shop, not confident enough, and not giving myself a good chance. But there wasn't much I could do about it. It was the turning of the tides. I should have either not run or maybe trained a bit harder for it. Having said that, if you get selected, then you go.'

In another twist of the knife, Sydney Maree then broke Ovett's world record for 1500 metres, in Cologne. Maree was something of an enigma, linked perhaps to his birth in South Africa, where he had tired of the apartheid boycott, which he felt was counter-productive (he's black). He tried to keep away from the debate as much as he could. That, according to white anti-apartheid campaigners in London, was because he was being sponsored by a South African brewery, who didn't want him sullying the waters. Anyway, Maree had 'escaped' to the USA and become an American citizen. He was more talented than Steve Scott, but, like Scott, few saw him as a winner. At least Scott was consistent, and was always in or close to the frame, whereas Maree, who raced much less, could just as easily finish half a lap down as come close to winning.

But Maree had at least one absolutely superb race per season. For example, in Oslo in 1985, he chased home Aouita and ran an unheralded 13 minutes 1.15 seconds, just behind the Moroccan's 5000 metres world record of 13 minutes 00.40 seconds. That was a special night. Cram took the world mile record, and Ingrid Kristiansen broke the women's 10,000 metres record, too. It was one of the greatest evenings of athletics I've ever attended. However, Maree's other great performance, equally out of the blue, was to break Ovett's 1500 record in 1983.

But Ovett was not down for long, because he was nowhere near 'out'. That third meeting in Oslo, prior to Maree's record, threw up a classic British double-header. It wasn't Ovett and Coe this time but Ovett–Cram. The youngster went first. He had taken precedence over Ovett for the first time in the European Cup the week after Helsinki, and had won the 1500 metres. In Oslo three days later, the man who still believed he was destined to be a 5000 metres runner tackled two laps, and came out with the fastest time of the year, 1 minute 43.61 seconds.

Ovett's riposte was more like the athlete of old. He sped around the mile, despatching his peers (including Maree) in a time of 3 minutes 50.49 seconds. As if that wasn't enough, Ovett paid an uninvited visit to the gents in the press box and announced he was going for a world record in the next few days, date and venue to be announced. Those of us who had endured the full ice-age of Ovett's boycott were torn between being enthralled by this new openness and hailing his revival, and seeing it as another cynical attempt to deflect attention from the recently crowned king, who was strolling languidly around the Bislet turf.

But Maree's record a few days later was just the extra impetus that Ovett needed, and he made good his promise, in the atmospheric surroundings of Rieti, a little town some seventy kilometres north of Rome, in the foothills of the central Appenines. It was close to Rieti, apparently, where the Sabine women were raped, and Rieti had a reputation for violating the norms of competition. It had, and still has, a reputation for fast times, belying the meeting's late-season date, which has raised much debate about whether the track is the correct circumference. One British journalist – no friend of Ovett – is alleged to have secured a chain and measured the kerb after Ovett's record. But a couple of years later, Coe also ran a very fast 1500 metres there. Criticism from the same quarter was, shall we say, muted on that occasion.

Ovett had hoped to break the record in Koblenz – probably his favourite venue – but a slow first lap had scuppered that. In Rieti, David Mack, a member of the Santa Monica Track Club, took Ovett round in 54 seconds. Mack had once distinguished himself in Oslo by having a punch-up on the infield with the Senegalese 800 metres runner Moussa Fall, but here the American was putting his pugnacity to better use. He was fighting a strong breeze, but still delivered Ovett to the 800 mark in just outside 1 minute 51 seconds. Ovett took over shortly afterwards, and shot through the breeze to a new record of 3 minutes 30.77 seconds. True to the Rieti tradition, his first reaction was bemusement: 'I knew I was fit enough, and ready to take the record, but in those conditions, I thought it was beyond my reach.' Maree had held the record for one week.

If Cram had been upset by Ovett's attention-grabbing in Oslo, he had further cause for annoyance after the latter's record. As he recalled in 2003, 'Seb Coe is then in the media, saying, "Well, Ovett has just run badly in the World Championships. He's still the world number one." ' If Cram needed any more assurance that he himself was really the best in the world, this was it. To have Ovett seeking to shadow his limelight was one thing; to have Coe then backing up his old enemy, thereby slagging off Cram in the process, vouchsafed it for the young Geordie. His riposte was going to enthrall millions, and be remembered as one of *the* great races.

It's an overused term, 'Mile of the Century'. There was one practically every year during the 1930s, when the Ivy League–Oxbridge fixtures were in vogue. And anyone who thinks that Bannister's first sub-4 qualifies should stop reading now. If Filbert Bayi's race against himself, the clock and John Walker (in that order) had been a mile rather than 1500 metres in the 1974 Commonwealth Games, that would make it a leading contender. Essentially, however, you need a worthy opponent to make it a real race, and I would hazard that Bayi didn't even know who Walker was in Christchurch. Walker admits he didn't know Bayi. The race between Cram and Ovett at Crystal Palace at the end of 1983 would qualify on every count, except a world record, but nobody at Crystal Palace that night cared about that. Nor need they have done. Twenty years later, in 2003, *Athletics Weekly* readers voted it the 'Race of the Century'. They could be right.

Initially, Cram did not see why he should run, and Brendan Foster agreed. But this time, after some thought, Cram finally contradicted his mentor. After his 1500 metres world record, Ovett had decided to make a last attempt to recoup the kudos he had lost in Helsinki. Cram was down to run the mile in the final meeting of the season at Crystal Palace, so Ovett decided to enter it, too. Andy Norman was getting closer to Cram, but, for the time being, he was still perceived as Ovett's man. In fairness, by this time, Norman was probably as sick of the evasive tactics as everyone else. He asked Cram to stay in the race, and accept Ovett to the field. To Cram's eternal credit, he did, eventually. 'Brendan was very much against it initially, [but] I was thinking, If I don't run against him, I might as well just pack up and accept that he's better than me. But I certainly believed I was better, and I think the only way to prove that to yourself, never mind everybody else, you can kid yourself as to how good you are, but you've got to go and put yourself on the line. I had done it once at the World Championships and I was happy to do it again.

'They [Ovett and Coe] had gone through this kind of thing about protecting their position – two number ones was better than one number one and one number two. I couldn't handle that. I would rather be the number one and the only number one. And I would actually rather be number two. Then you know what you have to do. So for those reasons I decided to run, even though the race was always going to be set up more for him than it was for me. But I was confident I could win.'

The race lived up to all the expectations, and more. Because Cram was so confident, he decided to have a bit of fun. Instead of going off with the pack at the gun, he settled in behind Ovett, something that the elder man couldn't handle at all. The détente lasted only 200 metres, with the pair dawdling 50 metres (and increasing) behind the fast-disappearing pack, before Cram took off. No one could have doubted that Ovett would have been content to stay there and let the rest go. It was another credit to Cram. Ovett, who had decided after Prague never to concentrate on just one opponent again, was doing exactly that. It was the supreme compliment to Cram.

He was in his element, for he too saw the mile as something special. 'I like the mile because you have to think. It is a bit of a game of chess at times, and guys like Ovett and Coe were great to run against, and even Aouita, because they made you think. Steve was the easiest to run against and I don't mean that in terms of how good he was, I mean in terms of what he was going to do. There wasn't that much variation: you knew he wasn't going to lead. Seb could on occasions take it out. So, yes, that night, I would say it was one of my favourite races, because of the result, but also [because] there was a real sense of cat and mouse. It was good fun, the first two hundred metres was a laugh. I'd decided I was going to run behind him in the early laps just to see how he felt about it, and he wasn't obviously having any of that. So we were running down the back straight, the pair of us looking at each other, while everybody hares off. Had anyone in the race had a bit of nous and gone after the pacemaker and opened up a thirty- or forty-yard lead on us, we might have been in trouble.'

Indeed, Pierre Delèze of Switzerland was no slouch, and he was leading the charge, but once Cram switched on the after-burners, it was clear that it was only a matter of time before the pair would be back in contention. The crowd was in no doubt. Although Cram and Ovett still had a lot of catching up to do, no one in the stadium ever believed that anyone other than Cram or Ovett would win. But which one? Ovett was the darling of the Crystal Palace crowd; the place was virtually his home stadium. He might have begun his career in Brighton, but his first big races had come at the Palace, and his fame and reputation had spread from there. The crowd loved him, and still saw him as a winner. They weren't antagonistic towards Cram, far from it, but Ovett was *their* man. Cram might have won the world title, but they'd seen Ovett run down 'Sir Henry' and give him a good pasting in the season that Rono had broken four world records. But nobody knew who was going to win. That's what made it the perfect match. Crowd anticipation was as palpable as the athletes' sweat.

Cram was probably the most confident man in the park. 'The race started from four hundred metres [from the finish], and there was an air of inevitability of what was going to happen. I knew when I was going to kick, and he knew when he was going to kick. I used to try and vary it, certainly between a hard run from maybe three hundred out or just before then, which is what I did that night.' They had caught the pack at halfway, and, with Cram still leading, as he'd done since picking up the pace, they gradually drew away from the rest. With the formalities out of the way, now they could just concentrate on each other. 'From the bell I picked it up and I kicked hard at three hundred and kicked hard at two hundred, and kicked in the home straight again. And then Steve had got no chance to use the acceleration that he had. The yard that I gained, particularly at three hundred to go, was what I won by in the end.'

By which time, the crowd was on its feet, yelling its heart out. Me included. The idea is that the media should maintain a bit of decorum had gone out of the picture windows of the press box. The worst charge you could have levelled against you by your colleagues in any sport was to be 'a fan with a notebook'. But this was something else. You didn't see this every meeting, or even every year. You might see something like this only once in a lifetime. I couldn't sit still or sit down. It was wonderful stuff. The only place to be was on your feet, applauding. For it was a special race, and I dare say that each generation has races like that. But what gave it the extra cachet was that it came in the wake of that era when Coe and Ovett wouldn't, for whatever reason, race each other outside the majors. Here was Cram saying, OK, 'I'm world champion. I beat you in Helsinki, you didn't even get a medal. But here you are, challenging me to race, when I thought my season was over. I could have stood aside and let you get on with it.' But he didn't, which is why Cram deserves all the kudos he received for this race, and this victory.

To Ovett's credit, he concurred. 'It was a good clash. I mean, I enjoyed it. OK, it was a defeat marginally, and I think for both of us, Steve having won the World Championships, and me coming back into form, it was probably the right combination. The fact that it was slow to start was probably a saving grace for me. If it was going to be an all-out world-record attempt, I would have been knocked to the back straight away. It developed into a two-horse race over the last lap, and I think that's what pulled the crowd to its feet. It was good to run against Steve. We'd run against each other quite a lot. It's not a case of avoiding people sometimes – if anything, I should have avoided that race, because it was probably one of the hardest ones at the end of the season to tackle, after being exhausted from the record attempt. I got beat, but it didn't worry me, because I thought I'd done my best. It was a good race, and everybody was happy. You can't win them all.'

Cram was going to struggle in 1984, with an even more serious injury than the one he'd had the previous year. It is credit to him, and to the previous level of fitness that he achieved, but more importantly to the depth of his self-belief, that he could go so unprepared to Los Angeles and come away with an Olympic silver medal. But his time was still to come, and when it did it would result in a wonderful year of world records in which he would finally overcome not only our heroes, but their times as well. But that would be after the final act of the greatest rivalry in the history of track and field athletics.

Revenge

Although he was pre-selected for the Olympic 800 metres – with Ovett and Cram pre-selected for the 1500 – it was far from obvious that Coe would even make it to the Games in Los Angeles, let alone create sporting history. After the Gateshead debacle, Bob Hague, on examining Coe, had known instantly that there was a serious problem. 'He was clearly out of sorts and he was rather pale,' recalls the doctor, 'and he drew my attention to some lymph nodes he'd got in his groin. He'd got a huge bunch of lymph nodes there that were grossly abnormal. You normally get a few in the groin, but nothing like that. There was obviously something going on. I put him in touch with a friend who was an expert in infectious diseases in Leicester. He investigated it, did biopsies and found it was toxoplasmosis.'

This was a relief to Hague. Although he had not said so to the Coes, he was worried that it might be leukaemia. But it was bad enough, for an elite athlete. It is one of the contradictions of being so fit that a minor ailment can bring you down. Toxoplasmosis is similar to glandular fever. It is something that a 'normal' person could have without knowing or noticing, apart from being a little more tired or debilitated than usual. But with a world-class athlete, it can stop them in their tracks. That is exactly what happened to Sebastian Coe in mid-1983. He may have got it from the family cat, notorious carriers of the disease, and his case was severe.

According to Bob Hague, 'It's an infective agent that gets into the lymphoid system and causes an illness. It can last for a long time and make you feel very below par. The majority of people who get it don't get it very badly. It frequently goes away on its own, but if people have a really severe illness, which he did, there are treatments, and he had a full course of injections. Clearly it was messing up his ambitions a great deal.'

Coe had obviously had the illness for some time, and in a burst of Ovett-itis had done little or nothing about it. Peter Coe was annoyed, but his son was now twenty-seven years of age, and Dad's influence was evidently waning, although his opinions were still being offered at full volume. 'That was the one time we came very close to really falling out,' says Peter. 'He tried all sorts of alternative stuff to get better. Very early on I said, "Look, it's not working, we need a really good analysis of what is wrong. You won't get it from physiotherapy, you won't get it from osteopaths or anybody." I was really arguing with Seb, I said, "Stop and get this thing done." Athletes are buggers for that.'

Despite that semi-jocular tone, there was going to be nothing remotely funny about the next six months, which would be the lowest of Coe's career. He couldn't run, something that had been his daily anchor for more than half his life, he was on a course of drugs which made him feel sick, and he was being written off on all sides, including by his peers, who may just have felt some degree of *Schadenfreude*, satisfaction at his demise. As Gore Vidal once said, 'It is not enough to succeed, others must fail.' I suspect that Vidal was sacrificing the truth for a memorably bitchy line, but you know what I mean. John Walker, who never shrank from offering a quote when asked, said, 'Great athletes get perhaps two years when they can do almost anything. Seb was maybe the finest middle-distance runner I've ever seen. But he's had his two years.'

Coe concedes that he might already have had the beginnings of the problem in Athens in 1982. 'I wasn't feeling well in Athens. I was lumpy under the arms, and some days I was feeling OK, and other days I was just feeling tired. The day of the [800 metres] final, I felt very ordinary. Looking back, the signs were very obvious. I remember having a good break, getting back into training, but never at any stage during that winter [1982–3] feeling anything other than a couple of degrees below most of the time.

'I remember one day driving down the motorway from Loughborough to London, I was finding it very difficult to stay awake. I thought I'd stop for forty minutes to sleep, and I woke up two hours later. I was working on something, and I just lay on Steve's [Mitchell] floor. Three hours later, I woke up. So the signs were there. Then the articles started appearing, you know – "Burn Out", "Mental Breakdown". We went through the whole lot.'

By now, Coe had definitively left Sheffield, a move he underlined by joining Haringey AC in north London. Granville Beckett, the *Yorkshire Post* journalist who had followed Coe's career from a child, remembers a typically grass-roots reaction to the news of the athlete's move. 'One chap who later became Hallamshire Harriers' secretary rang to say that Seb had joined Haringey. I said, "I'm sorry to hear that," and he said, "Well, he never did nowt for our club anyway." I thought, Just by being a member, you are attracting people to that club, aren't you? He was so short-sighted.' I was able to reassure Beckett that the only reason I knew Hallamshire was even in Sheffield was because of Coe's link to the club.

It would be close to six months before Coe could do any sort of training. A gap like that as a teenager would have been almost incidental, but Coe was entering his late twenties, with well over a decade of intensive training behind him. That background might serve him well ultimately, but it could also make it much more difficult to come back, both mentally and physically. He was fortunate in one sense that the illness prevented him putting on weight, so that wasn't an aspect he had to bother about when he began training in early 1984. He was also on massive doses of antibiotics, designed to kill off the virus.

'The hardest period was the weeks and weeks of very heavy drug treatment,' he says. 'I remember being at a book launch in one of the big bookshops in Dublin, and having to leave halfway through, and throwing up. I was just feeling like death warmed up, and that was the pattern of the day. Not long after Christmas, I started jogging with fourteen-year-old kids at Haringey, eight-minute-mile pace. Crammy and Ovett are running 3.33–3.34 [1500 metres races] in Melbourne, so if you ask at what point in the year did LA seem as remote as it possibly could be, it was probably that period.'

Peter Coe had enlisted the help of Dr David Martin, an exercise physiologist at the University of Atlanta, whom Peter had met at various coaching conferences. They would eventually collaborate on a book, *Better Middle Distance Running*, a volume which became a seminal work for serious students of coaching. Peter was going to send the results of all Coe's blood tests to Martin, who would use them to evaluate the amount of work that Seb could do without harming his immune system further.

'The thing about toxoplasmosis is that it can stay in your system for a good fifteen, twenty years,' says Seb. 'The risk was stressing the body too much, and dropping back into it [the virus]. There was also the risk of piling on the training so quickly that you ended up getting a stress fracture. It was probably Peter's finest hour, just managing that, and not on a day-by-day basis, that was hour by hour. And Dave Martin was fantastic, because he was doing all the blood chemistry analysis, so any time that the chemistries were looking like we were entering dangerous stress areas, we'd have to back off.'

Despite the dozen of more years of competition, there was still an element lacking which Peter sought to add. Seb was still uncomfortable in company in his races. He had been so good, and used what he calls the 'front-running tactic' to such good effect, that he had still not got used to the rough and tumble associated primarily with 800 metres running. Peter asked John Hovell, one of the Haringey AC officials and coaches, to supply relays of youngsters to accompany Coe during his speed/endurance sessions. Peter liked what he called, 'up and down the clock sessions'. Other coaches call them ladders or pyramids. This is the practice of running, say, 1200 metres at three-quarter race speed, taking anything up to two minutes rest/jog, then another 'effort' of 800 metres, rest, 600 metres, rest, and so on, down to 200 metres, then back up to 1200 metres. This has the additional benefit of teaching pace judgement at different distances, and getting the athlete used to using the shorter distances to effect mid-race surges.

'He [Hovell] knew quite well the strengths of the kids in the team,' Peter recalls, 'so I arranged that he could put me in a new face without interrupting the flow too much. Very short recoveries, just get another man in for the next time, going down or coming up. My job was to go into the stands in a position where I could see all the markers around the track. They [club runners] were instructed to get him into a bunch, rough him up a bit, it didn't matter, real racing conditions. People make a basic mistake: they train to train, they don't train to race.'

Coe repaid the debt to his new club-mates by turning out in the road relay season. These are major events on the club calendar, emphasising club spirit and solidarity, while being less stressful than either cross-country or track running, yet providing a good pointer to form. Coe will have been overjoyed, in his first race in eight months, to run the fastest leg in the Thames Valley Harriers road relay on 31 March. He was again fastest on the short (five-kilometre) leg of the Southern Counties 12-stage road relay the following week, and second fastest in the National 12-stage another couple of weeks later.

With Ovett and Cram in Australia, Coe would normally have been the centre of attention, but, although many of the national press attended those relays, there was something else to divert our gaze. It needed to be pretty extraordinary to keep us away from the prospect of Coe, Ovett and Cram at the Olympic Games. And it was. It was Zola Budd. The South African waif became a *cause célèbre* on and off the track. An eagle-eyed sub-editor on the *Daily Mail* had spotted that the teenage running phenomenon, barefooting around the bush in Bloemfontein, had a British grandparent. David English, the *Mail* editor with an eye for the main chance, had immediately done a deal with his Conservative government contacts for her to get a British passport in double-quick time. Depending on your politics, this was either one of the greatest coups of the Thatcher administration or a blatant disregard for the sporting boycott of apartheid South Africa.

Zola Budd is one of the greatest natural running talents I have ever seen – and on the testimony of several British internationals, men who ran with her, she trained harder than any woman athlete they had ever met. But the manner of her 'acquisition' for Britain was a disgrace to all right-thinking people. It was a passport of convenience, and it should never have been countenanced, but it was passed on the nod by the rump of the administrative 'old school', those who were being bypassed in the rush to professional athletics. And it *did* give us plenty to write about. I was one of the sternest critics of Budd during her time in the UK, something that she remarked upon in her autobiography, published after she returned to South Africa in 1988. But she also records in *Zola* that I was the first to tell her that she could win the World Cross Country title, something she did twice, 1985 and 1986. I would like to claim this as admirable foresight and qualitative judgement, but any fool could have told her that, and I was amazed no one else had done so.

I thought I was merely stating the obvious when she was expressing reservations about her chances a couple of weeks prior to the 1985 race in Lisbon. She won the 5-kilometre race by almost 200 metres. I was ambivalent. I knew how good she was, and I loved watching her race – she was as aggressive as any good runner should be – but she should never have even been in Britain. Budd, of course, would figure in one of the indelible memories of the Olympic Games in Los Angeles 1984 – the fall of America's darling, Mary Decker, in the 3000 metres final. That was something you couldn't make up, but so was the final act of the rivalry of Seb Coe and Steve Ovett. It was all going to keep us on our toes, and poised over our typewriters, throughout the summer.

Ovett was back from his Australian trip, where he had been edged out of victory in all three of his 1500 metres races. But the races had paid for the voyage, which was principally a training exercise, and he declared himself fitter than he had been in the two and a half years since the Church Railings Incident. He proved it with a welcome return to Paris, two years after he had dropped out of a race for the first time in his career. That had been due to the heat and humidity, something that was going to assail him again before the end of the season, but the spring weather in Paris was perfect for his demolition of a classy field in a road mile down the Avenue Foch.

The wave of big-city marathons over the previous decade had given rise to a parallel, albeit short-lived, fad for city-centre mile races. The Fifth Avenue Mile in New York was the model. It had been launched by Fred Lebow, the entrepreneur who had persuaded the city fathers to let him take the marathon out of Central Park and into the Five Boroughs. Lebow didn't know much about running, but he was a great salesman. He persuaded Mark McCormack's International Management Group, Coe's agents, to stage a series of mile races around the world. There was a lot of criticism of the events, since some were blatantly downhill. Mike Boit had won one in New Zealand in 1982 in 3 minutes 28 seconds, twenty seconds faster than the track record. Just about the only one remaining nowadays is the original, the Fifth Avenue Mile. Ovett was back to his magisterial best in Paris, dominating the Spanish stars, José-Luis Gonzalez and José-Manuel Abascal, in 3 minutes 56.12 seconds.

Coe might have had a good reintroduction to competition in the road relays, but track running is a very different matter. A month after Ovett's Parisian win, Coe was very edgy prior to his track comeback, and uncharacteristically didn't want to talk to journalists. His traditional county championship 'opener' was not in Yorkshire this time, but in Middlesex, at Enfield, north London. He was happy to talk afterwards, since in his first track race for ten months he led all the way in one of the stronger county races, winning the 800 metres in 1 minute 45.2 seconds, the year's fastest time. Cram won the North-East Counties 5000 metres on the same day back at Gateshead.

Everything looked to be on track for the trio to wheel up their preparation for Los Angeles, and both Ovett and Coe were being given the broadest latitude to qualify as well for their Olympic-title distances. But Ovett then went down with bronchitis and was still in bed when Coe strayed onto his territory and won the Southern Counties 1500 metres at Crystal Palace. He ran nowhere near the

Olympic qualifying time, but for the first time in three years things seemed to be conspiring in his favour. Graham Williamson was injured, and doubtful for the final selection race, the AAA Championships, again at Crystal Palace in late June.

Then, at the eleventh hour, a joker emerged from the pack, yet another world-class British middle-distance runner. Peter Elliott was already an accomplished 800 metres man. He had finished fourth as a twenty-year-old in the World Championships in Helsinki the previous year, a performance which had earned him a place alongside Coe in the line-up for the two-lap race in Los Angeles. But Elliott had been given impetus to attempt the same double, following a rare outing at 1500 metres when he had knocked ten seconds off his best by winning in 3 minutes 38.84 seconds in Australia in January, a race in which the far from fit Cram had been down the field. Elliott had a canny old coach in Wilf Paish, whose experience was second to none. Paish knew the sport in all its multi-disciplinary glory, proof of which was his coaching of Tessa Sanderson to victory in the Olympic javelin in Los Angeles.

There was a strong element of local rivalry in Paish and Elliot throwing their hats in the ring, because Elliott hailed from Rotherham, an area often referred to – because of its left-wing politics – as the Republic of South Yorkshire. Coe and his father lived in Sheffield, only a handful of miles away, and still in Yorkshire, but a very different political colour. What's more, as Coe admits, as transplanted Londoners they suffered from perceptions of snobbishness, added to which it was already abundantly clear that Coe himself was a Conservative.

Elliott feels that Coe was never really accepted as a Yorkshireman. 'He was born in London for a start, and supported Chelsea. He was based down in Loughborough. Things like that stick with people up our way. I had worked at the steelworks, I think that was why people got behind me, they could relate to that, they could relate to a working person.'

Since Elliott was a factory worker, who made a virtue of his status as a part-time athlete, this was a tabloid wet-dream, another Toff versus Tough scenario. The great English class divide swung into view, fuelled by Elliott's homespun philosophy of being a down-home boy from the backstreets who worked hard for a living, ran hard in training, then ran from the front in races. I would venture that only Paula Radcliffe (for similar reasons) has been more admired world-wide than Elliott. Nobody in their right mind could have disliked him. If Ovett was the Athletes' Athlete, Elliott was Everyman's Athlete. He was such a willing front-runner, you felt he was doing a horse out of a job. And while it is true that anyone with an accent as broad as Elliot's – sounding as if it had been hacked out of a coal-seam – is immediately identified as 'thick' in Britain, Elliot was clearly as sharp as a Sheffield knife. He now works in that town as the athlete services manager at the English Institute of Sport complex.

Like Cram, he admitted to being an Ovett fan, built on his early experiences training on the famous Merthyr Mawr sand-dunes in Wales with Harry Wilson's group. But he also admired Coe's support for the country championships, something which prompted him to turn out as often as possible in the Yorkshires. 'They were one of the reasons you were an 800 metres runner or a 1500 metres runner,' says Elliot. 'I always opened the season with the Yorkshire Championships, and the reason I did that was because Seb did that. But, although Seb was in Sheffield, and I worked in a Sheffield factory, I met Steve at Merthyr Mawr and I thought, what a character, what a great guy! And I became an Ovett fan. I remember at the [1980] Olympics, Seb was supposed to win the 800, and obviously Ovett won, and I was, like, "Ah!" and arms aloft. I worked at British Steel then, and on the day of the 1500, I was working outside, on the roof. I listened to it on the radio and Seb beat Steve and all the lads came out from the factory and they were, like, arms aloft and I'm, like, "Yeah, yeah." They took the ladder away and left me up there.'

Well, for a brief period during that summer of 1984, Elliott was going to leave Coe out to dry. But the week before Elliott's 'surprise' at the AAA Championships, a recuperating Ovett and a fit Cram appeared at a meeting in Loughborough, organised by Coe! The organiser himself didn't run, because, by now, he'd picked up a slight injury. Nevertheless, after Ovett won the 800 metres, complete with mandatory push and obligatory wave, and Cram the 1000 metres, the trio took to the track together – for a television interview. Ah, well . . .

Ovett won another 800 metres three days later, in Belfast, and decided to sit on his (Olympic) laurels, and miss the AAA Championships, billed as the final selection races. There were others vying for the vacant 800 metres spot in LA – Gary Cook, who had been a member of the 4×800 metres world record squad in 1982, and Ikem Billy, who had won the European Junior title the previous year, a decade after Ovett's international breakthrough. But Ovett had beaten Billy twice in three days, and he announced to journalists a message clearly intended for the selectors – 'There's more to come.'

Coe was less confident. He thought his muscle pull might not stand the rigours of heats and final of the 1500 metres the following weekend, but, since the Los Angeles team was being finalised on the evening after the AAA Championships, he had little option but to participate. He had reason to feel anxious. He was running into a minefield, with Sapper Elliott looking to trip him up. Elliott recalls arriving at Crystal Palace: 'I got the programme, and in the middle there was an article on me and Seb. It said, the "Apprentice takes on the Master." And I thought, Oooh. There was this buzz going around, because it was like people were building it up.'

But that wasn't the only attraction. Even without Ovett, the soap opera that was British athletics had an omnibus edition that weekend. Cram had given the selectors a bit of leeway by renouncing interest in the Olympic 800 metres, but, although he won the national title at the distance that weekend, he hobbled across the finish line, due to a torn Achilles tendon. He limped onto the infield and lay there, surrounded by photographers, for a half-hour while ice and strapping were applied. At least he had a grandstand view for the next drama. Neither Coe nor Elliott acquitted themselves well in the rough-house that was the 1500 metres.

In the Southern Counties race a month earlier, Coe had given the impression that he was staying in the pack, the better to experience the sort of hustle and bustle that he had so studiously and elegantly avoided for most of his career. He ultimately won the Southern with an extravagant burst that took him ten metres clear at the line. He would not have that privilege at Crystal Palace. Elliott was even less tactically astute than Coe, but with a better excuse: this was only his fourth race at the distance. The final lap was classic knockabout. Elliott, who had been bumped and boxed for most of the race, stormed around the pack to take the lead with 300 metres to run. Coe passed him on the final bend and took the inside lane, a little too abruptly in Elliott's estimation. Elliot sidestepped as neatly as any fly-half and came again. With the crowd on its feet, his final drive took him an ace past Coe, and he won in 3 minutes 39.66 seconds. The Olympic champion finished thirteen hundredths behind.

I felt and wrote at the time that Coe's congratulation to Elliott post-race was indicative of his acceptance that his chance of defending his title had gone. Coe said that Elliott saw him walk off with Andy Norman, and thought that he, Elliott, had not done enough. Coe says, 'If only he knew. It was Andy saying, "Look, you are not going to get the 1500, just concentrate on the 800 now." '

The selectors' meeting that night was as fraught as the race. Initially, they decided to give the last places to Ovett in the 800, and Elliott in the 1500. When the meeting broke up, that was still the consensus, and the news agencies, who were always given advance notice, were advised of the blow to Coe. But there was a spate of late night phone calls, and the team was changed early the following morning. Coe was in! 'I knew that they were picking the team. I can't even remember who I rang, from a phone box in Cromwell Road. I had just finished training, and he said, "You're in." I said, "What? The 800?" "No," he said, "both." Then, of course, all hell opened up, because Peter [Elliott] had been left out [of the 1500] – the North–South divide!'

There were a few days of media recrimination, briefly obscuring the fact that, once again, Coe and Ovett, while as distant yet as inseparable as North from South, were selected to defend their Olympic titles as well as their world-record distances. Cram, meanwhile, was in a plaster cast, however temporarily. It would later emerge that Elliott also had the beginnings of a stress fracture, which would ultimately eliminate him from the Olympic 800 metres final. Safely selected, Coe and Ovett went again to the Bislet Games in Oslo. No heroics this time; it was enough to stay out of trouble. Coe won the 800 metres in 1 minute 43.84 seconds, and Ovett won the 1500 in 3 minutes 34.5 seconds. Both times were the third fastest in the world at that stage.

Coe was overjoyed. His was a world-class performance, the first substantial indication that his comeback was on track. He went into Oslo to celebrate, an evening which would end up with Anne-Lise Hammer, the Oslo press officer, spending two weeks in gaol. Hammer is a political journalist who helped out at the Bislet Games during the great decade of record breaking. She went on to manage athletes, including Linford Christie for a while, and wrote a book on drugs in sport, which was never published in Britain for legal reasons. That evening in Oslo has been the subject of speculation for years. Dave Warren and Coe's agent Brad Hunt were also at the party, but there is collective amnesia on their part, and all Hammer will say is that Coe was so 'happy' that he was leaning out of the car window, arms outspread, yelling his satisfaction while she was driving round town.

'Seb had been injured for more than a year and he got his kick for the first time, so he was very, very happy,' she says. 'We had a car *incident*, that is true. I was the driver. Somebody accused us, or me, for having an *accident*, but we didn't actually have an accident. I would think that I was the most sober person, but I had to go to prison for drunk driving, for two weeks. It was a good story, of course, but I think Andy Norman was instrumental in stopping the story in the British newspapers because it was one month before the Olympic Games; it was kept under the lid. I had to promise my chief editor not to tell. I had to handle it. My chief editor did like Sebastian Coe very much, so when he heard that I had to go to prison, I got time off work during the Christmas break. It's a good story but actually nobody wants to remember that story.'

Coe had one last race in Britain, winning something called the Brigg Mile in a club meeting in north London in 3 minutes 54.6 seconds. There was a lot of history attached to the race. It was the event where Ovett had first broken 4 minutes in 1974. A decade later, Coe broke New Zealander Dick Quax's event record, set in 1972, the year that Ovett and Coe had had their only race in England, both beaten by Kirk Dumpleton in the English Schools Cross Country. That night, 4 July 1984, the man who finished second, some 100 metres behind Coe, in 4 minutes 8.1 seconds, was Kirk Dumpleton.

Coe felt that the British team was not giving itself sufficient time to acclimatise to the eight hours' time difference between the UK and Los Angeles, so he decided with Peter that he would go early to the USA, first to Chicago – six hours' difference – where he would complete their agreed training schedule, then the final hop to California. It would be the first time that Coe had spent so much prime time away from his coach, and it prompted much speculation of a rift. Both men deny that, claiming that it was a natural progression – the inevitable shift of balance between coach and maturing athlete, something that both Ovett and Cram agreed with, in respect of their own coaches, Harry Wilson and Jimmy Headley.

Peter Coe says, 'We were sitting in the car one evening, discussing the whole thing. I said, "So much has gone wrong for you in the last year or so, and you have been thinking about it too much now, Seb, that it's compounding it into a greater difficulty that it is. Only you can get it out, and would you prefer to sort this out yourself?" He thought about it, there was a sort of flickering that it would seem a bit disloyal, there was a certain reluctance at first, but I think that is really what he wanted to do.' Seb himself says, 'Peter's role had changed by that stage. He wasn't there at every training session, he was much more the dispassionate eye, watching and making suggestions and judgements. At fourteen, fifteen, sixteen, the coach makes all the judgements. If he is still making them by the time you're twenty-eight, there's something wrong with the relationship.'

Coe's time in the USA prior to such an astounding turnaround in fortunes in Los Angeles has given rise to more sinister rumours, too: that he went there to blood dope. He denies it, and says that he suffered those rumours every time he went training at altitude in Switzerland or Italy. Blood doping, or blood boosting, is the practice where an athlete has a pint of blood removed, which is then stored for a month. During that time, the body replenishes its blood supply, but the training is done under additional stress, another conditioning factor. The stored blood is then reintroduced, meaning that the athlete now has a surfeit of oxygen-carrying red-blood corpuscles. The result is similar to turbo-charging a car. Even with a 1 per cent advantage, a 10,000 metres runner could win a race by the length of the finishing straight.

Some would argue that it was no worse than going to altitude to train, and the practice was felt to be common in some countries during the seventies and eighties. Thomas Wessinghage said that it was a subject regularly debated by the milers, a tightly knit group on the circuit throughout the eighties. 'Yes, we had long discussions about that, and there were three questions that always stood there but couldn't be answered. The first question – Eastern Bloc athletes? Second question – Italians, middle- and long-distance runners? Third question – Finnish long-distance runners.'

Lasse Viren, the Finn who won the 5000 and 10,000 metres gold medals in both the 1972 and the 1976 Olympic Games, was a prime suspect, since he did little to impress outside of Olympic competition. He has never admitted it, and the only person to have done so is his compatriot, Kaarlo Maaninka, who won silver and bronze medals in the 1980 Olympics in Moscow. In Los Angeles, another Finn, Martti Vainio, was caught by a roundabout method after winning the Olympic silver medal in the 10,000 metres. Vainio tested positive for steroids, hitherto felt to be useless for distance runners, since water-based steroids bleed fairly quickly out of the system. But it seems that the blood that Vainio had had removed had contained traces of steroids, so when it was reintroduced in time for his race in LA, the steroids showed up in the post-race drug test. Or should that be dope-test?

Blood doping is banned by the IAAF and affiliated bodies, but there is no way of testing for it, especially if it is the athlete's own blood. It is possible to infuse blood from the same group as the athlete's, as happens in remedial medicine, but that is now old technology, overtaken by blood substitutes and plasmas, which are infinitely more frightening, both as performance-enhancers and as health hazards. I am not generally one of those who think that the drugs athletes use are necessarily dangerous – that was one of the first mistakes that the authorities made when banning performance-enhancers in the mid-seventies. The athletes knew they *weren't* dangerous when taken in properly monitored quantities. It is a question of ethics, much like pacing, on which I am equally old technology.

This is as good a place as any to air any suspicions about both Coe and Ovett. No book on athletics nowadays would be complete without a mention, an essay, a chapter or even the whole volume on performance-enhancing drugs. I have mentioned them in respect of Olaf Beyer and Jürgen Straub, and they have denied the accusations. Equally, I put the question to Ovett and Coe.

Matt Paterson, Ovett's long-time training partner, who, like Ovett, now lives in Australia, said that whenever he returned to Glasgow, his old mates always said that Ovett *had* to be on drugs to run as well, as frequently, as he did. Ovett says, 'I suppose at the time when we were knocking records off left, right and centre people must have thought, What the hell's going on here with these two? But I can put my hand on heart, and on my children's lives, that I never took an aspirin or a paracetamol at any stage in my career. I was frightened to death of doing a thing like that, and I'm very proud that I didn't. So, you know, they can say what they like because I know the true facts.'

Coe says, 'I used to hear those rumours: "Oh, he goes to Switzerland, to Italy, for his blood." I used to laugh it off, and Steve [Mitchell] and Malcolm [Williams] were mainly with me in Switzerland. I'm afraid it's the sadness of sport. This is where you've got to be so careful about pointing fingers at people making big breakthroughs, because only in public terms is it a big breakthrough. In reality, you've been slogging away, mile after mile, weight after weight, ten years at a time.'

Dr Wessinghage backs them up without question: 'I never had the feeling that any of the Brits or the Americans used performance-enhancing drugs. I had the feeling, as I said, with a few of the other nations; I wouldn't say athletes, nations. But not with them [Ovett and Coe], and that gave me a good feeling.'

Chicago was a haven for Coe. It must have seemed like heaven, without the British media breathing down his neck. He was staying with another coach that his father had met on the lecture circuit, Joe Newton, who was based at York High School. 'I was doing some good training sessions there, I was listening to a lot of jazz, which was nice, and I was just beginning to enjoy it. I remember running one evening on the golf course, and I was suddenly really excited about the thought of the championships. I thought, I've got a reasonable chance. I felt I was back in, feeling confident and competitive, and my kick had come back too. This was a huge thing.'

Back at home, things were not going so well for his rivals. Ovett was suffering a succession of problems – first the bronchitis, then a muscle pull, then a viral infection which caused a skin rash. He missed several race appointments, and contented himself with simply winning the races he did run. He was husbanding his resources. Cram, on the other hand, was having similar injury problems to the previous year. But, having come back so successfully in 1983, everyone was expecting him to do the same in 1984.

Saïd Aouita, the man who would become Cram's great rival the following year, was keeping everybody guessing. Aouita was a marvellous character, which is one of the reasons why I ultimately made a television documentary with him, in 1988. He talked as good a race as he could run, which, considering he went on to break five world records, was a storm of words. He had developed into a world-beater since finishing third to Cram at the World Championships in Helsinki the previous year, and was prevaricating between the Olympic 1500 and 5000 metres. He was unbeaten at all distances in 1984, and had run 3 minutes 31.54 seconds for 1500 metres, the fastest of the year, less than a month before the Games. Cram was particularly frank about the Moroccan's chances, saying, 'If he isn't in the 1500 metres, all well and good for me, but I think he'd be better off in the 1500 metres, because he's the guy I'd be afraid of in Los Angeles.' Aouita may have been tactically naïve in trying to run the legs off everyone, and providing a springboard for Cram's surge to victory in Helsinki, but the Moroccan wasn't stupid. In the end, sanity prevailed, and he won the Olympic 5000 metres at a stroll.

Many people expected Los Angeles to be a disaster. The Soviet Union and East Germany, the two strongest athletics nations apart from the USA, had boycotted the Olympic Games, in a riposte to the US boycott of Moscow. The infamous LA smog was widely feared by the runners, and the overcrowded highways were felt to pose a threat to stadium access and generally contribute to a hectically crowded Olympics. But the Angelinos, who didn't like the idea of the Olympics on their doorstep, left town in hordes, cutting down traffic and pollution to manageable levels. And the Games turned out to be a wonderful occasion for most people, from the moment the Rocket Man touched down in front of the main grandstand of the tarted-up Coliseum at the opening ceremony, and the eighty-four gleaming grand pianos slid out of the wings; to the last flag-waving hurrah at the closing ceremony with Lionel Ritchie's twenty-five-minute version of 'All Night Long', which would pop into my head unbidden all year long.

After his successful rehearsal at the World Championships the previous year, Carl Lewis was primed for his four-gold emulation of Jesse Owens. He won the medals but failed to win over either the crowd in the stadium or the millions watching the starspangled coverage on NBC. Lewis was a real conundrum – immensely talented, strongly competitive, handsome and articulate, but a complete turn-off. Those who had known him as 'the sweetest kid', in the words of one West Coast coach, blamed his manager Joe Douglas, a tiny, ebullient Texan. Douglas fostered an image of

'King Carl', another *L'Equipe* construction, and Lewis bought into it big-time. The result was that he was insufferable. His preening and posing alienated virtually everyone, from his rivals and other athletes to media and sponsors. In an autobiography, *Inside Track*, published half a dozen years later, Lewis comes over as petty, spiteful and mean-minded, quite an accomplishment for a book that was supposed to be an advert for his talents. He should have been an advertisers' dream, but nobody would touch him. Lewis blamed a bad press, but one US marketing executive I canvassed at the time simply said, 'Attitude.'

The ambivalence about his alleged homosexuality may have had a lot to do with it, and he was never clear on the subject. But that was undoubtedly one of the turn-offs in a country whose sporting image, born of the cowboy, is the ultimate macho man. The inimitably tasteless Daley Thompson went to his post-victory press conference in LA wearing a T-shirt bearing the legend, 'Is the World's Second-Best Athlete Gay?' But Thompson made an interesting contrast to Lewis in the arena of public perception. Despite his own nasty streak, to which many can testify, Thompson's flip attitude made him everybody's – including the US media's – surrogate hero, while Lewis' earnestness earned him only derision. But credit where it's due, Lewis was one of the greatest competitors I ever saw (then again, so was Thompson). I lost count of the times Lewis would pull out a victory under pressure in the long jump on the Grand Prix circuit throughout the eighties. But at the 1984 Olympics, another great competitor was having problems of a different kind.

As soon as Ovett arrived in Los Angeles he knew he was in trouble. There might have been less smog than usual, but the aftermath of his bronchitis, his inability to deal with heat, and the residual pollution all conspired to floor him, literally. 'I remember arriving in LA and almost straight away finding difficulty with breathing, even on a gentle run. I thought I was coming down with a cold, flu or something, which again is a worry when you arrive somewhere, but obviously it was a problem with the smog there. I was suffering from exercise-induced asthma, which is a restriction of the bronchial tube. But no one in Los Angeles wanted to label it as that, because you don't talk about the smog in Los Angeles at Olympics time. In the past I had one or two problems with asthma, but never as severe as that.'

Prepared or not, the Games must go on, and four years after what was probably the most eagerly awaited Olympic clash in history, Coe and Ovett again went to the line in the Olympic 800 metres final. This time, they were far from being favourites. Going into the competition, Coe was the year's third fastest with 1 minute 43.84 seconds, but much would depend on his capacity to do that repeatedly, which he had not shown for almost three years. Earl Jones and Johnny Gray had shared the national record of 1 minute 43.74 seconds in a sensational US Championships race, where John Marshall had edged James Robinson out of the third Olympic spot, despite sharing the time of 1 minute 43.92 seconds! Donato Sabia of Italy had also run under 1 minute 44 seconds, but lurking behind them on 1 minute 44.4 seconds was a tall, gangling figure with curly hair, not unlike Cram, but even bigger – a former basketball player, Joaquím Cruz of Brazil. Ovett was way down the lists, with 1 minute 46.15 seconds.

Coe breezed through the heats, showing little evidence of his two years of disappointment and indisposition. He won his first round in 1 minute 45.71 seconds, and finished a close second in the next to Billy Konchellah of Kenya (who had paced him in his world record in Florence), in 1 minute 46.71 seconds. Ovett finished second to Cruz in both rounds, in 1 minute 46.66 seconds and what looked like a promising 1 minute 45.72 seconds. But off the track he was in trouble. 'I just found I could not breathe and I was suffocating. I thought, I'd better get off the track, I am sure I'm going to pass out here. I remember just getting into the tunnel, sitting down, and then I passed out. And the next thing I knew, I came to, and Harry [Wilson] was standing there.

'I came to again in the hospital and I said, "What am I doing here?" He said, "I came to get you, you were about half an hour in that tunnel and no one knew where you were. And when I found you, you were just lying there." I think there were probably quite a few athletes lying around, but I was actually out. When I got to the hospital, they were saying, "You are OK, but we are going to have to look and take some readings from you." There was just disbelief that I was actually going through this sort of scenario. I mean, one minute you are super fit and you arrive in the city, and the next minute you are in the hospital. It didn't really sink in, I didn't realise how serious the problem was. They discharged me and I went back to the village, and the next day the same thing happened again.'

In Moscow, the Soviet invasion of Afghanistan had been the subtext of much of the reporting back in Britain. There was something much more insidious happening at home during Los Angeles – the Miners' Strike, and the commando tactics used by the Thatcher government to quash it. But such was the celebrity of the Olympic trio that the strike was knocked off the top of the television news agenda, to accommodate reports of Ovett's problems. It was obvious to everyone by now: every time Ovett went onto the track he looked dreadful. He had been floored in the tunnel after the second round, but he would floor himself in the semi-final in a desperate, successful, effort – which said much for his tenacity – to reach his third successive Olympic 800 metres final. Ovett was in Cruz's race yet again. And the Brazilian ran from the front with the same abandon he had demonstrated in the heats. Cruz had an untroubled win in an ominous 1 minute 43.82 seconds. Ovett seemed out of contention until the final strides, when he literally launched himself at the line in an effort to make the top four, and the final. He succeeded, by six hundredths of a second, but he was clearly in distress.

Coe, in contrast, stamped his authority on the second semi-final, winning in 1 minute 45.51 seconds. He had done everything right in all three races so far. There was a confidence about him, which came out in press briefings. Even socially he seemed different. He had finally become his own man. Only one athlete stood between him and his dream of a major 800 metres title – Joaquím Cruz. The tall, powerful Brazilian had taken over from Ovett, who was a shadow of his former self. The British team management was at the latter's hospital bedside, trying to persuade him not to run in the final.

'Harry was very cautious this time,' Ovett recalls. 'He was waiting for me and he got the doctors to me. I remember sitting in bed. I think it was Lynn Davies or Nick Whitehead came, and as I came to, they said, "Don't go on any more. You are being silly, don't go and push yourself," and this, that and the other. And I said, "Well, I have made the final." In my mind this thing came on so quickly, I had a funny feeling that it was going to go as quickly. Because it literally came on as I raced, or as I ran, and I thought it might go, I might run through it. I ran in the final, [but] it was a pathetic effort really. And I ended up again back in the hospital.'

Coe did everything right in the final too, but he came up against a *force majeure* in Cruz. The Brazilian altered his tactics and followed Edwin Koech of Kenya, a noted front-runner. When Cruz kicked off the final bend, there was nothing Coe could do. Cruz had run each round faster than the previous, and he won in 1 minute 43 seconds dead. Coe was an equally clear second, in 1 minute 43.64 seconds. Earl Jones was third. Ovett trailed in a disconsolate last, in 1 minute 52.28 seconds, and sank to his knees. Coe looked massively disappointed, but he had no reason to be. In contrast to Moscow, this was an Olympic silver medal hard earned and well deserved. He collected himself sufficiently to say afterwards, 'I'm half-delighted that I came back to win the silver, but half-disappointed because I know now that I will never win a major 800 metres championship.' He would turn out to be wrong about that. But there was something far more important to occupy him at that point – a successful defence of his 1500 metres title, something that had never been done before.

Prior to that, though, he had no small part to play in Ovett's drama. Ironically, immediately after the 800 metres, he would spend more time with Ovett than he had in the preceding dozen years. 'I hadn't realised at the end of the 800 what trouble he was in. I walked by and put my hand on his shoulder, because he's on all fours and I just laughed and said, "I think we are a bit too old to be playing with fire." And I then suddenly realised he wasn't even responding; he had gone white. They put him on a stretcher and then he started to lose colour. I yelled at the paramedic guys to get over because he just looked, frankly, like he was on his way out. So I hung around there in the tunnel with him for some time. I don't think he remembers much about what was going on. Rachel was in a state; Andy [Norman] looked quite shocked by it. When they took him off, I could not conceive that he was going to come back for the 1500.'

But he did, and amazingly won his 1500 metres heat three days later on 9 August, albeit in a pedestrian time of 3 minutes 49.23 seconds. But he was going to end up in hospital after each race. By this time, Rachel Ovett was frantic. 'I was pretty scared at that point,' she recalls, 'bearing in mind Dad's history [Mick Ovett's heart-attack]. Steve did have the symptoms of something far more serious. Steve had this steely determination, and no matter what, he was there, and he was going to do it. I can remember him saying he may not run the final, then Harry said, "Well, tomorrow, when you start . . ." And I said, "But he is not going to run tomorrow, is he, Harry?" Harry said, "Well, yes." I started crying and said I didn't want him to. Harry said, "Rachel, you can't say that," and at that point I realised, no, I actually couldn't. It seriously was wrong of me even to say it. I shouldn't have said it. If Steve wanted to do it, it was up to him. That was their decision. There we were, at the Olympics, with a coach and an athlete. No matter what I felt on a personal level, that wasn't going to change the job that they had to do.'

For a distraught wife, concerned for the health of her husband, this was an extraordinary recognition of the power of his ambition. She thought his life was in danger. And his life *was* in danger, because running was his life. This is what he did. This is what he was. He had to do it. He made the caveat that if he felt really bad, he would drop out of the final. Which is what happened. It was a desolate end to an Olympic career.

Ovett recalls, 'It was disappointing. I was coming towards the end of my career and I was in great shape. I trained very hard. I am not just saying that: Harry, if he had been alive, would have shown you facts and figures ... You know, I was probably in as good a shape as I have been in. When I got back to the British Olympic Medical Centre in London, they told me, your bronchii were restricting, your tubes. You were getting sixty per cent and you should have been getting a hundred per cent efficiency. I knew I was in trouble when I went through the bell and it was getting worse. I thought, No, you are going to have to stop. And it was the hardest decision of my life, I had never done that before. And that was it. That was the end of the Olympics for me.' Operating at 60 per cent of his capacity, Ovett had reached two Olympic finals.

Cram, too, was not 100 per cent. But you wouldn't know it. While Coe had almost given his father a heart-attack by throttling back too much when he saw he had qualified, and getting only the fourth of five automatic qualifying places in his 1500 metres semi-final, and Ovett was sensibly doing just enough to finish third in the other semi, up ahead of him Cram was winning. That was either a statement of intent or bravado intended to mask his lack of preparation.

There had been much trepidation about Cruz, following his dominating victory in the 800 metres, but the tall Brazilian just didn't have the same experience at 1500 metres, nor the background to accommodate seven fierce races in just over a week. After getting through his heat easily enough, he failed to show up for the semi-final. But Coe was operating on a different level now anyway. He felt good; he knew how well he was running; he didn't have to prove anything. He was going to do that in the final. 'I knew I was going to win on the day of the final,' he says. 'I knew I was going to win. The biggest issue was not before the race, it was two laps into it. If I had any niggling doubt at all, it was, at what point does the indicator light go yellow, and the engine start to splutter? This was my seventh race in nine days. So they had the advantage of coming there fresh. When I was on my seventh, they were only on their third. But were the problems of the last two years going to catch up with me spectacularly? If I had a slight off day, it was the semi the day before, [when] I eased off marginally too much, and allowed it to be a little too close in qualifying.

'I went in with one strategy and that was, there was no way that with six hundred metres to go was I going to let Crammy get in front of me, because by that stage of his career, he was at his best when he was making an uncluttered, unfettered run for home. He grew in confidence. Get him out in front and he was a difficult athlete to beat. He didn't have electric acceleration [like Ovett], but when he started to move, God, he really did! And he liked hitting the front. I sensed that he was an athlete that enjoyed taking it on from a distance.'

For those who remember Coe's grimace at the press box immediately after the finish line, I asked if revenge was a sufficient motivation. It was the one question out of the dozens I asked in our various interviews which Coe answered without reflection: 'Yes. Absolutely!' Eamonn Coghlan, who also felt that he'd had problems with the media, said the same thing, and just as quickly. Competition does not manifest itself simply on the track. Coe expanded: 'It's not just external, it's internal. It's the annoyance of missed training opportunities, it was the annoyance at having gone so long without diagnosis. It was just everything. It was articles in the newspapers, unfair comments about Peter, and my mum, even. All that sort of thing. Yes, absolutely!'

Steve Scott felt the onus more than anyone in the Olympic 1500 metres final in Los Angeles. Although he was from San Diego, over a hundred miles south, that was 'local' in US and Californian terms. He was the local boy, the home-town hero. Two decades later, Scott gave me a run-down of how he had foreseen the race. 'I was considered one of the favourites going into the Olympics. Unfortunately, I bought into it too. In 1983 I spent all year over in Europe. I would race and just have a fun time and a great attitude. Then, when the Olympics came along, it was like, Oh, I can't do that. Instead, I stayed here. I was so caught up in what was happening, reading the *LA Times* and seeing thirty-three days to go, thirty-two days to go to the Olympics. I just got caught up in the fact that, yes, I need to win for America, instead of just going and racing. I didn't stay in the village, I didn't go to any other races, didn't enjoy the experience. My memory of the Olympics is my heat, my semi, my final and the closing ceremonies. That is all I remember, and I barely remember that.

'I wasn't comfortable with the race plan, either, taking over that early. But I was committed to it, this was something we had decided a long time ago. I've taken the initiative before, but it was never planned; that was just not the way that I raced, I was very much a "feel" runner. The field was wide open, no one had really stood out. Coe did more so than anybody else, by how he ran the 800. I knew that Ovett wasn't going to be a factor, going through what he went through. I had respect for Cram, but he had had some injury problems and breaks in his training, so it was wide open in my mind, which created more anxiety, because then it was like, OK, now I can win this. Me and my coach's plan was to run 3.32, and if anybody can beat me, then great! So the winning time was 3.32, but unfortunately *everybody* beat me!'

That is pretty much what happened. Initially, Coe must have felt he was back at Loughborough on the first lap, because a Sudanese student, Omar Khalifa, who had blossomed into a world-class middle-distance man under George Gandy's tutelage, took the field through 400 metres in a businesslike 58.9 seconds. Then Scott, as promised, took over. He led for the best part of two laps, but it wasn't like Straub in Moscow: Scott was nowhere near that sort of form because he hadn't raced enough. Even before the bell, he had to concede the lead to the Spanish number two, José-Manuel Abascal, who was closely followed by Coe, Cram and Ovett. And that was the order as they hit the bell.

There are many things associated with a clanging bell – curfew, from the Old French *cuevrefeu*, the practice introduced to Britain following the Norman Conquest of extinguishing fires at night, prior to sleep. The ringing bell is also the last act in excommunication. After the book (of life) is closed, and the candle (like the fires) is extinguished, the bell of renunciation is tolled. The bell is also a summons to prayer, and communion. Running was their religion, their communion with nature, with their spirit, with their ego, with their ambition. All of that was going to come together for Sebastian Coe. And he knew it.

Making History

The Los Angeles Coliseum was the stage for many dramas during the 1984 Olympic Games. But few as riveting as this. The trio of English milers was poised to pounce with just 300 metres to run to the finish line. Then came the seismic shift. Coe had only been given the opportunity to come to Los Angeles to defend his title after an acrimonious debate over the final spot on the Olympic team. Cram, the reigning World, European and Commonwealth champion, had been so badly injured that his participation here was a minor miracle in itself. But if he had problems, what of Ovett? He had been stretchered out of the stadium five days earlier, after a fruitless attempt to defend his Olympic 800 metres crown, while Coe won silver again. Cardiac specialists had advised Ovett not to run, but he had threatened court action when the British team officials tried to stop him.

But the strain was too much. Ovett stepped off the track on the crown of the bend, and the stretchers were readied again. Up ahead, Coe looked fearfully over his shoulder, as he had done in Moscow four years earlier. That quick glance was invested with so much pain, anxiety, desire. This time when he looked back, though, he did not see Ovett, the man who had gone into Moscow having won forty-five consecutive 1500 metres and mile races. He did not see the man who had made his life, his career, a misery, the free spirit who had effortlessly taken the Olympic 800 title that the whole world had agreed was his.

....

He had endured the six worst days of his life, and then overcome his fear, to beat Ovett in the 1500 metres in Moscow. It was the single most defining race of his career. But now, there was still somebody right behind him. It was Cram, who had won the three titles that Coe had been unable to contest in the previous two years. While Coe had been indisposed, the world order had shifted, was still shifting inexorably, and was threatening to shift him into history. But Coe put that behind him as he put Cram behind him. The youngster would have his day, but for the moment it was Coe, gradually easing away as the pair ghosted past the Spaniard Abascal and headed for the haven of the finish line.

Entering the final straight, it looked as if the whole race had gone into slow-motion. Coe had often pointed out that an 800 metres race is won not in a sprint, but by the athlete who slows down the least in the final stages. Here the phenomenon translated to the 1500 metres, which had been run so fast at the start (unlike in Moscow) that it was to end in an Olympic record which lasted almost twenty years. In the absence of Ovett, Abascal's attempt to run the legs off the Brits would earn him the bronze medal. Cram's late entry to the fray after injury meant that he now began to wilt. The build-up of lactic acid in his muscles was drowning their capacity to function properly. He began 'treading water'. Even Coe was slowing down, but less so than Cram. The gap gradually opened as Cram's head began to roll with agonised, unfulfilled effort. He was destined for silver.

Now Coe was alone, on his way to becoming the only man in Olympic history to retain the 1500 metres title. Now he could savour it. He had beaten them all. Not just those here, but, more importantly, all the 'greats'. When their roll-call was read out, his name, Sebastian Coe, would be at the head of it. Ahead of Nurmi, the 'Flying Finn' who won nine Olympic golds, but never managed to win two consecutive 1500 metres; ahead of Lovelock, the 'Dark Destroyer'; ahead of Bannister, who 'broke' the 4-minute mile, but could never win an Olympic title; ahead of Elliott, who never lost as a senior; ahead of Snell, who won three golds, but never two 1500s; ahead of Ryun, fated never to win at the Olympics; ahead of Keino, who began the African tide; ahead of Bayi, who was denied Olympic glory by a boycott; ahead of Walker, the first man under 3 minutes 50 seconds for the mile; but most of all, ahead of Ovett.

A dozen years fell away in those final dozen strides to the line. Somewhere in the vaults of his memory bank, there was hidden the incongruous winter heat haze of that field at Hillingdon, when he could just about see that broad-shouldered figure way ahead of him; similarly submerged, the vain attempt to win from the front in Prague, before Ovett swept past; equally the shame of the Moscow 800 metres, when he was so scared, he couldn't even compete against Ovett; to the innumerable times he had watched Ovett win with panache. Gone now, the pain. He had won in Moscow, and now he was about to win in Los Angeles.

Suddenly, it was over. Coe wafted elegantly across the finish line, and the tumult finally broke through at the same time as the wave of emotion which washed over him. He'd done it. One hundred thousand people stood and saluted him as he crossed the line alone. He'd done it. Millions across the world marvelled at the repeat performance. He'd done it. The only man successfully to defend an Olympic 1500 metres title. He'd done it. After almost three years of illness, half an elite athlete's lifetime. He'd done it. Against all the odds. He had done it.

Legends

The following year, Cram would break Coe's 1500 metres and mile world records within a week, beating Coe in the process. Ovett looked finished. Bronchial pneumonia had weakened his strapping frame to the point of collapse. He was like a ghost. But he would amaze the track world by coming back to win Commonwealth gold at 5000 metres two years later, while Coe would strike back at Cram, and finally win a major 800 metres title, the European Championships in Stuttgart in 1986. But that was the swansong. The phenomenon was that 'Coe and Ovett' reached its apotheosis on the last lap of the Los Angeles Coliseum, and it was time to prepare the obituaries.

It had been the most extraordinary rivalry in British athletics, and the rest of the world had looked on in envy and admiration. In terms of titles and records, Coe comes out a clear 'winner', with two Olympic golds and two silvers, and eleven world records (three indoors). As Ovett told me without any prompting, 'Without question, Seb was the greatest middle-distance runner that we have had in the UK.'

Yet we can hardly call Ovett, who won Olympic, European and Commonwealth gold, and set half a dozen world records, a 'loser'. Furthermore, he made the march to his Olympic title look ridiculously easy. He was never quite the same after his church railings injury. Nevertheless, he did go on to set another world record. He may have benefited enormously from innate talent, but no one at that level in athletics – one of the most widely contested sports – achieves what Ovett achieved without extreme effort and application. And he overcame the most difficult transition: from being a junior winner who gets by without doing too much work to becoming a senior winner, which involves the hardest work.

There is a widespread fascination with people like Ovett, people who, for no apparent reason, display an abundance of what we call 'natural' talent. They are born with an inbuilt advantage, however unlikely that may be in many cases, and, given his parents' addiction to tobacco, certainly in the case of Ovett. Sometimes, as with the English footballer Paul Gascoigne, such natural talent will go hand in hand with a certain simplicity of character and/or intelligence. This was not the case with Ovett, who, by all accounts, was a very sharp youngster and is nowadays a very shrewd middle-aged man. But he was dyslexic, and left-handed, factors that maybe conspired to lend a sense of 'otherness'.

There is a clue in the terms we use to describe such natural talents – Child of God, Child of Nature, Nature Boy – as if they have some sort of hotline to the Creator; that if we could key into them, we would somehow better understand the Mysteries of the Universe. Ovett, of course, would scoff at such references, and rightly so. Nevertheless, I believe that this is why we are so intrigued and so drawn to such characters. And, despite – or because of – the bad-boy persona that the media created, with Ovett's complicity, he was widely loved. I was witness to it virtually every day of Ovett's career – among friends, family, neighbours, or anyone who knew that I was in the milieu.

And why aren't people like Coe appreciated more? He was a front-runner, and that's the bravest role of all. He was one of those people who make themselves what they are, having started from much further back, without that 'gift', or certainly not a *recognisable* gift. These are the people who are accused of being 'manufactured'. It's an insult to their foresight, to their acumen, to their application, to their bloody-minded hard work. Such single-mindedness is somehow an affront to us, because the majority of us know that we could never emulate it. So we begrudge, instead of acclaiming.

Ovett discovered a talent, and just ran with it, wherever it might take him, whereas the Coes, father and son, created a talent and drove it where they wanted. Ovett dared to be good right from the start, whereas Coe had to be shocked into it. Moscow did that. It could be argued that Coe's career truly began not with the European indoor victory in 1977, nor with the trio of world records in mid-summer 1979, but in the decisions that he took in the days following the 800 metres and prior to the 1500 metres in Moscow. And it was Coe's success which forced Ovett to change his whole competitive philosophy.

Coe did not have the obvious innate talent that Ovett possessed. Coe had to work to a goal that was not as immediately apparent. It takes an extraordinary amount of self-belief to nurture a dream against the odds that a character like Ovett presented. And Coe would have been aware of Ovett right from the start. Coe's career arc may have lacked the apparent *joie de vivre* of Ovett's, but, earnest as it was, it was nevertheless a glorious triumph, and a lesson and a model for generations to follow, even if they are unable to emulate it.

All of which makes the Coe and Ovett era strikingly different. And extraordinary. So extraordinary that people still remember it with an element of disbelief. Could they really have been so good? Well yes, they could have been. And they were. There was nobody like them. And they were so unlike each other, they were the perfect match.

Virtually everything, apart from the superlatives about the pair was different. But one thing Ovett and Coe had in common was the event they chose. Despite their success at 800 metres, with Ovett as Olympic champion and Coe as world record-holder, their true *raison d'être*, their *métier*, was the 1500 metres and the mile – the 'Perfect Distance'. And for an unforgettable, unrepeatable decade, through the start of the Afghan wars, through the socially and geographically divisive Miners' Strike, through the carnage of the Falklands conflict, which extended Margaret Thatcher's reign and permitted Coe ultimately to enter Parliament, two Englishmen ran the 'Perfect Distance' and held the sporting world to ransom.